Finding
A Path
To Flourish

A.E. Housman in 1911. This features in many biographies.

A.E. HOUSMAN

Finding A Path To Flourish

PETER WAINE

THE **BLACK SPRING**
PRESS GROUP

First published in 2021
by the Black Spring Press Group
Grantully Road, Maida Vale, London W9,
United Kingdom

Graphic design and typeset by Edwin Smet
Cover illustration by Nick Purser
Author photograph by Peter Waine
Printed in England by TJ Books Ltd, Padstow, Cornwall

First printing edition of 300 copies

Set in Bembo 13 / 16 pt
ISBN 978-1-913606-10-7

BLACKSPRINGPRESSGROUP.COM

MIX
Paper from responsible sources
FSC® C013056

To

Zoë Jasko
Who helped with this book in so many ways.

'The chief ambition of
my life has long been to be
invited to the Colchester
Oyster Festival.'

CONTENTS

A.E. Housman at Ruan Minor photograph by Mrs Grant Richards, 1916, published in G. Richards, *Housman, 1897–1936*, Oxford University Press 1st edition, 1941

INTRODUCTION

Alfred Edward Housman's life was full of contradictions: kind and unkind, friendly and rude, gregarious and painfully silent, reclusive and bon-viveur; his belief that life was dreadful and death welcome, but also that death ended one's enjoyment of cherry trees; a gourmand who lived frugally, a traditionalist who loved to fly to France in the dangerous days of pioneering aviation.

It is easy to love his poetry, to be impressed by his academic brilliance, to be fascinated by the contradictions so prevalent in his tormented character, to be sympathetic to his emotional plight – but to like him as a person is hard, and to understand him even harder. Perhaps we can hope only to reach a meaningful understanding, or, as one biographer put it: 'It became clear that there were some shadowy areas in his life... but I knew enough to have... a fairly shrewd idea of the truth.'[1] And yet, despite all, if Housman were to have befriended me I cannot be sure that I wouldn't have relished the prospect, perceived it as a rare and peculiar privilege and would have engaged with a generous heart, a lively wit and a stimulating raconteur, a brilliant mind and a loyal companion. Perhaps.

To his admirers he is a man who has penned some of the most sublime lines in the poetic lexicon of the English language, impossible to read in public without

1 Richard Perceval Graves, English biographer including *A.E. Housman: The Scholar-Poet*, Faber & Faber, 1979, poet and lecturer born 1945, best known for his three-volume biography of his uncle Robert Graves.

a tear or a gulp. Yet he was a strange man, offering different aspects of character to different audiences, ignoring some, generous and thoughtful to others, dry in presentation as a lecturer, but a noted after dinner speaker with a rarely experienced sense of humour and what he couldn't or wouldn't express in the spoken word or in prose – although he was 'one of the wittiest writers in the English language', 'the wit which flashes out here and there', 'the sharpness of his wit' – he managed to do with focus, deceptive simplicity and apparently effortlessly in verse, verse which came not from conscious effort but mysteriously.[2] He claimed it came unexpectedly, suddenly, he knew not where, adding that the final line or two might take a year to produce when the other lines, the spontaneous ones, the better ones in his view, took mere seconds – spontaneously from the pit of his stomach, leaving him exhausted. He wrote to his brother Laurence 'I hear that Kipling says I am "dead right" about the pit of the stomach.'[3] We shall see that this was not quite true as Housman often redrafted his poems, and in a few cases

2 D.R. Shackleton Bailey reviewing *Classical Papers* in Cambridge Review, 1973. A.S.F., Gow, *A.E. Housman: A Sketch*, Macmillan, 1936, p.5. D.S. Robertson in *The Classical Review*. There are plenty of examples of Housman's lovely prose style despite his instruction to his brother Laurence, 'I direct my brother Laurence Housman to destroy all my prose manuscripts in whatever language', (in Housman's will) *Times Literary Supplement*, 24 October, 1936.

3 Housman's 'The Name and Nature of Poetry', Leslie Stephen Lecture 1933. Letter Housman to Laurence, 24 May, 1933. Hereafter correspondence cited by date alone can be found in either A. Burnett, (ed.), *The Letters of A.E. Housman*, Oxford, 2007 or H. Maas, (ed.), *The Letters of A.E. Housman*, London, Rupert Hart-Davis, 1971.

many times. Producing poetry, for Housman, was as much a physical process as a mental one.

According to the poet Wilfred Scawen Blunt he 'refused absolutely' to read his poetry aloud.[4] He said to his brother Laurence, 'only the archangel Raphael could recite my poetry properly', and to his friend and publisher, Grant Richards, he wrote, 'I don't allow the wireless people to recite my poems.'[5] His poetic output was relatively meagre, yet he was offered the Poet Laureateship – which he declined – and the Order of Merit, which he also rejected, the former even more extraordinary for being offered at a stage when only *A Shropshire Lad* and *Last Poems* had been published.

He said that he lost his religious faith at 13 but he still acquired an encyclopaedic knowledge of the Bible which he used extensively in his poems; he never wished to be regarded as a war poet, but his verse lent solace to the bereaved in two world wars. Many of the most eminent contemporary composers attempted to put his poems to music but in Housman's eyes, at least, most failed.

He was homosexual but almost certainly repressed. A

4 Wilfred Scawen Blunt, 1840-1922, English poet and writer, inveterate traveller with his wife Lady Anne Blunt in the Middle East; they together were instrumental in preserving the Arabian horse bloodlines.

5 A. Burnett (ed.), *The Letters of A.E. Housman*, reviewed in *Housman Society Journal (HSJ)*, vol.33., 2007, pp.104-109. Letter Housman to Richards, 9 February, 1927.

Grant Richards, 1872-1948, British publisher and writer, established his own publishing firm at age 24, launched *The World's Classics* and published in addition to Housman, amongst others, George Bernard Shaw, Samuel Butler and James Joyce. Wrote his biography, *Housman 1897-1936*, London, Oxford University Press, H. Milford, 1941.

few argue strongly that he was not, others that if he was, why should the subject play such a central role in more recent biographies? Presumably, he still had homosexual emotions until the end, but any outward emotions had concealed themselves by the time he was 30. The subject of his affection was neither a homosexual nor even aware of the effect he had had on Housman. Reserved, hurt and cautious as the result of the pain he felt for unrequited love, Housman maintained a deep reserve for the rest of his days, allowing his true thoughts to be expressed generally in his poems and specifically to the very few friends he ever had.

Despite being one of the greatest philologists of modern times, he devoted 27 years to editing Manilius, a Latin poet of the third rank whom Housman himself summed up as 'a facile and frivolous poet, the brightest facet of whose genius was an eminent aptitude for doing sums in verse.'[6] In short, Housman is a subject worth a further look, in brief, because Housman liked brevity! Perhaps the key to Housman is what has hitherto been ignored; that he was surely placed somewhere on what we would today refer to as the autistic spectrum.

Cyril Clemens wrote:

---

6 A.S.F. Gow, *A.E. Housman: A Sketch,* Macmillan, 1936, p.13. A.S.F Gow, 1886-1978, English classical scholar and teacher, master at Eton College, Fellow at Trinity College, Cambridge. Close friend of Housman. Edited many scholarly volumes on Greek literature, published memoir on A.E. Housman. Marcus Manilius, FL 1st century AD, Roman poet, astrologer and author of a poem in 5 books called *Astronomica*. To an American correspondent Housman wrote 'I do not send you a copy, as it would shock you very much; it is so dull that few professed scholars can read it, probably not one in the whole United States.' Wikipedia. (https://en.wikipedia.org/wiki/Marcus_Manilius)

in appearance Housman was a striking man – one who would stand out in any crowd – five feet, nine inches tall... a fine Roman nose; keen, piercing, kindly eyes, grey eyes... his smile was a rare sweetness, and the twinkle in his eye gave evidence of a keen sense of humor [sic]. I shall always remember the stately manner in which he walked across the quadrangle to the dining hall.'[7] Another, however, conveyed a different impression, 'first scholar and poet; he looked the part of neither. In fact, he looked like what he started as – a competent, conscientious, scrutineer in the Patent Office, short, precise, neatly moustached, with thin, sensitive, probing fingers, and rather deep-set eyes.'[8] Blunt described his appearance as 'one of depression and indifferent health.'[9] Richards wrote 'look with your memory's eye... at the wiry frame of that man, at the lines and contours of his head' which suggest 'old-maidishness' or as A.C. Benson quipped he 'appeared to be descended from a long succession of maiden aunts'.[10] Housman was 'a small person

7 International Mark Twain Society, 1987, historical series 6. Cyril Clemens, 1902-1999, cousin of Mark Twain, President of the Mark Twain Society; Housman was invited to be an Honorary Vice President as too was Mussolini the Italian fascist leader.

8 Canon R.G. Lunt's address at the Housman Society dinner, 27 March 1981, who had sat beside Housman at High Table at Trinity in 1934.

9 W.S. Blunt, *My Diaries,* Part II, New York, Alfred A. Knopf, 1921, p.287.

10 Richards, *Housman,* p.300. A.C. Benson, 1862-1925, kindred spirit to Housman, academic, poet, man of letters and Master of Magdalene College Cambridge. He wrote the words of the song *Land of Hope and Glory*, as well as the popular Mapp and Lucia novels. Son of an Archbishop of Canterbury.

> with drooping moustaches and an undistinguished appearance.'[11] His friend Percy Withers referred to his 'chiselled speech, his stern and rather obdurate physiognomy in repose.'[12]

This book does not attempt to analyse his poetry nor his classical output except as a means of understanding this apparently enigmatic person.

I have chosen a thematic approach rather than a chronological one and therefore a brief chronology of Housman may prove helpful.

Housman was born in 1859 at Fockbury, near Bromsgrove, of a High Anglican family and his father was a solicitor. In 1871 his beloved mother died on his twelfth birthday. From 1870-1877 he attended Bromsgrove School as a Foundation Scholar and in 1877 won a scholarship to St John's College, Oxford.

Having gained a First Class Honours in the Classical Moderations Examination in 1879 he failed his Finals in 1881, leaving Oxford with no degree.

In 1882 he gained a clerkship in the Patent Office in London, sharing lodgings with his Oxford friend, Moses Jackson.[13]

---

11 *The Listener,* anonymous writer, 1936.

12 P. Withers, *A Buried Life: Personal Recollections of A.E. Housman*, London, Jonathan Cape, 1940. Percy Withers, 1867-1945, briefly practised as a GP. Writer, close friend of Housman.

13 Moses Jackson, 1858-1923, the subject of Housman's unrequited love, contemporary of his at St John's College, Oxford, unlike Housman gaining a First (but in Science); again unlike Housman a keen sportsman. Left England for India in 1887, married in 1889, returning only infrequently. Housman was Godfather to Jackson's fourth son.

In 1892 he became Professor of Latin at University College London leaving in 1911, aged only 33, to become Kennedy Professor of Latin at Cambridge University and a Fellow of Trinity College. Meanwhile, in 1896 he self-published his first and most famous collection of poems, *A Shropshire Lad*, and in 1903 published Volume 1 of *Manilius Astronomicon* and four more volumes followed until 1930.

In 1904 Sir Arthur Somervell composed his *Shropshire Lad* cycle, the first of many composers to set his verse to music.[14] In 1922 Housman published *Last Poems*. In the same year his great friend Moses Jackson died in Canada. In 1933 Housman delivered the Leslie Stephen Lecture 'The Name and Nature of Poetry'.

Housman died in 1936 and his brother Laurence, his literary executor, published the collection known as *More Poems*. The following year Laurence published his biography *A.E.H: Some Poems, Some Letters and a Personal Memoir by his Brother,* as well as a further collection of his brother's poems called *Additional Poems*.[15]

Those are the chronological basic facts of a very complex personality. The title of this book encapsulates the challenges Housman faced, the setbacks he endured and the extraordinary successes he achieved.

---

14 Sir Arthur Sommervell, 1863-1937, English composer and song writer, one of the most successful writers of Art Song in the English musical renaissance of the 1890s-1900s.

15 L. Housman, *A.E.H: Some Poems, Some Letters and A Personal Memoir by his Brother*, Jonathan Cape, 1937.

1. HIS POETRY DIVIDES

'Was reason for being born.'
'A minor poet.'

It is not easy to think of another poet who so divides opinion, who for some his output at its best is sublime but to others is immature and too pessimistic. At least the majority of the most important contemporary literary giants including Oscar Wilde, T.S. Eliot, Thomas Hardy, Sir John Betjeman and William Faulkner regarded his poetry as indisputably first rate.[16] Charles Brink, one of the greatest holders of the Kennedy chair of Latin at Cambridge, and a successor to Housman in that position, concluded 'nearly half a century after his death, he still goes on arousing attention, admiration, fear, imitation, criticism, evasion or downright detestation.'[17]

The extremes of reaction that Housman generated in respect of his poetry were replicated in all aspects of his life with the one exception; he is universally regarded as

16 Sir John Betjeman, 1906-1984, Poet Laureate 1972-1984, writer, broadcaster, founder member of the Victorian Society, helped to save St Pancras station from demolition, Vice President of the Housman Society. William Faulkner, 1897-1962, American writer, Nobel Prize for Literature 1949, wrote novels, short stories, screenplays, poetry, essays and a play. One of the greatest twentieth century writers, pioneered with Joyce the use of the stream of consciousness technique and great depth of characterisation. Amongst his best works are *The Sound and the Fury,* and *Absalom, Absalom!*

17 C. Brink, 'Historical Reflections on Bentley, Porson and Housman', *English Classical Scholarship,* 1986. Charles Brink, 1907-1994, distinguished holder of the Kennedy Chair of Latin at Cambridge, born in Berlin, refugee from Nazi Germany in 1938. On the occasion of the unveiling of the Housman memorial in Poets' Corner, Westminster Abbey.

possibly this country's preeminent classicist, an area which most today neither understand nor necessarily care about.

Housman was certainly in vogue at the time of his death even if some did not fully appreciate how highly he was regarded. 'As a youth I owned a first edition of Housman's famous *A Shropshire Lad* given by a great-aunt who had only bought it because she happened to live in Shropshire. Needing money, knowing vaguely that a slim grey volume was worth something, I took it to a London bookseller. He gave me £4 4/- for it. A few weeks later I read that a copy in good condition (as mine was) had been sold in US for about £50' (around £900 in today's value).[18]

Other comments have included, 'No one could mistake a Housman poem for a poem by any other writer' and 'The People who review the poetry which is being written to-day should read A.E. Housman ... If after reading his poems, they can still praise the rubbish which they mistake for poetry, they are even less intelligent than I imagine them to be.' 'The best of his lyrics are inimitable and imperishable', wrote T. S. Eliot adding that 'we would all write like Housman if we could.'[19] Thomas Hardy mentions that when *A Shropshire Lad* first came out he predicted that it would be a permanent addition to English literature. The admiration was mutual: Housman was a pallbearer at Hardy's funeral. He was in august company: the other pallbearers included the Prime Minister (Stanley

18 'An Appreciation' at the time of Housman's death, by William Hickey (Thomas Driberg) in the *Daily Express*.

19 T. Dudley Smith, 'Snakes and Ladders', *Hymn Society of Great Britain and Ireland*, Occasional Paper 3rd ser.1. 2008, p.12.

Baldwin), Ramsay MacDonald (soon to succeed Baldwin as Prime Minister), Kipling, George Bernard Shaw and Galsworthy.[20] Housman, for some unrecorded reason, heartily disliked Galsworthy. Withers, in his biography on Housman, referred to this as follows: '[Housman] told me how proudly he had accepted the office of pall-bearer... The following day he saw in the press that Galsworthy was to be one of the number, wrote immediately to decline the office and only capitulated as a consequence of Barrie's entreaties.'[21] Housman also seemed to heartily dislike Walter de la Mare and W.E. Henley stipulating that his poems must not be included in an anthology where poems from either of these two poets also appeared.[22] At the request of Siegfried Sassoon, Housman wrote a poem to celebrate Hardy's 80th birthday, known today as 'Last Poems XXXVIII'.[23] Housman referenced most of his poems by Roman numerals and we will follow that established custom. He also incorporated them, or they were subsequently collected into book form as *A Shropshire*

---

20 Stanley Baldwin, 1867-1947, KG, PC, FRS, 1st Earl, Prime Minister on three occasions, possibly unfairly criticised for inadequate preparation for the Second World War, considerable achievements in social welfare reform and had to contend with the General Strike. John Galsworthy, 1867-1933, OM, Nobel Prize for Literature 1932, English novelist and playwright especially renowned for *The Forsyte Saga*, a sequence of nine novels.
21 Withers, *Buried Life,* p.100. Sir James Barrie, 1860-1937, OM, Scottish novelist and playwright, principally remembered as creator of *Peter Pan.*
22 Richards, *Housman,* p.78. Walter de la Mare OM, CH, 1873-1956, English poet, short story writer, novelist. James Tait Black Memorial Prize 1921, Carnegie Medal 1947. W.E. Henley, 1849-1903, English poet, writer, critic and editor, especially known for his poem 'Invictus'.
23 Siegfried Sassoon, 1886-1967, English poet, writer and soldier, became one of the leading poets of the First World War.

Lad (*ASL*), *Last Poems* (*LP*), *More Poems* (*MP*) and *Additional Poems* (*AP*). When asked why he didn't give titles to more of his poems he replied, 'I found it a trouble to reinvent titles for poems and I do not think it worthwhile.'

Oh stay at home, my lad, and plough
The land and not the sea,
And leave the soldiers at their drill,
And all about the idle hill
Shepherd your sheep with me.

Oh stay with company and mirth
And daylight and the air;
Too full already is the grave
Of fellows that were good and brave
And died because they were.
(LP XXXVIII)

Did Hardy influence Housman? Certainly Housman was a sincere admirer of Hardy's poetry and in one letter it is clear that he was reading Hardy's *Collected Poems* of 1919 just before he completed *LP* in 1922.

To another his poetry is 'unmistakably modern' and 'complex, ambivalent and disquieting.'[24]

Oscar Wilde wrote to Housman's brother Laurence in 1897 on leaving Reading Gaol having served a sentence for gross indecency. 'I have lately been reading your brother's lovely lyrical poems… [and they have] given me that rare

24 M.H. Markel, 'A.E. Housman's Modern Love Poetry', *HSJ*, vol.2, 1975, p.41.

thing, happiness.'[25] Surely a powerful and meaningful endorsement.

William Faulkner was equally devotional, claiming that Housman's poetry, and especially *ASL*, 'was reason for being born, discovering splendour and fortitude.'[26] Faulkner's biographer adds that it seemed unlikely that any other collection of poetry had such an effect and lasting impact on him. Sir Stephen Spender, a contemporary, referred to the autobiographical nature of *ASL* – something Housman incidentally refuted – praising it for its clarity and candour with which it reveals 'the inmost secrets of the heart.'[27] Speaking 18 years after Housman's death, Brink said 'Housman had an extraordinary sensitivity and alertness that enabled him to use poetry to special effect, speaking in ways that few others had reached.' Alan Bennett commented 'though many of them are about love between men, they are all, gender apart, poems about the ineluctable inequity of loving.'[28]

The Times in its obituary on Housman commented that 'his simplicity in the simplest feeling is genuine; but it has passed through his impeccable intellect to come out on the far side a purer simplicity, the perfect product of head

25 M. Holland (ed.), *Complete Letters of Oscar Wilde,* Rupert Hart-Davis Fourth Estate, 2000. Letter from Oscar Wilde to Laurence Housman, 9 August, 1897.
26 J. Blotner, *Faulkner: A Biography*, London, Chatto & Windus, 1974.
27 Sir Stephen Spender, 1909-1995, English poet, novelist and essayist whose work concentrated on themes of social injustice and the class struggle.
28 Address at the Dedication of a memorial panel to Housman, Westminster Abbey, 17 September, 1996.

and of heart together.' In the same piece it asks whether he was a 'great poet' recognising that such an accolade is often reserved for those who have written a long poem but 'his little poems are no carved cherry-stones. They hold in simple, imperishable perfection of form, the simple, imperishable feelings of humanity.'

For good measure, but selected from many, two former Poet Laureates – Sir John Betjeman and Sir Andrew Motion – rate Housman's poetry amongst the very best.[29] Betjeman, for instance, learned most of *ASL* and *Last Poems* (*LP*) by heart, adding that he gained even greater fulfilment and a deeper understanding when discovering 'their skilful use of alliteration and sound vowels…'.[30]

Others, however, were dismissive. Dame Edith Sitwell called his poetry 'rhythmically dead.'[31] Calderon commented 'so far from believing that man wrote *The Shropshire Lad* I shouldn't even have thought him capable of reading it.'[32]

Some could be complimentary but lukewarm: 'almost by accident [Housman] produced a significant body of verse based on a wrong-headed theory of art.' Another

---

29 Sir Andrew Motion, b.1952, Poet Laureate 1999-2009 and novelist, founded the Poetry Archive, an online resource of poems and audio recordings of poets reading their own work. Vice President Housman Society.

30 J. Betjeman in 'The Influence of A.E.H.', quoted in *HSJ*, vol.7, 1981, p.16.

31 Dame Edith Sitwell, 1887-1964, English poet and critic, eldest of the three literary Sitwells – the others being Osbert and Sacheverell.

32 George Calderon, 1869-1915, English playwright, expert on Russian life and literature.

called Housman 'an electrifying minor poet.'[33] His long-standing friend and fellow Cambridge don, A. S. L. Gow – one of his very few friends – said 'in the hierarchy of scholars his name must stand higher than that of poets.'[34] Even Housman pondered whether he possessed the organ by which poetry is perceived and asked who had certified him as one of the minority who do. This, in turn, was partly contradicted by Brink: 'It may be doubted whether poetry which is both so poignantly simple and yet so complex at a deeper level, can rightly be called "minor"'.[35]

It is rare for one man to excel in two different and distinct ways. Brink thought Housman's achievement was quite extraordinary considering the sort of man he was: a 'seemingly contradictory character... and the combination in the same person of two such apparent incompatibles as pure poetry and pure scholarship.'[36] Brink's comments deserve special attention. Only very few, Gow and Enoch Powell included, understood Housman both as a classicist and as a poet.[37] Brink is perhaps the only one to analyse the personal and the biographical in Housman. He accused

33 Anonymous quotations.

34 Gow, *Sketch*.

35 From Brink's statement of support for the successful application for Housman's admission to Poets' Corner in Westminster Abbey. *Housman Society Publication*, 1996.

36 Brink, *Reflections*. The nine chapters of this book conclude with two on Housman.

37 Enoch Powell, 1912-1998, British politician, classical scholar (university professor at 25), author, linguist, soldier (Brigadier in his early 30s), philologist and poet, Conservative politician and Ulster Unionist MP. Powell attracted widespread attention and criticism following his speech in 1968 known as the 'Rivers of Blood' in which he criticised the then current rates of immigration.

others of practising 'amateur psychology', which has in turn invited over-emphasis on biography and he felt it undermined an understanding not only of the person but also of his poetry and of his scholarship. 'There is a relationship, but no simple and direct one, between the character of the person of genius and his production. Why is not immediately obvious. As a scholar he was, and is, hard to understand even to the tiny minority of the learned that can judge his work. As a poet he had his largest public in the First World War and the nineteen-twenties, and is now not much favoured except in 'historical perspective.'[38] Gow, however, never found this divide between Housman the poet and Housman the scholar an issue. He rather neatly said in 'the invectives against the follies and perversities of his fellow-scholars, it is not difficult to hear the voices of the Shropshire lad turned critic.'[39]

Housman's contemporary H.W. Garrod said Housman was 'a great scholar and, as I shall always think, a great poet – if with a range somewhat limited and special.' He noted the unhappiness in his scholarship, as well as in his poetry, adding 'he is a scholar because he hates poetry',[40] and reflected that bad poets are at least worse than bad scholars as well as being more numerous.

Between those who enthused and those who criticised there was, and is, a third group – those who did both. John Wain complained of Housman's 'immature and

38 R. Bloomfield, 'Charles Brink', *HSJ*, vol. 27, 2001, pp.74-76.

39 A.S.F Gow, 'A Sketch' quoted in *HSJ,* vol. 34.

40 H.W. Garrod, 'Mr A.E. Housman', *HSJ,* vol.40. p.104. Heathcote William Garrod, 1878-1960, British classical scholar and literary scholar.

commonplace nature of his subject matter.'[41] But Wain also wrote in his support for Housman to be included in Poets' Corner in Westminster Abbey, that Housman wrote lines that were a very poignant visual interpretation and very beautiful to the ear, quoting, in particular, Housman's lines 'on acres of the seeded grasses | the changing burnish heaves,' adding 'I don't think one can ask more of any poet, and yet he has more; he has, often, tragic poignancy.'[42]

George Orwell was another who was ambivalent.[43] He can pick up his pen and write – with the poem 'With rue my heart is laden' in mind (*ASL* LIV) – that such a poem could quite easily have been written 'expressly for adolescents', yet praises the same poem when writing about it during the Second World War.[44] Orwell had succumbed to the same evocative tug of the English countryside which made many who fought for King and Country feel that they were fighting for King and Countryside; odd, perhaps, considering that the nation had long been an urban society. (Edward Thomas, when asked in 1915 why he had enlisted to fight, merely picked up a handful of English soil and

41 J. Wain, *Housman Preliminary Essays*, Macmillan, 1957, p.115. John Wain, 1925-1994, English poet, novelist and critic, associated with the literary group known as The Movement, spending much of his life as a freelance journalist and author, writing and reviewing for newspapers and radio.

42 Supporting documentation for inclusion in Poets' Corner.

43 George Orwell, 1903-1950, Eric Blair (pen name George Orwell), English novelist, essayist, journalist and critic. His work constitutes biting social criticism, opposition to totalitarianism and strong support for democratic socialism. His notable novels include *Animal Farm, Nineteen Eighty-Four, Homage to Catalonia, Down and out in Paris and London* and *The Road to Wigan Pier*.

44 Tait, M.S., 'Hell-fire and the Beauties of Shropshire: the Poetry of A.E. Housman', *HSJ*, vol.31, 2005, p.41.

replied, 'for this.'[45]) Orwell draws comfort from the verse which had served well the previous generation, those who were in the trenches of the First World War. He says *ASL*, in which the poem appeared, is 'full of the charm of the buried villages, the nostalgia of place-names, Clunton and Clunbury, Knighton, Ludlow, 'On Wenlock Edge,' 'in summer time on Bredon,' 'thatched roofs and the jingle of smithies, the wild jonquils in the pastures of the "blue remembered hills."'. The years during and immediately after the war, the writer who had the deepest hold upon the thinking young was almost certainly Housman. In 1920, when I was about 17, I probably knew the whole of *A Shropshire Lad* by heart. These are the poems that I and my contemporaries used to recite to ourselves over and over, in a kind of ecstasy.' He ended by asking, but not answering 'what was there in them that appealed so deeply to a single generation, the generation born about 1900?'[46] But he also declared that Housman's poetry was, 'not tragic but merely querulous', and was subject to self-pity… 'the nobody loves me feeling' of *LP* XXVII which ends:

> The diamond tears adorning
> Thy low mound on the lea,

45 Edward Thomas, 1878 -1917, British poet, essayist and novelist, commonly regarded as a war poet but few of his poems deal directly with his war experience and his career in poetry commenced only after he had already been a successful writer and critic.

46 G. Orwell, *Inside the Whale and Other Essays,* Victor Gollancz, 1940.

Those are the tears of morning,
That weeps, but not for thee.

To this Orwell noted 'hard cheese old chap.'[47]

Garrod called some of the rural references 'fake pastoralism,' and another called it 'Georgian sham pastoral',[48] but the poems' rustic elements hold up well when viewed from the perspective of the illustrations. Interestingly, Richard Vicary commented when first reading Housman that he saw him as a rustic poet, depicting nineteenth-century English country life, albeit in a sometimes harsh manner, and noted that Housman's poetry possessed a wealth of visual imagery ranging from the brutal to the lyrical and from the urban to the rustic.[49] Housman's poetry is sprinkled with references to the English rural idyll: 'hanging woods and hamlets' and the 'windy weald', even 'those blue remembered hills' mentioned above. The first two verses of *ASL* and the last refer to sheep, shepherds and flocks, the heath being 'moonlit' and the 'sheep gleaming.'

John Bayley was also ambivalent towards the poetry: on the one hand a great admirer, writing that a shiver comes from 'the unexpected association of grave warning and relaxed familiarity', when referring to *AP* XII, 'An

47 Tait, 'Hellfire', p.41.
48 C. Connolly, 'A.E. Housman: A Controversy' in C. Ricks (ed.), *A Collection of Critical Essays*, Englewood Cliffs NJ, Prentice-Hall, 1968, p.35-40.
49 J.L Bradbury, 'Poetry and Place in A.E. Housman', *HSJ,* vol.5, 1979, pp.11-18. Richard Vicary, associate of the Royal Society of Painters, Etchers and Engravers, author of two books on the theory and practice of lithography.

Epitaph', he regarded *LP* XX as 'a clever poem, a touching poem, and a silly poem.'[50]

In later life Housman made it clear that he wished to be remembered as a classicist – though he was quite happy to add that, whereas nobody wished *Paradise Lost* to be a line longer, some had wished that *ASL* was and that he had obliged by his later collection, *LP*. In the advertisement for his edition of Juvenal he wanted 'no nonsense about Shropshire lads.'[51] Mary Anderson de Navarro was warned not to refer to his poetry, or to Shropshire, or even to Bredon Hill when she sat beside him at a lunch, a lunch she recorded that was eaten 'in utter silence.'[52]

Perhaps Housman was rather self-deceiving. He might say he wanted no nonsense about Shropshire lads but we know that he subscribed to a press cutting agency and we know for instance that the poem 'Illic Jacet' was sent to the editor of the *Academy* as early as 1900 suggesting that Housman had an interest in self-promotion despite denying it.[53]

This conundrum is at the heart of Housman's story, a man today known principally to a wider audience as a poet but amongst classicists still regarded highly; a man who knew surely that his poetry would determine and define

50 J. Bayley, 'Three Views of Some Housman Poems', *HSJ*, vol. 17, 1991, pp.27-31.
John Bayley, 1925-2015, British academic, literary critic and writer, Wharton Professor of English at Oxford, married Iris Murdoch who described him as 'the greatest critic since Coleridge.'
51 Letter, Housman to Richards, 13 June, 1905.
52 M.A. de Navarro, *A Few More Memories*, Hutchinson, 1936. Mary Anderson de Navarro, 1859-1940, American actress.
53 The *Academy,* February 24, 1900.

how he would be remembered – in his lifetime his poetry was well established in the public domain, even if used in ways which surprised him, such as in times of war.

Housman was critical and harsh about other poetry and poets. He put a line through 39 of the carefully selected poems included in Palgrave's *Golden Treasury*, a highly popular and admired collection of verse and literary gems first published in 1861 and which found a prominent place on many bookshelves of Victorian and Edwardian England.[54] It didn't seem to mean anything to Housman that the lofty reason why Palgrave wanted to publish his treasury was so that the best of English lyric poetry would find a ready and appreciative audience. Palgrave had written 'wherever the Poets of England are honoured, wherever the dominant language of the world is spoken, it is hoped that they will find fit audiences.'[55] On the whole Housman disliked verse which was contemporary to him in his later life and he famously condemned most verse from the eighteenth century.

Even his admirers were not blind; they agreed (but it need not be a criticism) that Housman's poetry was often heavy on descriptions of the wretchedness of the human condition, of sorrow, of nostalgia, of bitterness, of the gallows, suicide, churchyards and corpses, but also of the strength of the human spirit, of its capacity and courage to

54 Francis Turner Palgrave, 1824-1897, British critic, anthologist and poet. *The Golden Treasury of English Songs and Lyrics,* a popular anthology of English poetry originally excluding all poems by poets still alive. Regularly revised.

55 Introduction to *The Golden Treasury*.

endure. His poetry could indeed be morbid and Housman called some of it morbid secretions. When a poem starts all sunny and optimistic it can end with a mood change:

> Yonder see the morning blink:
> The sun is up, and up must I,
> To wash and dress and eat and drink
> And look at things and talk and think
> And work, and God knows why.

But it ends:

> Oh often have I washed and dressed
> And what's to show for all my pain?
> Let me lie abed and rest:
> Ten thousand times I've done my best
> And all's to do again.
>
> (*LP* XI)

One need look no further than *ASL* II rather than wait for *LP* XI to reflect on the melancholy of Housman's verse and the way it divides opinion: 'It has the freshness, the spontaneity, the seemingly artless but in fact highly polished art of simplicity [which is] the last phase of sophistication.'[56] It is 'too convoluted and verbose' and

56 R. Aldington, *A.E. Housman and W.B Yeats: Two Lectures,* The Peacock Press, 1955, p.13. The lectures were originally given in New York in 1938. Richard Aldington, 1892-1962, English writer and poet, an early associate of the Imagist Movement and married to the poet Hilda Doolittle. His works included poetry, novels, criticism and biography. Winner of the James Tait Black Memorial Prize 1946.

'attempts too obviously to delay by means of elementary arithmetic the super imposition of the two cherry trees', the one hung with summer blossoms and the other with winter snow.[57]

As a result of his poetry, Housman has been called a pessimist (perhaps nihilist is more apt) but this he refutes, saying that he didn't write his poems in a 'crisis of pessimism', calling himself a "pejorist", one who believes that the world is getting worse. Aldington tried to analyse pessimism as it relates to poets; he said it was prevalent amongst the nineteenth-century writers who were not religious or that other poets suffered accordingly even if for other reasons. He argued that in Shelley's case it was due to his pulmonary consumption, in Byron's case due to a liver which functioned imperfectly. He went further; Matthew Arnold and Thomas Hardy were also pessimists but at least Housman could, he concluded, write light-hearted and gloomy verse. 'And malt does more than Milton can' (*ASL* LXII) is one such example. The reason for the gloom, said Aldington, was that poets 'do not write what they want to write but what they must.'[58]

Housman explained his views on the subject in verse:

> They say my verse is sad; no wonder:
> Its narrow measure spans
> Tears of eternity, and sorrow,
> Not mine, but man's.

---

57 P.E. Firshow, 'The Land of Lost Content: Housman's Shropshire', *Mosaic*, XIII chapter 2, winter 1980, pp.103-122.

58 Aldington, *Housman and Yeats*, pp.17-18.

This is for all ill-treated fellows
Unborn and unbegot,
For them to read when they're in trouble
And I am not.
(*MP* preface)

Another example includes:

Ay, yonder lads are yet
The fools that we were then;
For oh, the sons we get
Are still the sons of men.
The sumless tale of sorrow
Is all unrolled in vain:
May comes to-morrow
And Ludlow fair again.
(*LP* XXXIV)

He grieves that man's life vanishes like the morning dew, he curses the inevitable finite nature of man's time on earth and he shows resignation to Heaven's will. He depicts himself standing alone surrounded by suffering in the evening twilight before the gloomy night presses in (*LP* XXXIX). One verse goes:

So here's an end of roaming
On eves when autumn nighs:
The ear too fondly listens
For summer's parting sighs,
And then the heart replies.

Included in *MP* XXXVIII is the stanza:

Now who sees night for ever,
He sees no happier sight:
Night and no moon and never
A star upon the night.

Whilst in *MP* XXI we have:

The stars of heaven are steady,
The founded hills remain,
Though I to earth and darkness
Return in blood and pain.

J. B. Priestley thought Housman was a pessimist.[59] Housman 'cannot write a little song in praise of spring without the sharp shadow of death following across the sunlit blossom.'[60] Perhaps Housman didn't regard this as a criticism; Keats warned against the poet excluding suffering and death for in so doing, he said, you kill the essence of great poetry.

Housman tried to define his likely audience: 'my chief object in publishing my verse was to give pleasure to a few young men here and there', insisting that his

59 J.B. Priestley, 1894-1984, O.M, English novelist, playwright, screenwriter, broadcaster and social commentator. *The Good Companions* brought him to wide public notice further enhanced by other successes such as *An Inspector Calls*.

60 J.B. Priestley, 'The Poetry of A.E. Housman,' *London Mercury*, VII, December 1922, pp.171-184.

poetry should be published in cheap pocket editions so that anyone could buy a copy. He wanted his poems to be enjoyed 'by the ordinary reader not the literary elite' – a goal he achieved.[61] Many of the Allies in the First World War and the enemy, the Japanese, in the Second, went into battle with their pocket edition of *ASL*. Housman hoped that the increased sales of *ASL* would enable the price to be reduced yet further and thereby increase sales so that 'a bullet, otherwise destined to have a fatal effect' would be 'deflected or weakened by the sure shield of his work.'[62]

Housman strongly cautioned against his poetry being analysed as some academic exercise; he made this abundantly clear in his lecture 'The Name and Nature of Poetry'. Indeed, his poetry cannot be slotted neatly into the pantheon of English literature. Some have said that his poems pointed to the modern, others that they are decidedly Victorian, some thought that they were Edwardian, others that his poems belonged to the 1920s, some even to the Romantic or neo- or post-Romantic! Housman commented 'to include me in an anthology of the Nineties would be just as technically correct and just as essentially inappropriate as to include Lot in a book on Sodomites…'.[63] One critic, Tom Burns Haber, concluded in *Manuscript Poems of A. E. Housman*, in which he analysed in depth the evolution and composition of Housman's verse for the first time via the notebooks that Housman

61 Letter from Housman to Miss Harvard, 3 June, 1903.

62 Richards, *Housman,* p.35.

63 Letter Housman to Richards, 9 October, 1928.

'belonged to no school.'[64]

Housman, however, is regarded as a 'war poet' but he never regarded himself as such and he never wanted to be labelled as one. Throughout his life though, Housman was in awe of military matters. As early as 1875, when he was only 15, he wrote to his stepmother after a visit to London: 'I think of all I have seen what has most impressed me is – the Guards. This may be barbarian, but it is true.'[65] As his sister Kate once said: 'he was ready to humble himself before the man who chose to go to fight and risk his life in doing so.'[66]

He regarded patriotism as a dangerous subject for poets. Laurence recalled that his brother thought 'of all the virtues... the one which had inspired the least amount of good poetry was patriotism because it is so easily degenerated into vice; when poets began by praising their own country, they commonly ended by insulting others.'[67] Despite frequent reference to soldiers marching and young lads dying, most of his poetry was written twenty years before the First World War, and if they refer to a specific conflict rather to the human condition in general it would be the Boer War of 1901 in which his brother Herbert died. Housman wrote a specific poem on that occasion – 'Farewell to a name and number' – which was published later as *MP* XL. At the outbreak of war in 1914 only *ASL*

64 T. Burns Haber, 'A.E. Housman', in S. Bowman (ed.), *Twayne's English Authors Series*, XLVI 1967, p.164.

65 Quoted by N. Marlow, *A.E. Housman: Scholar and Poet*, London, Routledge & Kegan Paul, 1958.

66 Maas, *Letters*, pp.5-6.

67 Housman, *A.E.H: Memoir*, pp.83-84.

had been published; the other poems, largely written around the same time, did not appear in print for a further decade or more. It is true, though, that the First World War boosted sales of *ASL*; hitherto if Housman was known at all outside the rarefied corridors of academia, it would have been as a poet of some standing but with only a select following.

Housman published one hitherto unpublished poem during the First World War; it had almost certainly been written before that conflict commenced. The soldiers billeted at Trinity College produced their own magazine *The Blunderbuss*. 'This will live in history as it was in it that Professor Housman, who was in residence, first published his well-known poem beginning:

> As I gird on for fighting
> My sword upon my thigh,
> I think on old ill fortunes
> Of better men than I.'

This became in due course *LP* II.[68]

However, in his poetry there are copious references to soldiers marching to their deaths, and being a classical scholar he added the understanding of death from the ancients and the concept of glory in dying young:

> Far I hear the bugle blow
> To call me where I would not go,
> And the guns begin the song,

68 Quoted by the Master of Trinity.

"Soldier, fly or stay for long."
(*ASL* LVI)

And again in *LP* XXIX:

Wake not for the world – heard thunder
Nor the chime that earthquakes toll.

And it ends:

Sleep, my lad; the French are landed,
London's burning, Windsor's down;
Clasp your cloak of earth about you,
We must man the ditch without you,
March unled and fight short-handed,
Charge to fall and swim to drown.
Duty, friendship, bravery o'er,
Sleep away, lad; wake no more.

Even the lads on the 'idle hill of summer' are depicted in uniform.

Kipling regarded Housman as a great poet and a first-rate war poet. 'The finest lines of poetry written during the war' said the great man of Empire when referring to Housman's poem 'Epitaph on An Army of Mercenaries'.[69]

These, in the day when heaven was falling,
The hour when earth's foundations fled,
Followed their mercenary calling
And took their wages and are dead.

69 P. Parker, *Housman Country*, Little, Brown, 2016, p.292.

Their shoulders held the sky suspended;
They stood, and earth's foundations stay;
What God abandoned, these defended,
And saved the sum of things for pay.
(*LP* XXXVII)

Whilst Housman knew Kipling's war poetry – he sent a copy of *Barrack-Room Ballads* to his brother Herbert in South Africa – Housman's poetry, even the implied war poems, is more sensitive and complex than Kipling's. *LP* XXXVII was also lauded by others, although it has none of the imperial jingoism of Kipling's verse. The lads who in peacetime 'in their hundreds to Ludlow come in for the fair' are not destined to march under an imperial banner, unlike Kipling's Tommy Atkins, but rather they 'held the sky suspended' on their shoulders. Gerald Bullett said Kipling's death left Housman 'the foremost poet in England, no two poets were ever more different but if Kipling had greater inspiration Housman certainly sang the loveliest songs.'[70] Garrod was less complimentary implying that 'Grenadier' was merely 'jaded Kiplingese.'[71]

One of the most evocative supposed 'War Poems' published as *MP* XXXVI, and therefore posthumously was:

70 Gerald Bullett, 1893-1958, British man of letters, novelist, essayist, short story writer, critic and poet, writing both supernatural fiction and some children's literature.

71 H.W. Garrod, 'Housman', *Essays & Studies*, XXV, 1939, pp.7-21.

Here dead lie we because we did not choose
To live and shame the land from which we sprung.
Life, to be sure, is nothing much to lose;
But young men think it is, and we were young.

Housman might have resisted publishing this in his lifetime because he realised, despite his classical scholarship, that most young men, given the choice, even if most of the 1914 generation were not offered that choice, would obviously not have wished to die! It is a surprise, though, that none of Housman's lines are carved on any public war memorial.

The praise for his supposed war poems continued to flow unabated and unwelcomed. The contemporary Scottish politician and writer, William Darling, said in 1931 that 'Epitaph on An Army of Mercenaries' 'does in eight lines what the official historians cannot do in volumes.'[72] The American poet Robert Lowell said it was as if Housman foresaw the Somme. [73] Therefore his poetry could be redefined, awkwardly for Housman, as war poetry of sorts.

We know that the lads who attended Ludlow fair did die young or as Housman said: 'they carry back bright to the coiner the mintage of man.'[74] That phrase gives us a glimpse of his technique of composition, of his tweaking a line or two, however spontaneous the original rendering.

72 W. Darling, *The Private Papers of a Bankrupt Bookseller*, Oliver and Boyd, 1931.
73 Robert Lowell, 1917-1977, American poet, Pulitzer Prize for Poetry 1947 and again 1974, one of the most important American poets of the post-war era.
74 *ASL* XXIII.

His earlier draft was: 'They carry unspoilt into darkness the honour of man:' not memorable and certainly not in the class of the final version. Indeed the final version was quotable and quoted widely. Cynthia Asquith, the daughter-in-law of the Prime Minister, Herbert Asquith, who lost two brothers, three first cousins, and one brother-in-law in the First World War, wrote to the mother of a friend who had been killed: 'It must be wonderful to think of [Julian] and his glamour as so utterly unassailable' and to know that he 'carries back brighter to the coiner the mintage of man'.[75] The full line was later inscribed on the gravestone of her brother killed in action aged 19, a private memorial, not a public one. Housman didn't use the 'mintage of man' which proved so comforting to others, when he wrote to his grieving sister for her loss but rather used his 'Illic Jacet' (*LP* IV) which begins:

> Oh hard is the bed they have made him,
> And common the blanket and cheap;
> But there he will lie as they laid him,
> Where else could you trust him to sleep?

Maybe Housman felt that the other words were in the public realm and not intimate for his sister Kate. Some claim incorrectly that 'Illic Jacet' was written on the

75 P. Parker, 'The Housman Lecture: May 2016, The Name and Nature of Poetry', in *HSJ,* vol. 42, 2016, pp.5-24. Cynthia Asquith, 1887-1960, English writer and socialist, best known today for her ghost stories and diaries, she also wrote novels and edited a number of anthologies as well as writing for children and on the British Royal family.

occasion of Herbert's death. It was written eighteen months previously.[76]

His poems gave comfort in times of war as they can equally do in peacetime. It can be difficult to recite many of them in public without feeling emotion. I found that the case when giving an address at the Memorial Service in Oxford's Christ Church Cathedral for Colin Dexter, a Housman enthusiast, and that was when reading 'Terence, this is stupid stuff' (*ASL* XX) which is by no means my favourite.[77] It was Dexter's, and it introduced the young Dexter to a lifelong love of Housman; some of the clues to his Morse mysteries are to be found in Housman's poems. He found Housman useful for a title of a book, *The Remorseful Day*, which was borrowed from *MP* XVI. Dexter wrote 'I have mentioned AEH many times, since along with cask-conditioned ale, fair women, Wagner, and crossword-puzzles, Housman is one of Morse's greatest joys.'[78] Both Sir Andrew Motion and Richard Dawkins – two very different careers – found the poem 'Tell me not here, it needs not saying' (*LP* XL) to have a similar effect on them.[79]

Housman is not unique in this regard. Other poems, by other poets, can have a similar effect, perhaps 'The Darkling Thrush' by Thomas Hardy being the best known.

76 *The Academy,* 24 February 1900, p.169.
77 Colin Dexter, 1930-2017, English crime writer, known for his Inspector Morse series of novels which were successfully adapted for television.
78 C. Dexter, 'Halley's Comet: No Sighting Yet', *HSJ,* vol.17, 1991, p.9.
79 Richard Dawkins b.1941, English ethologist, evolutionary biologist and author, Emeritus Fellow of New College, Oxford and formally Professor for Public Understanding of Science. Known as an outspoken atheist.

For Housman it was 'Diffugere Nives' from Horace's *Odes* IV.7: 'the snows are fled away', which he summed up as 'the most beautiful poem in ancient literature', adding that when a poem resonates like that it is 'a vibration.'[80] On one occasion, Housman referred to that poem in one of his lectures and an undergraduate attending recalled that he read it 'aloud with deep emotion, first in Latin, and then in an English translation of his own (*MP* V) and walked quickly out of the room... we had seen something not really meant for us... I was afraid the old fellow was going to cry.'[81]

He even had a fan in 'my old, dear, and intimate friend Princess Marie Louise, who is furnishing the Queen's dolls'-house [and] asked... to let 12 poems of mine [to be] copied small to form one volume in the library; and I selected the 12 shortest and simplest and least likely to fatigue the attention of dolls or members of the illustrious House of Hanover.'[82]

He incorporated his famously retentive memory, his deep encyclopaedic knowledge of the Bible and his proverbial grasp of the classics, mixed them together and created stanza after stanza, deceptively simple, always succinct, which gave satisfaction to a wide spectrum of people who could, and still do, access the poetry at a level at which they feel comfortable without feeling either patronised or deprived of further, deeper, meaning. We shall see that he

80 Housman's lecture course, Easter term 1914.
81 R. Bloomfield, 'A.E and Enoch Powell', *HSJ,* vol.24, 1998, p.35, with acknowledgements to the Literary Executors of Enoch Powell and to Robert Shepherd.
82 Housman to Richards, 4 May, 1923. Princess Marie Louise of Schleswig-Holstein, 1872-1956, granddaughter of Queen Victoria.

was not averse to adding further ingredients to the poetic mix, such as astrology and even palaeography – and the knowledge of the poetical practices of other great poets. There is a reflective, penetrating evocation of the human condition as portrayed by a tormented genius. Housman managed to offer a common touch, engaging with his diverse readership equally in times of war and peace and it didn't matter whether the reader was a lad at Ludlow fair or Master of a Cambridge college.

At times we are not sure how seriously Housman took himself as a poet or whether he wished to deflect attention from his poetry in the hope that his classical scholarship would gain the position and reputation which he felt it deserved, rather like an actor who is famous for a particular role but has a much wider repertoire. Either way, almost a century after his death we can enjoy his poetry, understand its effect on a generation which went to war and take advantage of the poetry in our own lives at moments of challenge and reflection and be divorced from the tormented poet himself and the times in which he lived. Does it matter whether he was bottom of the first division or top of the second in a poets' fictitious league? Those to whom he can speak in that sharp physical and focused way, into the soul, feel privileged and blessed and even sorry for those who cannot, for whatever reason, share such joy, that moment.

William Hyde, illustration to 'On the Teme', in *A Shropshire Lad*, Grant Richards, London, 8th reprint, 1908.

William Hyde, illustration to 'Wenlock Edge', in *A Shropshire Lad*, Grant Richards, London, 8th reprint, 1908.

2. SHROPSHIRE

'This is the land of lost content.'

Shropshire, the geographical entity, often landed Housman in trouble. How familiar was he with the county, how often did he visit it – if at all – and if he did, at what stage in the composition of the poems which became *ASL*? What was the source of his knowledge of the county; how symbolic was the Shropshire of the poems? Was it a symbolic evocation of a place beyond his distant youthful horizon, the emotive symbol of lost youth, especially poignant in later life when he was living in the great metropolis of London? Housman doesn't help us; his answers are often bland, evasive and contradictory.

Garrod in his J.H. Gray lectures regarded Housman's Shropshire as an 'utterly false world'; 'This false-pastoral twist is altogether too tiresome, and it pervades nine-tenths of the Shropshire Lad.' As if that wasn't enough, he goes on to add that it is 'an astonishing medley of false and true'. However, for good measure, if one opened Housman's heart one would find written not Cambridge but Clunbury and Clun and that Shropshire was the 'stuff of a real experience.'[83]

Shropshire may be beautiful and a fitting farewell to England, but it was not a county with a placid history of easy living but rather a crossroads for warring armies, of Celts, of Teutons, of Romans and latterly of the English, and Housman knew that too.

83 J.H. Gray lectures, Cambridge, 1946.

When Severn down to Buildwas ran
Coloured with the death of man,
Couched upon her brother's grave
The Saxon got me on the slave.
(*ASL* XXVIII)

Or:

The blood that warms an English yeoman,
The thoughts that hurt him, they were there.
(*ASL* XXXI)

Housman would say that his knowledge of the county was scanty: 'I do not know the county well.'[84] He told Withers that he had written six of the poems before he set foot in the county but having changed the title to *ASL* he felt he should visit 'to gain local colour.'[85] On one of the rare but cherished occasions when Housman was expansive and communicative at High Table at Trinity, 'there was one author, whose name I have forgotten, who wrote about a city without having been there, and when he finally did visit the place found he had nothing to change!'[86]

In 1933, Housman told the French scholar, Maurice Pollet, that it was a county 'where I have never spent much time.'[87] He said, 'I had a sentimental feeling for Shropshire because its hills were our western horizon.' He

84 For this and the general understanding of Housman's attitude towards Shropshire see Richards, *Housman,* p.39 and p.195.

85 Withers, *Buried Life*, p.67.

86 *International Mark Twain Society*, 1937, series 6.

87 Maas, *Letters,* p.328.

also said, 'The Shropshire Lad is an imaginary figure, with something of my temper and view of life, very little in there is biographical.'[88] An interesting discovery, as recent as 2009, shows that Housman stayed for nearly a month in July 1899 at a hotel in Church Stretton; this was three years after the publication of *ASL*. He did not disguise his name and was probably unaccompanied. The visit would not have been for the purpose of adding to his knowledge of the area because he had already written the majority of the poems with a Shropshire theme and the visit might have been a one-off, but to discover such a visit and so recently is interesting and shows that on occasion we should temper our conclusions in case there is still more to be discovered. Perhaps he was enjoying himself and at the same time becoming better acquainted with the landscape he had already portrayed in *ASL*.

The Times obituary on Housman, almost certainly written by A. C. Benson, noted that, 'The Shropshire of Housman's imagination is at once curiously romantic and realistic – a land of fair and of solid earth, somewhat like that depicted on the Shield of Achilles in the Iliad.'[89] 16 of the poems refer to specific parts of Shropshire: thirteen are in *ASL*, three in *LP* but none in *MP* or *AP* and 13 of them can be placed in the southern half of the county. Some earlier critics, however, argue that *ASL* suffers from being based on too specific a geographical location, but only 18 of 177 pieces actually have definitive references to specific spots. He might have told others that he didn't

88 Reply given by Housman to the questionnaire sent by Pollet in 1933.
89 Richards, *Housman,* p.287.

know the county well, but he seemed to have had an in-depth knowledge of certain places, especially the southern part where *ASL* is placed, if his comments on possible illustrations for *ASL* are anything to go by.

He held strong views about which illustrations were appropriate for the 1908 edition. His poems lend themselves to illustrations and especially those of *ASL*. The strong black and white woodcuts are ideal for the visual imagery and the lithography is equally ideal for the cherished moments when Housman explores the gentler human sentiments. To combine the moods of the poems with a varied and appropriate form of illustration produces a powerful mixture and enriches the original words. His poems also lend themselves to authors in search of a good title, incongruous, perhaps, as Housman didn't bother about titles for the majority of his poems. Nevil Shute's *The Far Country,* and James T. Farrell's *A World I Never Made* are but two of many examples, and we have already noted Colin Dexter's borrowings.[90]

In the 1908 edition there were eight colour illustrations. Housman saw four before publication, liked three, those of Clee Hill, Ludlow and Wenlock Edge, but not the fourth *On the Teme* which, he said, 'might have been anywhere.'[91] He suggested that a better view would be 'from under Whitecliff just opposite Ludlow' (Possibly the illustrations

90 Nevil Shute, 1899-1960, English novelist and aeronautical engineer who spent the latter part of his life in Australia. Best known novels include *A Town Like Alice, On the Beach* and *No Highway*. James T. Farrell, 1904-1979, American novelist, short story writer and poet, most remembered for the *Studs Lonigan* trilogy.
91 *Housman 1897-1936*, p.75.

by Agnes Miller Parker, in the 1940 edition, are the best, never seen, of course, by Housman, who died in 1936 – see plates).[92] He also revealed that he must have had more than a passing knowledge of the county from the descriptions in the poems:

> They hang us now in Shrewsbury jail:
> The whistles blow forlorn,
> And trains all night groan on the rail
> To men that die at morn.
>
> (*ASL* IX)

That is precisely how the railway lines curve near Shrewsbury jail.

His rendering of Abdon under Clee in 'Fancy's Knell' (*LP* XLI), with dancing on the green, looks implausible, but the village declined in the mid-nineteenth century, from a population of 172, when it had a school, knowledge which Housman put to special effect in this poem:

> When lads were home from labour
> At Abdon under Clee,
> A man would call his neighbour
> And both would send for me.
> And where the light in lances
> Across the mead was laid,

92 Agnes Miller Parker, 1895-1980, British engraver and illustrator. The main body of her work consists of wood engravings which demonstrate fine draughtsmanship and skilful use of black and white design. Interestingly, since the 1940s very few editions of Housman's poems have been illustrated.

There to the dances
I fetched my flute and played.

In the same poem he adds mood to the description:

Wenlock Edge was umbered,
And bright was Abdon Burf,
And warm between them slumbered
The smooth green miles of turf;
Until from grass and clover
The upshot beam would fade,
And England over
Advanced the lofty shade.

The sun does drop behind the ridge of Wenlock Edge leaving Corvedale in darkness, the eastern face of the Edge is umbered and the upshot beam strikes in midsummer on Abdon Burf. Also, Housman is sound on describing the topography of Shropshire, or at least the parts where he placed *ASL*. 'Valleys of springs and rivers' describes perfectly the Teme, just as he correctly depicts the different topography of the uplands of the 'wild green hills of Wyre.'

As through the wild green hills of Wyre
The train ran, changing sky and shire,
And far behind, a fading crest,
Low in the forsaken west
Sank the high-reared head of Clee,

(*ASL* XXXVII)

Or again:

In midnights of November,
When Dead Man's Fair is nigh.
(*LP* XIX)

There is a fair at Church Stretton on St Andrew's Day, which is November 30th.

Housman's usage of the unfamiliar place names of Shropshire is further evidence of a wider knowledge of the real county. Corve is a pre-English name:

And if my foot returns no more
To Teme nor Corve nor Severn shore,
(*ASL* XXXVII)

But *The Times* was dismissive. 'A Shropshire Lad, a book of poems about Shropshire by a man who knew nothing of the county' and neither Kate nor Laurence mention that he had visited the county in their respective writings on their brother.[93] The critic Norman Nicholson added 'you might as well use *A Shropshire Lad* as a guide to the county as use Rossetti's *Blessed Damozel* as a guide to Heaven'.[94] This is perhaps rather unfair. The disputed issue is how he acquired his knowledge. Pevsner, in his authoritative series, *The Buildings of England*, noted that

93 *The Times Literary Supplement*, 20 March 1953.
94 Betjeman, 'The influence of AEH', p16.

Housman visited the excavation at Uricon and Housman himself confirms his visit in a letter to Laurence. Pevsner wrote '[Uricon's] ruins still possess the ability to move and impress the imaginative spectator, much as they impressed A.E. Housman when he visited them…'.[95] On another occasion, he wrote to his brother regarding Hughley church after he had viewed it from Wenlock Edge, and he goes into greater detail in a letter to Houston Martin.[96] Furthermore, he wrote accurately about Shrewsbury, the names of its bridges, its position on the River Severn and the proximity of the jail to the railway station. He wrote about Ludlow, giving the local name for Ludlow church tower; he knew the market day for Ludlow (*LP* XIX) and the timing and toll of its carillon of bells.

Of course, some of this knowledge could have been acquired from a reference book and we know that Housman owned a copy of the *Handbook to Shropshire, Cheshire and Lancashire* (J. Murray 1879 edition). Indeed, he annotated various sections; for example, against 'Dead Man's Fair' he wrote 'last Thursday in November'. The guide even contains the rhyme which Housman included as the epigram to *ASL* L. But even the handbook could not have given the insight and feel that Housman so successfully inculcates into the very essence and vibrancy of *ASL* and of the other poems with a Shropshire reference.

When *ASL* was reviewed in 1898 in the *Fortnightly Review* by the critic William Archer, Archer didn't know

95 Maas (ed), *Letters*, p.39. N. Pevsner, *Buildings of England – Shropshire*, Yale, Yale University Press, 1958, p.328.

96 E. Haynes, 'Housman's Shropshire', *HSJ*, vol.20, 1994, p.19.

that Housman had by then been Professor of Latin for six years at University College, London. 'Mr. Housman writes… under the guise of 'A Shropshire Lad' – the rustic name for his book. But this is evidently a mere mask. Mr. Housman is no Shropshire Burns singing at his plough. He is a man of culture… I think he has an Elzevir classic in the pocket of his smock frock… I rather take it to be Lucretius.'[97]

Famously, he gave Hughley church a steeple when it doesn't have one. When asked why he replied that the place he had in mind had an ugly name, so he substituted Hughley. A few suggest the actual place intended is not in Shropshire but was Bromsgrove church, his Parish church. That church does have a steeple, which divides the graveyard into two parts, the shadow side and the sunny, as in the poem, but Bromsgrove isn't an obviously ugly name. Perhaps we can be a little clever here. Assuming that Housman had an ear for music, which we shall revisit, 'Bromsgrove' to him and in that context would be an awkward word, if not technically ugly. It is the imbalance of consonants to vowels which makes 'Bromsgrove' an ugly word for Housman the poet. Bromsgrove is less elegant to sing or say than the word he chose, namely Hughley; the former has a large number of consonants whereas the latter flows with easy vowels.

The vane on Hughley steeple

97 Quoted in Parker, *Housman Country,* p.96-7. Elzevir, Dutch publishing house of the seventeenth and eighteenth centuries, specialising in pocket editions of classical texts.

Veers bright, a far-known sign,
And there lie Hughley people,
And there lie friends of mine.
Tall in their midst the tower
Divides the shade and sun,
And the clock strikes the hour
And tells the time to none.

To south the headstones cluster,
The sunny mounds lie thick;
(*ASL* LXI)

Surely, what matters is how Housman's Shropshire, real, imaginary, or a bit of both, inspired him; how it became his Shropshire that facilitated some of the most wonderful poetry ever written:

Into my heart an air that kills
From yon far country blows:
What are those blue remembered hills,
What spires, what farms are those?

That is the land of lost content,
I see it shining plain,
The happy highways where I went
And cannot come again.
(*ASL* XL)

Practically every child has been introduced to Housman

via those eight lines, even if that remains the sum total of their knowledge of his poetry.

To the north, the views of the Clent and Lickey hills and west the distant Shropshire hills, seen from his childhood homes, whether visited or not, became images which served Housman well:

> The weathercock at sunset
> Would lose the slanted ray,
> And I would climb the beacon
> That looked to Wales away
> And saw the last of day.
>
> (*LP* XXXIX)

Terence, the narrator in *ASL*, is nostalgic for those 'blue remembered hills' and in particular for the 'sighing poplars of home' (*ASL* LII).

> Far in a western brookland
> That bred me long ago
> The poplars stand and tremble
> By pools I used to know.

The nostalgia for youth and for the western brookland is compounded by the realisation by the narrator that he is forgotten in the land of his childhood, for the poem continues:

> He hears: no more remembered

In fields where I was known,
Here I lie down in London
And turn to rest alone.

London, the great metropolis, comes to symbolise the loss of innocence that comes with age.

It seems unlikely that Housman's knowledges of Shropshire was via more than an occasional visit to part of the county. However, despite this he acquired an emotional insight, a feeling for the chosen rural idyll which served more than adequately as the geographical background to his most famous and endearing collection of poetry. If the visits were few then it is even more of an achievement to have grasped so comprehensively the historical and topographical nature of the terrain and to have superimposed a poetic layer over the land of 'lost content', his childhood's 'western brookland' – and with such a sure touch.

3. *A SHROPSHIRE LAD*
'Oh I have been to Ludlow Fair.'

Although never out of print, *ASL* had an inconspicuous start. Initially Housman was compelled to self-publish having been rejected by Macmillan. He spent £500 for five hundred copies, and two years later a number were still unsold. Indeed he made a mere £2 5s 3d on sales from the first edition of *ASL*.[98] Not an encouraging start. This didn't surprise his friend Sir William Rothenstein; 'perhaps success [in respect of *ASL*] is not the right word, for rarely has a work of genius been at once accepted at its true value.' Whilst never doubting the poem's merits Rothenstein added, 'here was fine poetry, and a poet taking his place quickly as an immortal...'.[99] Richards reminds us that at the time of the publication of *ASL* 'no one seemed to know anything about [Housman], save that he was Laurence Housman's brother.'[100]

The first known review of the poems appeared in *The*

98 Richards, *Housman*, p.16. Housman came from a supposedly poetic family. His mother wrote poetry, but none survives, as too did his maternal grandfather John Williams: 'He would sometimes indulge an hour in sweet commerce with the muses.' *HSL* vol. 25, 1999. 'Far from haunts of busy men, | Pairing wood-doves in yon glen, | Cupid spent his noon-day hours, | Till extinct his fairy pow'rs.' It proceeds for a further 114 lines. Perhaps a pity it survived.

99 Sir William Rothenstein, 1872-1945, friend of Housman and great admirer of his verse, drew three sketches of Housman, became Trustee of the Tate and Principal of the Ruskin School of Art. W. Rothenstein, *Men and Memories: Recollections of William Rothenstein*, vol.1, London, 1931.

100 Richards, *Housman*, p.15.

Times and was encouraging if somewhat qualified. 'Mr Housman has a true sense of the sweetness of country life and of its tragedies too, and his gift of melodious expression is genuine.'[101] (We will note that *The Times* was not always complimentary.) However, the review which gave Housman the greatest pleasure was one by the American Hubert Bland: 'the best review I ever saw of my poems... in a weekly paper.' Bland goes on to add 'a shelf of modern poets resembles a case of trinkets in the window of a jeweller's shop... the total effect is one of dead and even dismal sameness' and ends 'Mr Housman's poetry is wanting in the note of gladness; that is to say, it is not the highest poetry. But it comes astonishingly near the highest.'[102]

Another review states, 'Here is a writer who stands outside all the poetical vogues of to-day... I have seen no book of verses for years that breathes at least more spontaneity, and very few with as much individuality. Mr Housman's technical merits might easily be surpassed, but his rhythms and forms call for no criticism... there are lyrics here that might have come out of Heine's Song Book. The exquisiteness of Heine and his poisonous sting are both absent...'[103] True – Heine was indeed a major influence on Housman.

101 *The Times*, March 27, 1896.

102 *The New Age 1896*, quoted in a letter from Housman to Laurence 27 August, 1896.

103 *Bookman*, August 1896. Heinrich Heine, 1797-1856, German poet, writer and literary critic, best known outside Germany for his early lyric poetry, which was set to music by Schuman and Schubert.

With poor sales, despite promising reviews, enter Grant Richards, a publisher, who persuaded Housman (almost certainly the approach was via Laurence rather than directly) to let him take all the unsold copies and to publish a second edition, this time at Richards' own expense. It was a stroke of luck. Without this intervention it is not idle to speculate that *ASL* would have languished and eventually been lost.

Richards described his first encounter with Housman. 'My visitor, seeing me for the first time, and on a matter of business, had no reason to be other than remote. He was polite but not genial. Dry? No, not dry, but adequate to the occasion. Unenthusiastic? There was nothing for him to be enthusiastic about: he was a poet... Unkindling? Well, why should he show himself otherwise at this first interview? I fell back, back on the word 'precise.' ... And economical – economical of words.' Richards added surprisingly perhaps 'he was certainly not difficult to talk to on that occasion... I believe we had settled our business in a quarter of an hour or less... I was adding to my list a work of genius.'[104]

ASL was still not a bestseller – we know it took the onset of the First World War and cheap editions for that to happen. It enjoyed greater initial success in America, and so much so that it was reported that Housman Societies were springing up there. The reason is possibly the publication of *ASL* in the very popular magazine *McClure's Magazine* which at the time enjoyed a wide circulation and there was

104 Richards, *Housman*, pp.29-30.

no similar magazine to boost the early sales in England. It is rather endearing, perhaps, that there were Americans walking through Manhattan soon after *ASL* was published, with a copy of Housman's poems in their pockets or at home, with no real prospect of ever visiting those faraway places – those valleys of springs and rivers – and seeing 'far behind, a fading crest, low in the forsaken west... the high-reared head of Clee', – as they crossed busy Fifth Avenue.

The popularity of *ASL* in America so early after publication was quaintly illustrated by Beverley Nichols: 'Then there was another man, heavy-jowled and extremely plain... He had manufactured... a depressingly large number of braces – ... which in America are whimsically termed 'suspenders'. We sat in the same hotel, while I informed him of the braces situation in Europe. He was not very interested until he learned... that I wrote books... He ran into the hall, got his bag, and produced from a nest of braces, a first edition of *A Shropshire Lad*, which he knew by heart.'[105]

18 years passed between its publication and effective release from the grip of pending oblivion. Oddly, as we said, both *ASL* and *LP* were translated into Japanese in 1940, another time of world conflict, and sustained both sides. Housman remains particularly popular in Japan to this day. Was it a shared love of the cherry tree and the symbolism of that tree in Japanese culture? That is the most likely supposition.

It was his friend Pollard who suggested the name

105 Beverley Nichols, 1898-1983, English writer, playwright, composer, wrote more than 60 books and plays. Quoted in Richards, *Housman,* p.55.

change from *The Poems of Terence Hearsay* to *A Shropshire Lad*, pointing out that 'Terence was not an attractive title, and that in the phrase "A Shropshire Lad" which he had used in the poem, he had a much better one. He agreed at once, and I think the change helped.'[106] It might have done but 'A Shropshire Lad' doesn't appear in the poems! With the change of name, the reference to Terence in *ASL* ('Terence this is stupid stuff') makes rather strange reading. Housman left the name change to the very last moment. The manuscript had already been submitted to Kegan Paul, Trench, Trübner & Co. (an introduction made by Pollard – in fact Pollard attended on Housman's behalf) with the original title which was also retained previously when the manuscript was first sent to Macmillan. Withers claimed that the book had been rejected by up to four publishers before being accepted by Kegan Paul and then only at Housman's own expense.[107] Housman refuted this.[108]

ASL has a sequence and storyline which seemed more obvious to Housman than to most of us, and it was this link, however opaque and tenuous, connecting the stanzas, which Housman used as the principal reason why he never gave his blessing for any of the poems in this collection to be included separately in anthologies. He was not short of such requests. Edward Thomas, writing in 1915 when compiling his anthology, *This England* and referring to *ASL* – the other collections had not yet been published

106 Quoted to the author over a cup of tea by the grandson of Pollard, Professor Henry Woudhuysen, Rector of Lincoln College Oxford and also quoted in Graves, *Scholar-Poet*, p.101.
107 Withers, *Buried Life*, p.68.
108 Maas (ed), *Letters*, p.350.

– recorded, 'A.E. Housman can't let me use him in my anthology because he has always said no to anthologists but he atoned by praising my Swinburne, which is the highest compliment I have had yet.'[109] Another example of a literary great being in awe of Housman.

Housman made clear his general views on anthologies to Richards. 'You must not treat my immortal works as quarries to be used at will by the various hacks whom you may employ to compile anthologies' – but this was only to apply to *ASL*.[110] 'I have never laid down any general rule against the inclusion of poems from *Last Poems* in anthologies... the rule regarding *A Shropshire Lad* still holds good.'[111] Of course, over the years *ASL* has become the staple of many anthologies. It was not only in the case of anthologies that Housman was protective of his poems. He would not allow them to be altered by publishers or composers either. Writing to Richards in 1898 he said, 'I think it best not to make any alterations, even the slightest, after one has once printed a thing. It was Shelley's plan, and is much wiser than Wordsworth's perpetual tinkering, as it makes the public fancy one is inspired.'[112] He did in fact make two changes, which he called minor, to *ASL*, 18 years after they were first published, and 'Illic Jacet' had a makeover too: 'chamber' for the word 'beside'; and another change, 'and low is the roof' for 'thin is the guilt'.

There is a conundrum here: Housman excluded some

109 In Eleanor Farjeon, *Edward Thomas the Last Four Years*, London, Faber & Faber, 1958, p.118.

110 Maas, *Letters*, p.91.

111 Housman to Richards, 14 March, 1924.

112 Letter Housman to Richards, 24 July, 1898.

poems from *ASL* because he felt they didn't meet this narrative criterion, and these were eventually found a home in *LP*, *MP* and *AP*. Yet some could quite easily have been included and some that were could equally have been excluded. Some in *ASL* don't even refer to Shropshire; others elsewhere do. To me the following is one of his best poems, an example of one with a Shropshire theme which was not included by Housman in *ASL*. It starts with a lovely notion:

> When summer's end is nighing
> And skies at evening cloud,
> I muse on change and fortune
> And all the feats I vowed
> When I was young and proud.
>
> (*LP* XXXIX)

ASL gives us a brief introduction to how Housman composed. For example, in the initial drafts of *ASL* XXI, 'Bredon Hill', we can see his process of composition, which resulted in 'the coloured counties': 'And see the sunny counties' changed to 'And see the pleasant counties' then 'checkered', 'patterned', 'English' – and finally 'coloured' – the one word, the only one, which really works. Housman explained, 'when I wrote the poem I put down, just to fill up for the time, a quite ordinary adjective, which didn't satisfy me; others followed. Then with the poem in my head, I went to bed and dreamed, and in my dream I hit on the word "painted"; when I woke up I saw that "painted" wouldn't do but it gave me "coloured" as the right word.' It would be interesting to know which stanzas came to him 'just as they are printed' and which with 'a little coaxing after tea' – and, indeed, which came after a year of hard graft during which it had to be rewritten 13 times?[113] In fact we know the answer to the last question: after some deliberation it was the final verse to *ASL*. There was nothing random about which verse Housman wanted to end *ASL* and he made his final choice after a bit of juggling:

I hoed and trenched and weeded,
And took the flowers to fair:
I brought them home unheeded;
The hue was not the wear.
(*ASL* LXIII)

Originally, he thought of *ASL* LXII 'Terence this is stupid stuff' as the ending, but felt it would have meant ending on a frivolous note. It is a poem which includes lines such as:

Oh I have been to Ludlow fair
And left my necktie God knows where.

In other words, the narrator is drunk, and being almost semi-autobiographical, we get the image of the Kennedy

113 For a good introductory analysis of the evolution of the poems see T. Burns Haber. (ed), *The Manuscript Poems of A.E. Housman,* University of Minnesota, Minnesota Press and OUP, 1955.

Professor of Latin at Cambridge wallowing drunk in the mud!

In *ASL* Housman is especially poignant about departure. In *ASL* XXXII he encapsulates every feeling, whether momentary or permanent:

From far, from eve and morning
And yon twelve-winded sky,
The stuff of life to knit me
Blew hither: here am I.

Now – for a breath I tarry
Nor yet disperse apart –
Take my hand quick and tell me,
What have you in your heart.

Speak now, and I will answer;
How shall I help you, say;
Ere to the wind's twelve quarters
I take my endless way.

Few need look further than his poems to find a verse which speaks directly to their own condition and experience. If *ASL* XXXII is not the full treatment, then try *ASL* III:

Leave your home behind, lad,
And reach your friends your hand,
And go, and luck go with you
While Ludlow tower shall stand.

Or again, that well known poem *ASL* XXXVII, already quoted, begins:

> As through the wild green hills of Wyre
> The train ran, changing sky and shire,

And ends:

> About your work in town and farm
> Still you'll keep my head from harm,
> Still you'll help me, hands that gave
> A grasp to friend me to the grave.

As we know, John Wain was ambivalent about Housman's poems and about *ASL* in particular. He regarded many of them as immature and full of self-pity, of grumbling and of a lack of any development, but surely that is grossly unfair.[114] W.H Auden rebutted Wain: 'to grow up does not mean to outgrow either childhood or adolescence but to make use of them in an adult way.'[115] If we take the poem 'When I was one-and-twenty' to be about youth and the ever-evocative emotional saga-the end of love, we see layers of meaning. So too in 'Bredon Hill' (*ASL* XXI). Its symbolism is powerful, and the ability to combine few words so effectively requires a true wordsmith. Here the

114 J. Wain, *Housman Preliminary Essays,* Macmillan, 1957, p.115.

115 W.H. Auden, 1907-1973, Anglo-American poet, poetry noted for its stylistic and technical achievements, its variety of tone and form and its varied content – politics, morals, love and religion. Won Pulitzer Prize 1948, Professor of Poetry at Oxford. 'Straw Without Bricks', *The New Statesman*, 18 May 1957, p.644.

church bells which in happier times produced 'a happy noise to hear' now intone the woman's funeral. All will come to the churchyard, as all will die in the end.

In 'Is my team ploughing' the dead man discusses with his friend what has become of the world. Housman is making a big statement; man has little impact on the world and the world reacts to his death by carrying on. Meanwhile, his sweetheart finds a new lover who is the dead man's friend:

> 'Is my girl happy,
> That I thought hard to leave,
> And has she tired of weeping
> As she lies down at eve?'
>
> (*ASL* XXVII)

Hardly immature.

In fairness to Wain, he argued that Housman's poetry did not develop, that he had in effect rewritten the same poetry for forty years, almost that he rewrote the border ballads. But then we know that Housman composed most of his poetry in a very short time period, with hardly time to develop! Garrod, again in his Gray lectures, surmises that *ASL* is marred by what he called 'sham masculinity'. He felt that one or two of the poems in *LP* were, in contrast, 'softer, more tender, more feminine.' An interesting observation considering that they were largely written at the same time or nearly so.

Whilst *ASL* is recognised as the pivotal achievement of

Housman's poetic output, it is not quite the sum total of all that was best in his stable. *ASL*'s poetry might be heavy at times, dark in places, and the narrators sometimes offer strange, unconventional utterances and insights, but the sheer scope and emotional meaning of the stanzas, against the backdrop of Housman's Shropshire, is majestic and cuts to the soul of those on his wavelength. That *ASL* had to be self-published initially is odd to say the least; that it has never subsequently been out of print is no surprise to many.

4. THE OTHER POEMS

'The farms of home lie lost in even.'

There was a gap of nearly 30 years between *ASL* and the publication of *LP* despite the fact that most of the poems included in *LP* were written between 1895 and 1910. 'I wrote verse at eight but very little till I was thirty-five'[116] – not quite true; in the meantime, he wrote plenty of nonsense verse:

> At the door of my own little hovel
> Reading a novel I sat
> And as I was reading the word
> A gnat flew away with my hat

There is evidence that he was writing nonsense verse when an undergraduate at Oxford. Housman, for example, wrote to M.R. James:[117]

> The Figures you do not perceive
> Are those of Adam and Eve.
> To draw them would not do at all:
> How providential was the Fall.[118]

---

116 Letter Housman to M. Pollett, 30 January, 1933 in reply to the latter's questionnaire.

117 M.R. James, 1862-1936, OM, English author, medievalist, Provost of King's College, Cambridge and of Eton College, Vice Chancellor Cambridge University, particularly well known for writing ghost stories.

118 Recalled by Sir Brian Young, 'The Queen of Air and Darkness and a Letter on Genesis, *HSJ,* vol.33, 2007, p.97.

Perhaps adequate as nonsense verse – and there is quite a lot where that came from – but he wouldn't have been offered the position of Poet Laureate based on them!

Housman was often urged to bring out another collection after *ASL* but he said that he didn't have enough additional material, and the notebooks confirm that whilst there was worthy material for a further volume, the majority of the quality verse had gone in to compiling *ASL*. He did change his mind in 1920, however, asking Richards how long it would take to publish another volume of poetry.

He then held back, and *LP* wasn't published until 1922. When Richards, as his publisher, broached the subject again a mere three months later, Housman curtly replied, '"My new book" does not exist and possibly never may... What I asked you was a question inspired by an unusually bright and sanguine mood, which has not at present been justified.'[119] Richards claimed that between 1896 when *ASL* was published and 1922 when *LP* came out there was never a week and seldom a day when somebody didn't ask him when it would have a successor.

This delay is perhaps rather odd considering that most of the poetry had already been written. Perhaps it is because he regarded his day job as a Latin Professor as more important. As early as 1903 Housman had said 'I wrote the book [*ASL*] when I was thirty-five, and I expect to write another when I am seventy... My trade is that of Professor of Latin.'[120] The delay, as we shall note, was because each

119 Letter from Housman to Richards, 5 January, 1921.

120 Letter from Housman to Witter Bynner, 3 June, 1903.

subsequent book of poems revealed a little more openly his homosexuality. The last two, with even more implied homosexuality, were only published posthumously.

In fact, Housman published *LP* in his lifetime for the benefit of the dying Jackson and, as he said in the preface to *LP*, by so doing he could also check for any spelling and punctuation mistakes. With a combination of impatience and reproach he told Richards, his publisher, 'It will save the printers trouble if you tell them that they had better not try to improve my spelling and punctuation.'[121]

But despite these endeavours *LP* suffered the inevitable and proverbial problems. 'I find the same set of blunders in punctuation and ordering of lines, some of which I have corrected again and again, and the filthy beasts of printers for ever introduce them anew.' This was written about *ASL* but in the year of publication of *LP* and is one of many similar tirades. Again, specifically in respect of *LP* and after the inevitable mistakes, fewer in number than was initially with *ASL*, Housman wrote, 'Don't put in an errata slip. The blunder will probably enhance the value of the first edition in the eyes of bibliophiles, an idiotic class.'[122]

Richards tried to excuse himself. 'Such things, [printing mistakes] in my experience, happen too often with the books of which one is most proud and in which one most wishes to prevent errors. Malignant fate! I was as the years rolled on justly to be reproached again and again.'[123] There

121 Letter from Housman to Richards, 19 June, 1922.
122 Letter fr. Housman to Richards, 3 October, 1922 and 14 October, 1922.
123 Richards, *Housman,* p.77.

might have been a little more reason, if still no excuse, for the printing errors at the time of the first edition of *ASL* as Richards had only been in business as a publisher for a year.

It is easy to have sympathy for his publisher; Housman's punctuation was often complicated to say the least. There was even a misprint in the Bible reading for his funeral service – not in the verse he had written (plagued therefore to the end, and beyond the grave). To make matters worse there was also one in *The Times* obituary notice!

We will note that Housman didn't want Laurence to illustrate any of his books; when Richards asked about a possible design for the cover of *LP* and suggested one previously considered, but subsequently rejected for *ASL*, Housman wrote, 'I am no judge of this sort of thing, but there is nothing in the design which I much object to, except the portrait of a tramp sucking a stick.'[124] Surely a design considered in 1896 would not be an ideal choice in 1922 with all that had happened in the world generally and in the world of art in particular in the meantime, unless it was to reference *ASL* and thereby in modern parlance capitalise on brand recognition.

There was another occasion when Housman showed his lack of appreciation for Laurence's ability to design book covers. Laurence designed the cover for his own book of poems, *Green Arras*. Many years later Housman wrote to Laurence and recalled a conversation he had with a dinner companion who had said that *ASL* had a pretty cover. This dinner companion did not say that *Green Arras*

124 Letter Housman to Richards, 9 July, 1922.

had, and Housman was quick to stress to Laurence 'nor has it.' However, Housman had been very helpful to Laurence on the contents of the book offering 'kind and caustic' comments.[125]

The initial print run for *LP* was 4,000 – Housman had suggested 10,000 – and most were sold on the day of publication with 21,000 copies sold by the end of 1922. It was reprinted five times before the end of the following year. Housman himself regarded *LP* as a credible collection, writing to the dying Jackson, 'I feel sure it will do you more good than doctors.'[126] Touchingly, Jackson, replying from his hospital bed 'to my dear old Hous' wrote in a weak hand in pencil and Housman painstakingly inked over the letter in order to maintain the wording but also, as suggested in a recent biography, in order to follow the action of his dying Jackson.[127]

LP received encouraging reviews from the outset to complement the equally encouraging sales. *The Bookman* noted that 'if the permanence of poetry be in proportion to the intelligent emotion it evokes, Housman's poetry should certainly endure.'[128] *The Londoner,* along with others, was equally enthusiastic. Richards said 'as much as I loved *A Shropshire Lad* this manuscript seemed to be on the whole, finer, more important work and include poems

125 L. Housman, *The Unexpected Years*, Jonathan Cape, London, 1937, p.162.

126 Letter from Housman to Jackson, November 1922.

127 E. Vincent, *A. E. Housman: Hero of the Hidden Life*, Boydell & Brewer, 2018.

128 W.R. Benêt, 'A.E. Housman's *Last Poems*', *The Bookman*, March 1923, pp.83-85.

of greater beauty and distinction'.[129]

In the introduction to *LP*, Housman reminds us of the emotional price composing poetry exacted from him: 'It is not likely that I shall ever be impelled to write much more. I can no longer expect to be revisited by the continuous excitement under which in the early months of 1895 I wrote the greater part of my other book, nor indeed could I well sustain it...'[130]

Laurence has come in for a lot of criticism for the way he published the unpublished poems as *MP* and *AP* but he had been given a tough remit as Housman's literary executor, and if the litmus test was sales then he did an excellent job. Laurence was keen to publish as many of the remaining poems as possible and as quickly as possible. After *MP* comes *AP* – originally titled *A.E.H. Some Poems, Some Letters and a Personal Memoir by his Brother.*

But there was no excuse for Laurence to allow textual mistakes to creep into the published versions of these later collections, caused by rushing to publish. For instance, *MP* XXXIII – a very fine poem – there are three textual errors, one in the final verse refers to 'an evening wretched in Wales'; it should have been 'on Wales.' That one word spoils the image of the Welsh hills standing out against the crimson sunsets, an instantaneously recognisable part of Housman's poetry. Carelessness in the printed word in one form or another seemed to have plagued both brothers. In the index of *My Diaries* by Wilfred Scawen Blunt, *ASL* is attributed to Laurence!

129 Richards, *Housman,* p.197.

130 A.E. Housman, *Last Poems*, New York, Henry Holt & Co., 1922, p.5.

Housman made it clear to Laurence that he wasn't to publish any poems 'inferior in quality to the average of my published poems'.[131] Laurence struggled to interpret what was of 'minor merit', and it is quite possible with such an instruction to get it wrong, tending to give a poem the benefit of the doubt, admitting to err on the side of leniency when he felt his brother would have erred 'on the side of severity.' Laurence explains his conundrum in his preface to both *MP* and in his biography, *A.E.H. Some poems, some letters and a Personal Memoir by his Brother Laurence Housman.*[132] Housman was really very unhelpful in this respect. Two years before Housman died Laurence asked him to sort out the remaining poems – the 'sheep and the goats' – but there is no evidence that he obliged, and Housman had only crossed out one unfinished unpublished poem in his notebooks, so Laurence understandably assumed that the others could be published. Laurence had asked three Cambridge advisers which poems to publish in the collection which became *MP* but Gow said that any advice was of little use for Laurence went ahead and printed everything, excluding only one.

Laurence wasted no time in getting *MP* published; from the instruction in May 1936, it was a mere five months with a print run of 13,937, which was followed by a second print run of 7500 in November and with similar numbers in America. Some argue that Housman knew that Laurence would make mistakes as his literary executor. Perhaps Housman felt Laurence would do an adequate job and that any lapses of judgement or taste would be laid at Laurence's

131 The will of A.E. Housman dated 19 November 1932.

132 Housman, *A.E.H: Memoir.*

door and any hidden gems unearthed would reflect well on Housman himself. We don't know. Laurence felt it was for a more lofty reason that he was chosen namely to let him know the secret of his life and to give him permission to reveal Housman's homosexuality to a wider audience.

To some, *MP* fails the test Housman set but the bar was high and there are real gems in the book. 'On forelands high in heaven' (*MP* XXXIII) and 'Parta Quies' (*MP* XLVIII), are both first-class, as too is *MP* VIII which starts:

> Give me a land of boughs in leaf,
> A land of trees that stand;
> Where trees are fallen, there is grief;
> I love no leafless land.

And then there is *MP* IX:

> When green buds hang in the elm like dust
> And sprinkle the lime like rain,
> Forth I wander, forth I must,
> And drink of life again.
> Forth I must by hedgerow bowers
> To look at the leaves uncurled,
> And stand in the fields where cuckoo-flowers
> Are lying about the world.

MP XIV is, to me at least, one of his best in any of his collections:

The farms of home lie lost in even,
I see far off the steeple stand;
West and away from here to heaven
Still is the land.

There if I go no girl will greet me,
No comrade hollo from the hill,
No dog run down the yard to meet me:
The land is still.

The land is still by farm and steeple,
And still for me the land may stay:
There I was friends with perished people,
And there lie they.

The line 'no dog run down the yard to meet me' is pure genius – a neat touch.

'Parta Quies' was only published late and in *MP* despite being the first poem of Housman's established work to have been published originally in *Waifs and Strays* in 1881.[133] It is a poem of great quality, noted for its inherent maturity, written poignantly as a tribute to his mother who, as we know, died on his twelfth birthday and written when he was therefore only twenty-two. The opening lines 'good-night; ensured release, imperishable peace', are on his own memorial tablet in Ludlow.

However, the critics were lukewarm. *The Dublin Review* predicted 'The new volume will not supplant, or even accompany, its predecessors in our pockets or our

133 *Waifs and Strays; a Terminal Magazine of Oxford Poetry*, 1881.

affections' but strangely added, 'it contains more beauty and at the same time more sadness than any other poetry of modern times.'[134] *The Observer* said, 'it was not, of course, to be expected that these last poems would enhance a name already great. They are his own rejected.' As with the previous review, *The Observer* couldn't leave it at that; 'if all the chips on the floor of English poetry were of this quality, our wealth would exceed all bounds.' In short, those who were disappointed in *MP* were impressed by some of its quality. In a letter from Jackson to Housman the former added 'the *Morning Post* is about the only other paper to count. The old woman's *D. Telegraph* and the screamingly radical press, with Bosh-writers... don't count.'[135]

Laurence was undeterred. He went on to publish a further collection, known as *Additional Poems* (*AP*) and most of these were also written in those frenzied earlier years but hitherto unpublished. Again, there are gems, fewer still in number, but there, nonetheless. For example, *AP* VI is one of his most famous and poignant – a heartfelt rendering of a suppressed homosexual:

Ask me no more, for fear I should reply;

Also to be found in *AP* is another harrowing verse with an equally appropriate homosexual rendering but beautiful in itself:

134 Neville Watts in *The Dublin Review*.

135 Letter Jackson to Housman, 23 November, 1922.

He would not stay for me; and who can wonder?
He would not stay for me to stand and gaze.
I shook his hand and tore my heart in sunder
And went with half my life about my ways.
(*AP* VII)

No wonder they were published posthumously. Housman wanted them to see the light of day but not while he lived; they were found in a drawer, and he could easily have destroyed them.

Laurence's excuse to publish *AP* was pretty feeble. He said he had consulted others who were mildly against, as he admitted, confessing that he too was not that enthusiastic, yet a mere twelve months later he stated that despite opinion being divided he was going to publish nevertheless and with a clear conscience.

Part of the interest and fascination of these other poems is what Housman wanted to convey via them. What voices, messages about himself, about his homosexuality, his personality generally, did he want ultimately to ensure was left revealed after his death for posterity? Whilst *ASL* is supreme the best of the others are better, or as good as the average in *ASL*. One could only guess what might have happened to these later poems if Laurence had not published them before his own death. Hopefully, but we are not sure, it would have meant only a delayed publication rather than confinement to perpetual obscurity. Finally, Housman stipulated in his literary instructions that the idea of all his poems being published in a single volume was 'a silly notion' but it was soon done.

He might have appointed an unreliable literary midwife in his brother, but Laurence's choice of poems which he included in later collections have over the passing years been vindicated, a difficult task made no easier by Housman himself. At least Laurence guaranteed that there was a little more of the same, or nearly so, which otherwise if only *ASL* and *LP* were published might have constituted too small a legacy for many of us.

5. HIS TECHNIQUE

Turning the routine into the special.

Housman claimed that most of his poetry was composed in a frenzied period of a few months and it is usually argued that the rejected, unrequited love for Jackson was the principal inspiration for this poetic outpouring. In 1922, when Jackson was dying, and so many years after their Oxford days, Jackson provided the stimulus for the publication of *LP.* So Housman was *still* trying to impress Jackson and he was honest enough to write 'you are largely responsible for my writing poetry and you ought to take the consequences.'[136] Jackson never read the letter as he died before its arrival, a sad final twist as Housman had said the essence of poetry is 'to transfuse emotion – not to transmit thought.'[137]

Housman's notebooks, even the edited ones, challenge Housman's comment that most of the poems were composed in a frenzy. Nor did he regard the verse which followed the physical excursion as necessarily the final version. The one we are familiar with might be a redraft. We have commented earlier on what became the final poem of *ASL* which was rewritten 13 times – and on others. Indeed, Housman refers to the 'genesis of the piece which stands last in my first volume. Two of the stanzas... came into my head just as they are printed, while I was crossing the corners of Hampstead Heath between Spaniard's Inn

136 Letter Housman to Jackson, 4 January, 1923.
137 'The Name and Nature of Poetry' lecture.

and the footpath to Temple Fortune. A third stanza came with a little coercing after tea, one more was needed, but it did not come. I had to turn and compose it myself and that was a laborious business. I wrote it thirteen times and it was more than a twelvemonth before I got it right.'[138] As we will note with prose, so with poetry, Housman often struggled to complete the acceptable final format that met his exceptionally high standards. His notebooks more than hint that he was not in fact, and perhaps surprisingly, a naturally fluent writer. Even his second and third drafts can be somewhat laboured.

In the five months of 1895, according to his notebook, he wrote 23 of the verses of *ASL*, but *ASL* in its final version had 63. Admittedly of the 23, 19 were never rewritten so they could be regarded as spontaneous and in their final format from the start. These 23 poems cover the themes associated with Housman: the war-sick soldier, the love-sick youth, portrayals of pastoral beauty, homesickness, the predictable pessimistic end of things.

In the first draft of his Preface to *ASL* Housman said he wrote the 'greater part' in the opening months of 1895. To Withers he revealed that some of the verses were composed in 1886 and that about a third were down in some form on paper before the onset of the 'continuous excitement' which apparently overwhelmed him in early 1895.[139] His notes inform us that some lines started as a standalone or two; for example the germ of 'Along the field as we came by' (*ASL* XXVI) is jotted down in two lines in the

138 'Name and Nature' lecture.

139 Withers, *Buried Life*.

notebook as:

> But she shall lie with earth above,
> And he beside another love.

Or again, in his notebooks we see his constant redrafting:

> And you with colours gay
> And martial music swelling
> Walk the resounding way
> To the still dwelling.

This later became *LP* VII. Then eight years later he wrote 'And both are sighing' as the last line of the penultimate stanza. A further twenty plus years later this stanza with its alterations was eventually published.

We also know that 44 verses in *ASL* were rewritten three times and 18 in *AP* were rewritten twice. Others were slotted into different collections from the one originally intended. 'Her strong enchantments failing' was earmarked to be *ASL* XLIII but was withdrawn at proof stage to become *LP* III. Burns Haber concluded that when all the redrafting is taken into account relatively few came from the pit of the stomach perfectly formed but agreed that most of *ASL* was written in August and September 1895 and that by the end of 1895 'the high tides of inspiration had subsided, and the next few pages are filled with the flotsam of the ebb.'[140] Housman did not destroy these notebooks so he must have been willing for

140 Burns Haber, *Manuscript Poems*.

them to be available in the public domain. He did edit, though, some of what he called his 'foul papers' resulting in some secrets of composition going to his grave, as he must have wished.

Housman stated in his 1892 inaugural lecture at UCL that thinking can be detrimental to contentment: 'The pursuit of truth in some directions is even injurious to happiness, because it compels us to take leave of delusions which were pleasant while they lasted.' We know that he argued, unsuccessfully, against the over-analysing of his own 'spontaneous' poetry.

Housman enjoyed playing with words and with their different meanings. He spent time mastering the style of other poets, both classical and modern, and he was not averse to borrowing from those from whom he had a low opinion such as Tibullus. Tibullus, he said was almost the worst in the world. He was also happy to adapt the techniques of others, to beg, steal and borrow wherever possible and whenever suitable, from Horace to Wordsworth, via Pope.

He raided Wordsworth, about whom he could be quite rude, both as an undergraduate at Cambridge and as a poet, but by so doing he turned a lovely line into something quite exceptional and to many much more memorable: 'The wild green landscape' of Wordsworth becomes 'the wild green woods among' (*LP* XXXII) of Housman.[141] Both are great poets but Wordsworth, unlike Housman, has been constantly in vogue – Housman has never been out of print – yet surely Housman's treatment

141 C. Dexter, 'Housman's Wordsworth', *HSJ*, vol.32, 2006, p.54.

here is the more ethereal and is indisputably poetry; is that so with Wordsworth's rendering? Housman dipped into Wordsworth's *Prelude*. Wordsworth wrote 'the orange sky evening' but Housman metamorphoses it into 'the orange band of eve,' turning the routine into something very, very special. To me, at least, those last two lines are among the loveliest in the English language:

> And silent hills indenting
> The orange band of eve.
>
> (*MP* XXXIII)

On other occasions Housman borrowed a whole line from a poet: 'The queen of air and darkness' (*LP* III), is from Coventry Patmore's 'the powers of darkness and the air'; borrowed but surely bettered?[142] Or did both borrow it from the Bible? In the Bible it is 'the prince of the power of the air' (Ephesians II:2). In 'Hell Gate' Housman draws on Dante, Milton and others.

It was surely Housman's exceptional memory which allowed him to draw on such diverse sources for his poems. Laurence in his autobiography refers to his brother's exceptional memory. He recalls 'I happen to have mentioned the hymn which begins "Son of my Soul," saying that it only formed part of a whole hymn, the first verse of which I was unable to remember. Immediately he quoted it with unhesitating correctness.' Laurence gives another example; Housman didn't care much for Landor and said he had read very little of his work 'yet when I sent

142 Letter from Housman to Geoffrey Wethered, 13 September, 1933.

him a quotation I could not identify, he placed it for me at once in one of the *Imaginary Conversations*'. [143]

Another trick of Housman's was to adapt and distil the classical and the modern, the ordinary with the extraordinary. In *ASL*, the cherry tree, the 'loveliest of trees' (actually not so in his estimation; he told Joan Thomson it was the English pear 'that possibly the blossom of a pear tree has the purest beauty of any of the English fruits'[144]) was 'wearing white for Eastertide.'[145] The cherry tree is a symbol adopted by others as well. The metaphor of snow for white flowers may be a well-known ingredient in Housman's poetry. But Heine, a source for Housman's poetic inspiration, wrote that 'white flakes are falling... as though some forgetful tree discharged a heavy snowdrift | ...it is no snowdrift | ...'Tis an avalanche of petals | Loosed by spring.'[146] Horace, similarly, refers to snow at the beginning of 'Diffugere nives' with 'The snows are fled away.' Tennyson was also inspired by the cherry tree: 'all about the thorn will blow | In tufts of rosy-tinted snow.' And then we have Browning, 'Now comes the story of the white blossoms on her.'[147] The great, mad John Clare used

---

143 L. Housman, *Unexpected Years*, p.384. Walter Savage Landor, 1775-1864, English writer, poet and activist. Best known for his volume of prose *Imaginary Conversations*, imaginary dialogues between the ancients from Greece and Rome.

144 Thomson worked as her father's secretary when he was Master at Trinity, said to have written juvenilia and also books on Russia. She struck up a special, certainly unique for a woman, relationship with Housman, and Housman must have known how highly she regarded him and this was possibly a reason why he opened up to her on many personal matters.

145 Housman was christened on Easter Day.

146 T. Burns Haber, 'Heine and Housman', *JEGP xlii*, (1944), pp. 326-32.

147 'Pippa Passes'.

the symbolism of the cherry tree too.[148] Where Housman seems to be unique is in his rendering of the cherry tree as somehow a melancholy thing. The cherry tree symbolises the value and brevity of beauty, which are two strong and persistent themes in Housman's poetry. Both blossom and snow are transitory, with blossom symbolising youth and spring and snow the end of the year and death.

Another technique was to combine words in ways which could so easily have degenerated into ridicule, but not with Housman.

> The happy highways where I went
> And cannot come again.
>
> (*ASL* XL)

The highway itself cannot be happy but words together create a deeper meaning without the reader laughing or putting the poem down, a clever combination of alliteration and personification. Indeed, this is one of his most quoted poems. Furthermore, Housman could use words in other ways too to great effect, as in *ASL* LIV, 'The lightfoot boys...', 'the rose-lipt girls': all odd but effective, creating emotion coupled with atmosphere.

We referred to his technique of using a word's different meanings. He played with death and dying, but he also liked the word 'wind' or its effects and uses it in at least six different ways to convey human passion, death and desolation, geographical isolation, the indifference of nature and the plight of man:

148 'The Winter's Spring'.

'Tis time, I think, by Wenlock town
The golden broom should blow;
(*ASL* XXXIX)

The golden broom symbolises loss and decay.

In addition, he could make the mundane poetic. I cannot fathom how he does it, why it should work, but it does:

When smoke stood up from Ludlow,
And mist blew off from Teme,
(*ASL* VII)

The second line is a traditional scenario but treated differently; the first line is a routine event, but it works and complements the second.

He can link words that are incompatible and produce poetry that has never been out of print. He can use a concept to link verses like a poetic daisy chain. The sound of church bells floats across his 'western brookland,' a call to prayer, but equally the death knell to a dead girl, the symbol of a lover's grief or the human longing for silence and contemplation. We have already quoted:

The diamond tears adorning
Thy low mound on the lea,
Those are the tears of morning,
That weeps, but not for thee.
(*LP* XXVII)

The poems touched on Housman's friends who were absent; the 'Dead clay that did me kindness' (*LP* XXX); on the lads 'That shepherded the moonlight sheep – A hundred years ago' (*ASL* IX); on the Roman, no more than 'ashes under Uricon' (*ASL* XXXI). Some are even more distant; 'Unborn and unbegot' who will read him 'when they're in trouble – And I am not' (*MP* un-numbered).

His poetry – and also his prose – flows effortlessly, the envy of many, but in order to produce such divine and fulfilling touches of the pen Housman had to endure, more frequently than some assume, the hard grind which is the lot of mere mortals.

6. ON POETRY

'Poetry is to harmonise the sadness of the universe.'

On 9th May 1933 Housman gave the Leslie Stephen lecture – 'The Name and Nature of Poetry'. He was 75 years old. This showed a more emotional Housman than the one locked away during the previous years. One eyewitness recalls, 'you could have heard a pin drop.' Another said, 'I heard that lecture. It was moving beyond belief,' adding, 'And I lived on the next staircase but never spoke.'[149] Interestingly, Housman was able to convey emotion in a semi-public lecture on poetry and hold his audience in a way that he didn't manage, as we shall see, when lecturing on classics, where he achieved the respect and silence of the lecture room through a combination of fear of interrupting and the intellectual intensity of the subject matter.

He wasn't the first poet to attempt an analysis of the name and nature of poetry. Wordsworth gave it a pretty good go in his Preface to the *Lyrical Ballads*, Coleridge in his *Biographia Literaria* and Shelley in his *Defence of Poetry*. T. S. Eliot did the same in his Clark lectures in 1926 and earlier still in his *The Sacred Wood: Essays on Poetry and Criticism* in 1920.

Housman wanted to keep intellect out of poetry, a hard act in his case – 'to set up in the reader's sense a vibration corresponding to what was felt by the writer'; 'Poetry is not the thing said but a way of saying it'; 'Poetry's aim

149 Young, 'Queen of Air', p.99.

and nature was one of communication, not of thought but of emotion'; Poetry is 'to harmonise the sadness of the universe.'[150] He could have added that poetry for him was also a means of escape, emotional outpourings behind the comfort of the mask of the Shropshire Lad and that of the narrators. Laurence said that his brother had invented this '"fig-leaf" of a fictitious character, which he pretended was not his own' and 'Alfred was able to let himself go.'[151]

As noted, Housman didn't spare eighteenth century poets, referring to most of their efforts as pseudo-poetic diction and 'A deadening of language which deadened perception.' In the eighteenth century 'man ceased to live from the depths of his nature; he occupied himself for choice with the thoughts which do not range beyond the sphere of understanding.' Much of their effort was little more than 'sham poetry, a counterfeit deliberately manufactured and offered as a substitution.'[152]

He spared only four eighteenth century poets: Collins, Smart, Cowper and Blake. What those four had in common was their greater or lesser degree of insanity. Housman added that both Collins and Cowper saw 'the inside of madhouses. [They] are not supposed to have written any of their poetry there; and Blake was never mad enough to be locked up.'[153] Plato concluded that all poets are mad

150 'The Name and Nature of Poetry' lecture.

151 Graves, *Scholar-Poet,* p.67.

152 'The Name and Nature of Poetry'.

153 Point made by Colin Dexter in his Housman lecture 2004. William Collins, 1721-1759, English poet, confined to a madhouse in Chelsea in 1754. Christopher Smart, 1722-1771, English poet, High-Church Anglican, a friend of influential cultural icons such as Samuel Johnson and Henry

and, of course, Housman would have known his Plato. Even Pope was not spared: 'that Pope was a poet is true; but it is one of those truths which are beloved of liars, because they serve so well the cause of falsehood.'[154]

Does it matter if a poet happens to be mad? John Clare was, ending his life in an asylum; he thought he could almost talk to birds, animals and plants as he roamed the English countryside before the enclosures largely put a stop to it. His poetry is of the highest rank, although Housman deleted all three of Clare's poems in Palgrave's *Golden Treasury*, including the very special one which has the line 'I am! Yet what I am who cares or knows!' No wonder Colin Dexter had a high opinion of Housman's poetry but a low opinion of Housman's assessment of other poets.

Housman continued, his audience in silence: 'If what you want to do is state an idea do it in prose.' He then analysed the difference between prose and poetry. Poetry is to 'transfuse emotion' – transfuse the feeling the poet had when the poetry suddenly emerged within him.

Fielding, who often wrote under the pseudonym Mrs Mary Midnight: locked away in a mental asylum by his father-in-law. William Cowper, 1731-1800, English poet and hymn writer, one of the most popular poets of his time, one of the forerunners of Romantic Poetry. Sent to an asylum in St Albans in a period of depression and insanity, but later recovered through his Evangelical Christianity. Wrote many hymns including *Amazing Grace*. William Blake, 1757-1827, poet, painter and printmaker, seminal figure in the history of poetry, mainly posthumous recognition. Often mistakenly said that Blake wrote the words to 'Jerusalem'; the song's text is taken from his long poem 'Jerusalem'. Less evidence of genuine madness than with the others quoted by Housman but he was certainly misunderstood by contemporaries.

154 'The Name and Nature of Poetry' lecture.

Coleridge said the same: 'poetry gives most pleasure when only generally and not perfectly understood.' Eliot talked of translating ideas into sensations.

We noted also that Housman had said that poetry was more physical than intellectual and that he could recognise it by the symptoms which were provoked in him. It was more a natural rather than a manufactured process. 'Experience has taught me when I am shaving of a morning to keep watch over my thoughts because, if a line of poetry strays into my memory, my skin bristles so that the razor ceases to act. [...] The particular symptom is accompanied by a shiver down the spine...'.[155] Wordsworth said something similar: 'all good poetry is the spontaneous overflow of powerful feelings', adding 'there would flow into my mind, with sudden and unaccountable emotion a line or two of verse, or a whole stanza', describing poetry also as 'emotion recollected in tranquillity.'[156] Coleridge felt the same: 'a more than usual state of emotion, with more than usual order,' referring to the need to let go so that he might be the reciprocal of the original lines.[157] Emily Dickinson touched on poetry and emotion not from the perspective of composition, but from reading, when she said that poetry 'should take the top of your head off'.[158]

It is not only the exclusive preserve of poetry where sudden emotional impulses are felt. It is a feeling noted and shared in other art forms. Leigh Hunt's 'the flowers of any

155 Burnett, *Letters*.

156 Preface to his *Lyrical Ballads,* 1802.

157 Samuel Taylor Coleridge, *Biographia Literaria*.

158 Emily Dickinson, 1830-1886, prolific American poet. The Housman Lecture, Hay Festival, 2009.

kind of experience, rooted in truth, and issuing forth in beauty' and Ruskin's 'the suggestion, by the imagination, of noble grounds for the noble emotions' are of the same persuasion but referring to different art forms.[159]

Housman knew that some poets had to defend their poetry from accusations of being prose. He thought the debate was better defined not as poetry versus prose, but as poetic verses compared to non-poetic. He never tried in the lecture to distinguish between what he regarded as good and bad poetry, adding 'I could no more define poetry than a terrier can define a rat, but that I thought we both recognised the object by the symptoms which it provokes in us.' Housman sat down.

He had just been responsible for producing one of the seismic literary events. The impression, the furore produced was instant and lasting. Initially he was rather proud of his achievement, writing to Laurence, 'success here has taken me aback' adding 'the leader of our doctrinaire teachers of youth [F. R. Leavis] is reported to say that it will take more than 12 years to undo the harm I have done in an hour.'[160] Leavis did not, however, criticise Housman directly but rather via his own literary journal *Scrutiny.*[161] The lecture received mixed reviews in the US, ranging from 'disappointing' to 'there is no better survey

---

159 A. Burnett, 'The Housman Lecture', *HSJ*, vol. 33, 2007, pp.8-9.
160 Quoted in G. Watson, *Never One's for Theory: England and the War of Ideas*, James Clarke & Co. Ltd., 2000. As a family we are familiar with the effect of being at the receiving end of literary criticism from Leavis; when Leavis was provoked he was devastating. When my wife's uncle, C.P. Snow, delivered his lecture 'The Two Cultures', Leavis was venomous.
161 *Scrutiny: A Quarterly Review.*

of what has been wrong with poetry for some eight or more years...'; of course dividing opinion is a typical reaction in the case of Housman.[162]

Housman had to defend some of his views: 'I did not say that poetry was better for having no meaning, only that it can best be detected so.' Again, nothing especially original here; Coleridge neatly wrote, 'Prose = words in their best order; poetry = best words in the best order.'[163] A good example of Coleridge's statement is found in his own poetry:

> For he on honey-dew hath fed
> And drunk the milk of Paradise.
> ('Kubla Khan')

To get the very best out of these strange lines of poetry depends on how it is said rather than what is said; honey-dew is a sugar secretion from plant lice.

In time, Housman regretted giving the lecture or accepting the original invitation, referring to it as 'that infernal lecture' even before delivering it.[164] In a letter to H. E. Butler, Professor of Latin at UCL, he wrote, 'I am not proud of this, which I wrote against my will, and am not sending copies outside the family.'[165] When Richards asked him to sign a copy he replied, 'I'm damned if I will. I

162 *The Saturday Review of Literature.*

163 Henry N Coleridge (ed.), *Specimens of the small oak Table talk of Samuel Taylor Coleridge*, London, 1835, vol.1, p.76.

164 Letter Housman to Richards, 28 March, 1933.

165 A.S. Roberts, *Adventures with Authors*, Cambridge, Cambridge University Press, 1966.

don't like the lecture. I was over-persuaded into writing it. I wrote every line against my will. I shall inscribe no copy to anyone.' He even said the lecture was 'rhetorical and not wholly sincere' and that having taken an emotional toll on him, 'the painful episode is closed.'[166] Sir Frank Kermode said of the lecture, 'For so reticent a man it was a surprising performance. It possibly upset his health and he came to regard [its] date, May 1933 as an ominous moment in his life.'[167]

In a way it is extraordinary that he delivered the lecture in the first place. According to a faculty teacher, Basil Willey, by then 'old literary luminaries were sinking below the horizon, and others rising into the sky.'[168] It is a little surprising, therefore, that the ageing Housman was even invited. It is remarkable that he accepted. Earlier that year he had declined to write an essay for Laurence on the poet Coventry Patmore saying that the endeavour 'would give me more trouble than you can imagine, whereas I want peace in my declining years; and the result would not be good enough to yield one pride of satisfaction.'[169]

Ezra Pound did not mince his words saying the lecture was full of bathos, was ambiguous and, for good measure, accused Housman of word twisting.[170] T.S Eliot

---

166 Letter Housman to Laurence, 24 May, 1933.

167 *London Review of Books,* 2007.

168 Basil Willey, *Cambridge and other Memories 1920–1953*, London, Chatto & Windus, New York, Norton, 1970.

169 Graves, *Scholar Poet,* p.235.

170 Ezra Weston Loomis Pound, 1885 -1972, expat American poet, critic in the early modernist poetry movement, fascist collaborator in the Second World War.

was kinder: 'Mr. Housman's quotations, in this lecture, show about as much sensitive and refined a perception as any human being can aspire to. But in this way, is he quite fair to Dryden?'[171] By 1933 Eliot represented the contemporary poetic scene; Housman did not. Eliot in a kind but academically truthful way complimented the lecture where he was in agreement and politely expressed reservations where he was not. Eliot, in *The use of Poetry and the Use of Criticism* reflected that 'criticism, of course, never does find out what poetry is, in the sense of arriving at an adequate definition; but I do not know of what use such a definition would be if it were found.'[172] I think Housman might have settled for that and turned the page on an awkward saga.

171 T.S Eliot in *The Criterion*, October 1933.
172 T.S Eliot, 'The Use of Poetry and Use of Criticism: Studies in the Relation of Criticism to Poetry in England', *The Charles Eliot Norton Lectures*, Harvard University Press, 1933.

7. THE POEMS' NARRATORS

'Who in despair laments the futility
of their general lot.'

Housman grants a central role to narrators in his poems. There are a number of them and they constitute an eclectic group – a tone of sadness, some possessing wisdom, others overwhelmed by the transience of this world, and others affected by love, youth and the inevitability of death.

Some are resigned to death. In 'On the idle hill of summer' (*ASL* XXXV) the narrator resigns himself to death in war simply because he was born. 'Woman bore me, I will rise.' Other narrators cannot differentiate between illusion and reality:

Good creatures, do you love your lives
And have you ears for sense?
Here is a knife like other knives,
That cost me eighteen pence.

I need but stick it in my heart
And down will come the sky,
And earth's foundations will depart
And all you folk will die.

(*MP* XXVI)

The narrator in the 'loveliest of trees' is determined to enjoy life to the full because he believes that time is running out. Even, therefore, in one of his most beautiful and powerful poems there is a melancholy vein running through it:

> Loveliest of trees, the cherry now
> Is hung with bloom along the bough,
> And stands about the woodland ride
> Wearing white for Eastertide.
>
> Now, of my threescore years and ten,
> Twenty will not come again,
> And take from seventy springs a score,
> It only leaves me fifty more.
>
> And since to look at things in bloom
> Fifty springs are little room,
> About the woodlands I will go
> To see the cherry hung with snow.
>
> (*ASL* II)

Some narrators are killers whose punishment gives Housman scope to incorporate concepts of death. Others offer no specific reason for their actions: 'Farewell to barn and stack and tree' (*ASL* VII) offers no reason whatsoever for the narrator murdering his brother, Maurice.

Others behave very oddly. In 'The True Lover' (*ASL* LIII), we get a thin justification for his behaviour. He kills himself because his lover should have felt his heart beating for her. Many are dreamers:

There, when hueless is the west
And the darkness hushes wide,
Where the lad lies down to rest
Stands the troubled dream beside.

(*ASL* LV)

When the eye of day is shut,
And the stars deny their beams,
And about the forest hut
Blows the roaring wood of dreams.

(*LP* XXXIII)

He has another go via a dreaming narrator in:

My dreams are of a field afar
And blood and smoke and shot.
There in their graves my comrades are,
In my grave I am not.

(*MP* XXXIX)

A few of the narrators seem to display a two-sided personality, for instance in *ASL* XXVIII 'The Welsh Marches'. This is a lovely poem, and the antics of the narrator need not detract from the apparently simple, almost catchy, tone of this well-known verse, which starts with the lines:

High the vanes of Shrewsbury gleam
Islanded in Severn stream;
The bridges from the steepled crest

Cross the water east and west.
(*ASL* XXVIII)

But the narrator in a later stanza relates:

Here the truceless armies yet
Trample, rolled in blood and sweat;
They kill and kill and never die;
And I think that each is I.

On another occasion, the narrator has a conversation with himself:

– I waste my time in talking,
No heed at all takes he,
My kind and foolish comrade
That breathes all night for me.
(*MP* XIII)

The narrator of *AP* XII 'An Epitaph', despite some ambiguity is almost certainly mad:

Stay, if you list, O passer by the way;
Yet night approaches; better not to stay.
I never sigh, nor flush, not knit the brow,
Nor grieve to think how ill God made me, now.
Here, with one balm for many fevers found,
Whole of an ancient evil, I sleep sound.

We have narrators, therefore, who are in despair, who lament the futility of their lot especially in respect of death. Those that are deranged fortunately seem only to harm themselves. In the case of 'Hell Gate' (*LP* XXXI) – a challenging poem – even Housman agreed that the narrator was 'on the edge of the absurd.'[173] There are indeed some rather strange reflections here. In the first we have:

> And my dark conductor broke
> Silence at my side and spoke,
> Saying, 'You conjecture well:
> Yonder is the gate of hell.'

In the second verse we have:

> And again the sombre guide
> Knew my question, and replied:
> 'At hell gate the damned in turn
> Pace for sentinel and burn.'

In each verse – there are seven, making this one of Housman's longest poems – we are treated to similar reflections. Even Housman confessed that he struggled with this poem: 'About "Hell Gate" my troubles were, first that the whole thing is on the edge of the absurd: if it does not topple over, that is well so far. Secondly, ... the texture of the diction, especially in the parts I had to

173 Housman draws on other great poets, including Dante and Milton, and details the story of hell's destruction.

compose, is not what it should be.'[174]

Sometimes the narrator is in the first person giving advice – he watches the 'beacons burn' in 1887 (*ASL* I), advises the recruit to 'leave your home behind, lad' (*ASL* III) and go off and fight, returning, hopefully, as a hero. Although Housman said *ASL* was hardly autobiographical, Laurence thought the narrator in *ASL* was his brother and that the poems enabled Housman to speak through the narrator and thereby remove his natural inhibitions.

The role of narrator doesn't appear central in the works of most poets, but it does with Housman – and yet the narrator's role is usually passed over or touched on only briefly when analysing Housman's work and poems. The narrator after all is partly Housman speaking, the poet breathing life into his stanzas in the very special way in which he chooses. To ignore the narrator is to interpret the poems at one level removed. However, to over-indulge and over-analyse their roles is to become distracted. We are reminded that Housman's poetry resonated equally with the lad attending Ludlow Fair as it did with the academic in a Cambridge college. It is a matter to each according to his needs, merely two sides of the same coin.

174 Letter to J.W. Mackail who also helped Housman in his choice of poems for *LP*.

8. POEMS PUT TO MUSIC

'He hoped I'd never set any of his poems'

Housman's poetry with its quality, its brevity, clarity, and emotiveness, has inspired some beautiful musical renderings from his greatest of contemporary composers. There are almost 400 musical settings to his poetry.[175] Butterworth, and in particular his exquisite treatment of 'Loveliest of Trees' from his *Six Songs from A Shropshire Lad*, composed in 1911, remain especially popular.[176] Gurney is also regularly performed, as is, in particular Vaughan Williams' *On Wenlock Edge*.[177]

Sir Arthur Somervell's cycle of ten songs, *A Shropshire Lad*, was published in 1904 and these are the earliest surviving musical renderings of Housman's poems. They were rather quaintly referred to in *The Musical Times* as depicting 'memorable incidents, in the career of a lad who starts life in a village and ultimately becomes a soldier'.[178]

In general Housman was ambivalent about whether his poetry should be put to music. Withers recalls the occasion when Housman was a visitor and he put on a new recording of a composition by Vaughan Williams. It

175 An impressive number but not unique by any means; de la Mare had over 500, Yeats over 350, Hardy 300 plus, but Housman's poems are probably sung more than the others in the concert halls today.
176 George Butterworth, 1885-1916, many rate his potential so highly that, had he lived, he might have been compared to Elgar.
177 Ivor Gurney, 1890-1937, English poet and composer particularly of songs. He suffered from depression caused by his experience in the First World War and spent his last fifteen years in psychiatric hospitals.
178 *The Musical Times*, xlvi. 1905, p.188.

proved a big mistake... '[Housman's] reaction was so violent that my wife, who was sitting near him, was momentarily expecting him to spring from his chair and rush headlong out of the room...'.[179] This was strange behaviour in more ways than one. Housman claimed that, 'I never hear the music, so I do not suffer.'[180]

He tolerated composers attempting to set his poems to music – even saying that it was one way of achieving immortality – but he objected to the poems being printed in the programme. Graham Peel, a popular composer at the time, composed over 100 accompaniments to Housman's poetry – 'in summer time on Bredon' is the only setting of his still played. Its success is due not to the unhappy lot of the lovers on Bredon Hill but rather to his capturing of the hill itself, of the 'coloured counties' and of the distant towers and spires – and, of course, the bells! Peel rated the efforts of Vaughan Williams the most highly: 'Here, in a haze of muted strings, in blurred piano chords, in the chill of open fifths on the violins, was the remote hillside, familiar yet unattainable, the wind blowing through the grasses, the snow lying so still at Christmas, the vague, forlorn sound of bells from the plain below.'[181] Housman did not agree.

Another composer who had success but who is now largely forgotten was Muriel Herbert, who also wrote musical and song settings for other poets including

179 Withers, *Buried Life.*

180 Housman to Richards, 2 July, 1914.

181 G.Tree, 'A. E. Housman As Lyricist?', *HSJ,* vol. 8, 1982, pp. 16-23.

Herrick, Browning, Bridges and Christina Rossetti.[182] Herbert's relative success, albeit transitory, was due partly to her balance between straightforward melody and an accompaniment – a sensitive musical interpretation of the stanzas.

Would-be composers were tempted – like bees to nectar – by the distinct, evocative rural nature, the pastoral innocence and doomed youth which permeate the poems. The rural idyll was being rediscovered at the time, mainly in the immediate inter-war years and the very names given by the composers for their pieces are a constant reminder: Vaughan Williams and his *Norfolk Rhapsody, In the Fen Country* and the *Lark Ascending*; Butterworth with his *Banks of Green Willow* and the *English Idylls*. Vaughan Williams, however, also wrote some of his most memorable Housman accompaniments pre-war; his cycle *On Wenlock Edge* was first performed in 1909. Oddly, neither Elgar, Holst nor Delius, a trio of the other great contemporary

182 Muriel Herbert, 1897-1984, British composer, mainly for solo voice and piano. Robert Herrick, 1591-1674, English lyric poet and cleric, best known for *Hesperides,* a book of poems. He penned such immortal lines as 'gather ye rosebuds while ye may.' Robert Browning, 1812-1899, English poet and playwright whose dramatic monologues made him one of the foremost Victorian poets. Noted for his irony, characterisations, dark humour, social commentary, historical settings and challenging vocabulary and syntax. Married the poet Elizabeth Barrett. Robert Bridges, 1844-1930, OM, Poet Laureate 1913-1930, achieved literary fame late in life, his poems reflecting a deep Christian faith, author of well-known hymns, including 'Jesu, Joy of Man's Desiring'. His poems set to music by Holst and Parry amongst others. Christina Rossetti, 1830-1894, English poet wrote mainly devotional and children's poems, including the popular carol 'In The Bleak Midwinter'.

English composers, attempted Housman – especially odd in the case of Elgar who wrote that the English landscape, and the Malvern Hills in particular, adjacent to those of Shropshire, were often his inspiration. It was, for instance, so integral to the composition of his *Cello Concerto* that he said, 'if its melodies ever seemed to float across the hills don't be frightened – it's only me.'[183] The discovery of the English rural idyll in the inter-war years was partly due to the easier access to the countryside as a result of the increase in car ownership and to the successful campaign of the right to roam. Also, English folk music, collected by Cecil Sharp – and just in time – added further to this rediscovery of the English countryside.[184] Vaughan Williams made full use of these almost forgotten pieces which could so easily have been lost; he was influenced by Sharp who in turn influenced Butterworth.

Others were attracted to Housman's poems because of their expression of human suffering. Ivor Gurney, who served in the trenches and was gassed at Passchendaele was one such, but he fell foul of Housman.He wrote to Housman asking permission to set some of his poems, writing on Gloucester Cathedral notepaper. Housman replied, 'Mr. I. B. Gurney (who resides in Gloucester Cathedral along with St Peter and Almighty God) must NOT print.'[185] But in the same letter he allowed him to

183 Quoted in P. Waine and O. Hilliam, *22 Ideas That Saved the English Countryside*, Frances Lincoln, 2016, p.115.
184 Cecil James Sharp, 1859-1924, founding father of the folksong revival in England. He gathered thousands of tunes both from rural England and the USA and wrote an influential work *English Folk Song*.
185 Letter Housman to Richards, May 16, 1908.

attempt composition. Gurney, however, was aware of the inherent obstacles of setting Housman's poetry to music. Writing in 1917, he said, 'I feel rather incapable of setting them. Such precise and measured verses are too easy to set [and] do not give the scope that [Robert] Bridges' songs offer one.'[186] Gurney was being very clever and astute. He was equally competent as a poet as he was as a composer, but even that didn't endear him to Housman. Within two years of writing his cycle in 1919, he was admitted to the City of London Mental Hospital. Gurney had had a nervous breakdown as a result of his horrific wartime experiences, writing suicide notes to friends shortly before starting to compose *Ludlow and Teme* in 1919.

Another composer who fell foul of Housman was Frank Lambert, who, in asking permission spelt Housman's name incorrectly; 'The conditions on which Mr Lambert may print my words to his music is that he should spell my name correctly.'[187] Among the lesser known largely contemporary composers who attempted composition was C. W. Orr (24 poems in all between 1921 and 1925).[188] Each composer's setting adds a different dimension. Gurney's setting of 'Far in a western brookland' (1919) from his *Ludlow and Teme* has the sighing poplars and glimmering weirs and Orr's 'Along the field' (1927) captures the whispering aspen.

On one occasion a would-be composer wrote asking

186 Ivor Gurney in R.K.R. Thornton (ed.), *Collected Letters*, Carcanet, 1991.

187 Letter Housman to Richards, 11 November, 1909.

188 C.W. Orr, 1893-1976, English composer, Delius became his mentor, mainly composition of songs accompanied by the piano.

permission and Housman responded, 'The applicant may publish the songs as far as I am concerned, but I had rather that you should tell her so, as I do not want to write letters to a lady whose name is Birdie!'[189]

Commenting on a programme of English songs given in 1938, one music critic wrote that part of the programme was 'a series of "Shropshire Lad" lyrics set by Ivor Gurney, Vaughan Williams, John Ireland, George Butterworth and Arthur Sommervell. Housman did a tremendous service to English composers when he wrote those wayward, passionate, disturbing lyrics... I am tempted to think that the Housman lyrics, except for Vaughan Williams' *On Wenlock Edge*, are more effective when sung by a baritone. The darker voice suits the dark melancholy of the verses.'[190]

Only six of the 63 poems in *ASL* have not been set to music at least once, and often many times with 'Loveliest of Trees' perhaps the most popular overall; 12 out of 41 in *LP*, 31 out of 48 in *MP* and 14 out of 27 in *AP*. Why fewer attempts in the latter collections when there are some equally tempting morsels? For instance, neither 'Because I liked you better' (*MP* XXXI) nor 'Ask me no more, for fear I should reply' (*AP* VI) has ever been attempted. It is not difficult to see why the six from *ASL* that have not been given a musical rendering were excluded even by the unwary composer. For instance, XXVIII, 'The Welsh Marches', is about battles and skirmishes; XLI is about an

189 Letter Housman to Richards, 1 March, 1905.

190 Stephen Williams, Music critic *Evening Standard,* 17 June 1938. John Ireland, 1879-1962, English composer and teacher of music, known principally for piano miniatures and for songs with piano.

encounter with a Grecian statue and XLIII ends with the lover cutting his throat!

There was a clear divide between the music composed pre-1914 by Butterworth and others and the inter-war years in which the gassed Gurney composed. The Second World War stopped the process in its tracks and Housman's poems would only thereafter attract a trickle of composers, including, though, one of the most eminent, Tippett.

More recently still both jazz and folk treatments have been tried, especially in the 1980s – the folk singer Dave Weller, 'Is me [sic] team a-ploughing' and jazz musician John Dankworth, 'When I was one-and-twenty.' There were even blues inflections sung by Cleo Laine and 13 settings by folk musician Michael Raven, sung by Joan Mills in the 1990s.

When the composer Herbert Howells sat beside Housman at High Table he recorded, 'I knew of his reputation as the most renowned Latinist in Cambridge and also as one of the most feared men in Cambridge. After regaling us for the first half of the meal with a lecture on suicide, he turned to me, knowing I was a composer, and said he hoped I'd never set any of his poems. I said I hadn't, although only that week I'd set 'Far in a Western Brookland.' There followed a vituperative dismissal of all that Vaughan Williams and Butterworth had done for all his verse in 'On Wenlock Edge' and the 'Shropshire Lad' songs and orchestral rhapsody which I did have the courage to counter; but resolved that Housman should never see any of my settings during his lifetime, and later

I destroyed them.'[191]

Housman was on the lookout for composers changing his poems. We have noted how possessive he was about his poems – no publisher should dare suggest any changes and no verse from *ASL* should be included in anthologies – but also over how and when they could be published. In a letter to Richards referring to Vaughan Williams, Housman laments, 'I am told that composers have in some cases mutilated my poems – that Vaughan Williams cut two verses out of 'Is my team ploughing'. I wonder how he would like it if I cut two bars out of his music.'[192] Vaughan Williams couldn't have picked a worse poem to make the cut: 'Is my team ploughing' was Housman's own favourite – as it was incidentally Hardy's.

Vaughan Williams defended himself; the composer has 'a perfect right artistically' to set any piece he likes as long as he doesn't render a different meaning, adding in the case of Housman that 'a poet should be grateful to anyone who fails to perpetuate such lines as':

> The goal stands up, the keeper
> Stands up to keep the goal.[193]
> (*ASL* XXVII)

Housman did not spare illustrators in his criticism either:

191 Herbert Howells, 1892-1983, CH, English composer, organist and teacher, most famous for his large output of Anglian Church music. C. Palmer, *Herbert Howells: A Centenary Celebration,* Thames & Hudson, 1992, p. 16.

192 Letter Housman to Richards, 20 December, 1920.

193 Richards, *Housman*, p.221.

'Neither illustrators nor composers care two pence about words and generally don't understand them.'[194] They are 'completely wrapped up in their own art and selves, and regard the author merely as a peg to hang things on, but that they seem to have less than the ordinary human allowance of sense and feeling.'[195]

Even when Housman allowed his poems to be put to music he stipulated, with a single exception, that the poem should not be printed in the accompanying programme – the one exception being, perhaps surprisingly, in the case of Vaughan Williams. But so exceptional was the dispensation that Housman felt compelled to write to Richards: 'As Mr. Vaughan Williams... came to see me and made representations and entreaties, so that I said he might print the verse he wanted on his programme. I mention this lest his action should come to your ears and cause you to set the police after him.'[196]

Despite the awkward, slightly cantankerous attitude towards composers, and contrary to what some say – and even Housman himself – Housman did have a musical ear, a point made by his sister. Housman said that on the previous three times he visited a music hall he found the music harrowingly dull and wondered whether the halls were deteriorating or his musical standards were rising. 'My taste in music is rather vulgar', Housman said to Withers. Or was it that, as Withers said, he might have had a musical ear, as Kate also implied, but that he had

194 Burnett, *Letters,* Vol.2, pp.68-69, letter dated 6 May, 1928.

195 Letter Housman to Richards, 20 December 1920.

196 Letter Housman to Richards, 11 November 1909.

little musical feeling.

The final analysis is that Housman has been treated well by composers, even if he did not always see it that way. Perhaps his attitude, on occasion, can be explained by his wish to defend the integrity of the text, to warn would-be composers that the material wasn't as appetizing as it might appear and that on no account should a composer change a word or reposition a line of his original, whether thereby changing the meaning or not.

9. AS A CLASSICIST

'A vague legend attached to a man.'

'The one was the scholar as all the world knows; the other a countryman all his days.'[197] Being a classicist was what Housman called his 'day job.' He referred on more than one occasion to what he regarded as his true priorities. In the Leslie Stephen lecture he concluded by saying, 'I shall go back with relief and thankfulness to my proper job.'[198]

Today we tend rather to skim over this aspect of his life, perhaps understandably at a time when the study of classics is so rarely pursued. The only part of Housman's life where there is almost complete consensus, though, is that he was a pre-eminent classicist, perhaps the greatest we have produced, and it was as a classicist Housman claims, with reasonable conviction, that he wanted to be remembered. When Gow was told by R.S. Woods that J.J. Thomson, the Master of Trinity, had said that Housman was the greatest Latin scholar in the world, Gow asked 'who said that?' 'The Master,' responded Woods. Gow replied that Thomson was only a physicist but that, 'I, who *am* a Classicist, can tell you that he is perfectly right!'[199] Garrod said that Housman told him that 'he thinks more highly of scholarship than of poetry, that he prefers to be immortal along that line' and that 'it is not often that a man

197Appreciation by Kidd in *The Times* at the time of Housman's death.
198 'The Name and Nature of Poetry' concluding comment.
199 R.S. Woods, 1891-1986, GP and Olympic athlete.

may sit and choose which of two immortalities he will.'[200] Auden as a poet could be cutting and rude about Housman the poet but he nonetheless acknowledged his classical reputation even though he wasn't himself a classicist – and he expressed that admiration, being a poet, in a poem:

> No one, not even Cambridge was to blame
> (Blame if you like the human situation):
> Heart-injured in North London, he became
> The Latin Scholar of his generation. [201]

We will not analyse the merits nor the techniques of Housman's classical prowess. Few today would be interested and fewer still qualified to do so. We will concentrate instead largely on seeing how the classics influenced Housman's poetry and what it tells us about his character. It was the classics which contributed to the insightful richness of his poems, poems which straddle the ancient and modern worlds, uniting the best to reflect on the constants of human nature.

Housman might have wished to be remembered as a classicist but it is as a poet that his reputation lies today, even if Housman the classicist has woven the classics into his poetry with an intricate thread. Classical words and phrases adorn the poems: 'threshold', 'the laurels', 'fleet foot' and 'low linted'. In *ASL* XIX, 'To An Athlete Dying

200 H.W. Garrod, 'The Profession of Poetry and other Lectures', Oxford, 1929, pp.211-224.

201 Quoted by Adrian Poole and Angela Leighton (ed.), *Trinity Poets: An Anthology of Poems by members of Trinity College*, Carcanet, 2017.

Young', Housman writes about a young victorious athlete carried shoulder high, his body in a coffin, removed from this world, 'where glory does not stay', destined, in turn, for Elysian fields where glory is everlasting. *ASL* LVI, which he named 'The Day of Battle', is a straight take on a speech by Sarpedon in Homer's *Iliad,* although it doesn't seem to add much to the poem itself. When asked about this, Housman merely shrugged his shoulders. In the Latin dedication in *Manilius* to Jackson, Housman alludes to Ovid's exile poetry, suggesting the deep hurt he felt from his separation from Jackson; it translates as, 'To my comrade M.J. Jackson, who cares nothing for these writings.'[202]

One of the common conceptual figures in classical literature is the dreamer. Housman makes use of the dreamer in the guise of his poetic speakers; it is a way of allowing a deceptively simple poem to engage with an extra ingredient, an insight into the basic issues of life and truth, of appearance and reality:

> When shall this slough of sense be cast,
> The dust of thoughts be laid at last,
> The man of flesh and soul be slain
> And the man of bone remain.
>
> (*ASL* XLIII, 'The Immortal Part')

And again:

202 Preface to A.E. Housman (ed.), *M. Manilii Astronomicon Liber Primus,* London, 1903.

This tongue that talks, these lungs that shout,
These thews that hustle us about,
This brain that fills the skull with schemes,
And its humming hive of dreams, –

The influence of Cicero, Horace, Propertius and Ovid on his poetry is both real and frequent.

Moses Jackson's grandson wrote that Housman had an unmatched ability to analyse classical verse, to focus on each and every line and aspect, to glean the true meaning and to present his textual investigative efforts in a logical and clear way.

Housman, as a classicist, was one of the greatest of all time. His classical technique and criticism drew the admiration of fellow classical scholars and created awe amongst his students. On occasion, however, it also drew other responses. A review of Housman's *Lucan* evoked a mixed response from Eduard Fraenkel: 'the editor tickles and teases his reader with a vengeance; at times it looks as if his very object were to make [the reader] lose patience' but 'beneath the mummery of an often madcap wantonness, an astonishing achievement of scholarly criticism is achieved.[203] Fraenkel later added 'although we Germans know Housman to be a rabid Germanophobe, we nevertheless pronounce him to be the greatest living authority in both Latin and Greek in the English-speaking

203 Eduard Fraenkel, 1888-1970, German-British philogist. Professor of Latin, Corpus Christie College, Oxford, *Classical Review* vol.40, 1926, p.146. Housman gave Fraenkel a positive reference for the Oxford Professorship, hoping he would be appointed because he wanted Fraenkel to succeed him at Cambridge. *Classical Review* vol.41, p.83.

world.' Housman had died a few days before this letter was published in *The Times* on 5th May 1936.

Housman had his fan club, not least Enoch Powell and, whatever one might think of Powell's subsequent political career, he was a first class classicist himself. At the end of his second term at Cambridge, Powell said, 'At his feet, I wrote greatly daring, to offer him a conjecture of my own in a line of Virgil's Aeneid.'[204]

> 'Dear Mr. Powell
> You analyse the difficulties of the passage correctly, and your emendation removes them.
> Yours sincerely
> A. E. Housman'[205]

For that Powell said, 'No praise in the next forty years was ever to be so intoxicating.'[206]

When reflecting on the great influence Housman had had on his life, Powell realised that his personal contact with Housman – if personal it can be described as – equalled a mere two years or six terms of twice-weekly lectures of which no word ever passed between lecturer and student and only twelve months' dining at the same Fellows' table, and after dinner Housman was not approachable in the high-backed crimson leather chair he requisitioned by the fireplace in the Combination Room.

---

204 Bloomfield, 'Housman and Powell', pp.30-36.
205 Powell went on to publish his suggestions in *Philologus* 89, 1934.
206 E. Powell, 'A Personal Recollection of A.E. Housman', *HSJ*, vol.1, 1974, p.28. Amended by the joint editor Graham Speke.

Powell was almost besotted by Housman, even echoing Housman's Introductory Lecture at UCL of 1892 in his own Inaugural Lecture at Sydney University in 1938.[207] Powell records his first encounter with Housman in 1931 when term started, and he briefly saw a 'sudden gleam of light as the Fellows' door into the cloister opened; and a taut figure strode rapidly to a nearby staircase and disappeared up the wooden stairs with a twitch of the gown. Housman then was no more to me than a vague legend attached to a man.'[208]

Housman might have held the chair of Latin at both UCL and later at Cambridge, but he continued to study the Greek works almost as a mere mental exercise. It is not certain that Housman would have even put himself forward for the Kennedy Chair had it not been for pressure from such as Henry Jackson, then Regius Professor of Greek and a Fellow of Trinity. Housman seemed perfectly happy at UCL. His principal classical work was editing Manilius, a minor Roman astronomer poet, in five volumes and only published initially, as we noted, as was *ASL*, at his own expense. A labour of 27 years and another 27 years to sell all 400 copies of Volume I. Housman said the reason it didn't take even longer is that it was rumoured that it had a scurrilous preface which might offer low enjoyment to the unlearned. Garrod said that Housman and he alone had read Manilius from cover to cover and that only Housman

207 Enoch Powell, 'Greek in the University', Inaugural Lecture University of Sydney, 7 May 1938.
208 Powell, 'Recollection', p.28.

understood him.[209]

Housman admitted that Manilius was a third-rate Roman poet but seems to have gained satisfaction by thereby becoming the pre-eminent authority on him. According to Gow, Housman's ruling ambition was 'to build himself a monument' and Manilius was probably that monument.[210] In the meantime Housman had abandoned work on Propertius, who was a major Roman poet and one whom he admired.

When in 1926 the former Prime Minister, Herbert Asquith, who had recently been ennobled as the Earl of Oxford and Asquith, chose for his Presidential Address to the Scottish Classical Association at Edinburgh Joseph Justus Scaliger, Housman had a field day. Asquith described Scaliger as 'the greatest scholar of the sixteenth century.' Housman read the address, disagreed with much of it, made his views public, and in so doing criticised in one go a former Prime Minister, a peer of the realm, a former Rector of Exeter College, Oxford, and a former Public Orator of the University of Cambridge.

According to *The Oxford Magazine* in an article on Housman's appointment at Cambridge, there should be no doubt about the shrewdness of his appointment. 'Electors to Professorships never elect the best man is a truth which all the best men (i.e., all the candidates save the Professor, in his blindness) clearly recognise... But nothing went wrong at Cambridge last week, when the Electors... elected Mr.

209 Garrod lecture 1928 printed in Garrod, *Profession*, pp.211-224.
210 Gow is quoting Housman's reflections on another scholar, Arthur Platt, as quoted by E.J. Kenny, *HSJ*, vol.3, 1977, p.9.

A. E. Housman. Mr. Housman is the greatest living critic on Latin poetry... If we bred a great man, yet it took us a long time to find it out... [Remember Housman was a failed undergraduate from Oxford.] Perhaps, indeed, Mr. Housman did not always give us a fair chance. His mordant wit sometimes played among us to wound... We have heard it said by many persons during the last week that Cambridge has done an adventurous thing. That is a shallow judgement. Cambridge has invested in genius; and that, after all, is of all investments the safest.'[211] Housman once said that Oxford had not much effect on him except that he met Moses Jackson there.[212]

Housman's rudeness to others made it even more surprising that he was duly elected to Cambridge. 'I asked Herbert Richards if Housman had any chance of election. "None whatever," was the reply; "more's the pity. He's the man for the place, of course, but he's been too rude to the men he didn't like."'[213]

There has been a great deal of speculation over why Housman failed his Greats when he had been expected to get a First, and in the light of his subsequent pre-eminent classical career. Laurence said that he thought it was inconceivable that his brother hadn't studied sufficiently to get at least a Pass. In the Finals Housman went up for more paper and his friend Pollard congratulated him on having so much to say. Housman replied gruffly that he

---

211 Anon, 'Notes and News,' *The Oxford Magazine*, 26 January 1911.

212 R. Graves, Ludlow Commemorative Lecture, 30 April, 2008.

213 Richards, *Housman*, p.98. Herbert Richards was the uncle of Grant Richards.

was tired of sitting still. Theories abound on reasons for that monumental failing: he miscalculated the amount of work and so prepared inadequately; the examiner punished him for showing 'contempt' in his scrappy answers; because of his distaste for the intellectual systematising of ancient philosophy. Another theory is that his tutors failed to inspire him and so he spent his time not on the set curriculum but on the Roman poet Propertius, who was not on the syllabus.[214] Another theory is that he was somehow incapacitated by his discovery of his sexual orientation. Tom Stoppard, whilst admitting it was only a hunch, suggested that when Housman realised that he wasn't going to get a 'certain' First, he contrived a total humiliation.[215]

Whatever the reason, the consequences were dire. His family had shielded him from the full extent of the declining fortunes of their home life, hoping thereby to prevent Housman from being distracted from his studies and Finals. However, only a mere six days before Housman sat his Finals he was informed that his father had suffered a major stroke. They were depending on him to help cushion this inexorable decline.

Housman was unaware of the full extent of the domestic

---

214 M. Davies, 'Housman and Murray: A Syncrisis', *HSJ*, vol.41, 2015, p.69.

215 Housman's journey to the pinnacle of English classical eminence met obstacles even before he failed his Greats. A little known fact from his step-mother's diary tells us he was rejected as an undergraduate by Corpus Christi College and only gained a scholarship to St. John's on the strength of his essay on 'Compare Horace and Juvenal as writers of satire'. At the time he wrote the essay he had not read a single satire of Horace's!

nightmare and that an inheritance he was expecting and which would have made him comfortable for life was not to be. He responded in poetry, in one of the few poems he gave a title, 'An Epitaph':

> I never sigh, nor flush, nor knit the brow,
> Nor grieve to think how ill God made me, now.
> (*AP* XII)

Acknowledgement of Housman's undoubted genius was frequent; Gow said it was impossible to listen attentively to Housman for long without becoming aware that one was in contact with a mind of extraordinary distinction, whilst Powell said, 'The exhilaration was produced by watching what seemed to be a mental machine of great power and precision applied to material at first sight unexpectedly.'[216]

Housman produced the weighty tome of his 'Classical Papers,' felt his way through the poets of Greece and Rome, the writings of the Church Fathers, of medieval scholastics, of the Elizabethan-era dramatists and all with the same monumental intellect and focus. By the end he had contributed to the understanding of over 170 ancient Greek and Roman writers and was expert on both Juvenal and Lucan.

Housman, the great textual critic (rather than a literary one), was, in turn, critical of many English classicists.[217] He claimed that good literary critics were less common than

216 Gow, *Sketch,* p44. Graves, *Scholar-Poet,* p.249.
217 The textual critic aims to restore the texts of the ancient authors to what was actually written some 2000 years ago.

returns of Halley's Comet – that is, once every seventy-five years – adding that poets were almost as common as gooseberries.[218]

The centre of classical scholarship during most of the nineteenth century was Germany; even Oxbridge didn't have professorships in Latin until the middle of that century. Housman felt that the English classicists largely lacked rigour. 'Munro, it must be remembered, was editing Lucretius at a time when his countrymen were content with such books as Connington's Virgil.' This is a bold assertion – Munro was an extremely eminent and highly respected classicist. Housman wrote, 'Haupt and Meineke however betake themselves to the coward's remedy of declaring the stanza spurious.' He was only 23 years old when he wrote that and had recently failed his Oxford Finals. Whilst still an undergraduate he wrote, 'I will not try to learn anything from such an ignoramus', referring to Jowett: he vowed never to attend Jowett's lectures again![219]

Few seemed to have escaped his criticism: Gilbert Wakefield (1751-1801), 'a clever, but shallow and careless scholar... ready to explain everything and unable to explain anything, contradicting and abusing his readers with ridiculous confidence.'[220] On Alfred Earnout (1879-1973)

218 A & B. Holden, *Poems That Make Grown Men Cry*, Simon & Schuster, 2014.

219 J. Carter (ed.), *A.E. Housman: Selected Prose*, Cambridge, Cambridge University Press 1961. Benjamin Jowett, 1817-1893, influential tutor, administrative reformer, theologian, Anglican cleric, translator of Plato and Thucydides, Regius Professor of Greek Oxford and Master of Balliol.

220 Introduction to the history of the editing of Lucretius,' *De Rerum Natura* (Ms. add. 6895, delivered in 1928-9) quoted in D. Butterfield, 'Housman's Public Use of Reproof', *HSJ*, vol.36, 2010, p.161.

who edited Lucretius, Housman says, 'he is a good Latinist, and his text is not a bad one; but his preface is a disgusting and memorable example of the pollution of scholarship by politics.'[221] Having complimented Hermann Diels (1853-1933) he said his translation of Lucretius is 'a rather repulsive one' whilst the American edition of Lucretius by W.A Merrill in 1906 was 'a nightmare of a book.'[222] In 1892 he had been at it again, commentating on other editors on *Oedipus Coloneus*. 'But of the notes themselves it would be hard to speak too severely. They are vicious to a degree which well-nigh protects them from refutation. So intricate is the triangle of error...'.[223] That didn't stop others from continuing to praise Housman's standards; one has to search far to uncover extended criticism of his scholarly malpractice.

'In early years he had been the bad boy of scholarship, who had made fun of his elders and embarrassed scholars by what were thought deplorable exhibitions of bad taste. But he grew old, and age brought, as it will in England, respect. The rowdy of yesterday became the sage. His paradoxes were accepted as dogmas; his casual sayings were circulated with a hushed reverence, and he became a figure of legend. Even the Germans knew of him...'[224]

Housman, the lecturer, is a topic in itself – it reflects on his character and on the attitude others had on him both

221 Carter, *Selected Prose*.
222 J. Diggle and F.R.D. Goodyear (eds.), *The Classical Papers of A.E. Housman*, Cambridge, Cambridge University Press, 1972 and MS Add. 6895,36
223 Carter, *Selected Prose*.
224 'An Appreciation' at the time of his death by C.M. Bowra, Warden of Wadham College *Spectator,* Oxford, 19 June, 1936.

as a scholar and as a man. He was a conscientious don, delivering, according to David Butterfield, a Cambridge don himself, over 1000 lectures between the ages of 52 and 77, equal to 37 days and three hours of continuous talk.[225] The lectures delivered outside the weekly series were regarded as more lively and his ambience more welcoming. His two inaugural discourses on being appointed to the chairs at UCL and Cambridge and his address to the Cambridge Classical Association in 1921 fall into that category. The word 'insightful' was used to describe one of them. Powell attended every lecture until he graduated, unlike others who were motivated initially by curiosity, to see what a great poet looked like, then stopped attending after a lecture or two. The only movement detected during the lectures, according to Powell, was a 'prefatory wielding of the window pole to exclude the hated draught from above his rostrum!'[226] His lectures were precisely 50 minutes long, then he would don his mortarboard and stalk out.

He hardly missed a lecture, in fact only twice, in 1928 when he was ill and in the week when he died. When Housman returned to lecturing from the nursing home for the Lent Term of 1936 his manner was different from the norm. He paused from time to time to enquire if the students had understood him – something he had never done before. He was dying. Even Housman realised that he had adopted a more becoming attitude. In a letter to

---

225 D. Butterfield, 'Housman's Cambridge Lectures', *HSJ*, vol.35, 2009, p.131.
226 Butterfield, 'Housman's Cambridge Lectures'.

a member of his family he agreed that this lighter touch, albeit adopted so late in life, was the best he had used. He died a few weeks later.

The classics also touched his prose, not much commented on today, as it resides in the shadow of his other achievements. It possessed the same DNA as his poetry: both were pragmatic, possessing streaks of satire, using everyday words with remarkable clarity. E.H. Carr, the British historian of the Soviet Union and a contemporary, said, 'I should like to think that I had learned something of his flair for cutting through a load of nonsense and getting straight to the point,' adding that he thought Housman was the most powerful intellectual machine he had ever seen in action – an oft-reached conclusion.[227] Bacon also commented, 'There is not another who has written with such devastating and magnificent fury concerning his author, the rigmarole of critical method, and the folly of man – The sentences scorch your brain as you read.'[228]

Housman kept Selden's *Table-Talk* at hand, often referring to it: 'When engaged in writing, I have made constant use of it as a corrective, both of slipshod and flummery, as a guide to follow as faithfully as can be.'[229] Furthermore, Housman had a notebook for his prose jottings, just as he did for his poetry. 'If Mr. – were a postage-stamp he would be a very good postage-stamp; but adhesiveness is not the virtue of a critic. A critic is

227 J. Haslam II, *The Vices of Integrity: E.H. Carr, 1892–1982*, London, Verso, 2000.

228 Leonard Bacon on the Preface 6 *Manilius*.

229 Withers, *Buried Life*, p.98.

free and detached.'[230] On this occasion a jotting made but never used.

As with his poetry, likewise with his prose, he was willing to borrow from others including Homer, Pliny, Herbert Spencer, W.S. Gilbert, Matthew Arnold and the Bible. Housman regarded as one of the greatest achievements of the eighteenth century the invention and then the establishing of a healthy, workmanlike, athletic prose to supersede the cumbrous, decorated and self-admiring prose of a Milton or a Jeremy Taylor.[231]

Just as he complained about the sheer physical effort of writing poetry, so too does he reflect on the toil associated with formulating quality prose. On declining the office of Public Orator at Cambridge he said, 'you none of you know... what a trouble composition is to me.' Poetry he said was either easy or impossible and it is likely that the best of his prose came likewise – in short bursts – sometimes to be used immediately but often kept in a notebook for possible future purpose.

The reason for the partial eclipse of his prose despite its high standards is that the prose is largely to be found only in learned journals and dusty biographies. At least he was chosen as official lapidarist, as a composer of ceremonial pieces by Trinity and by Cambridge University. The gems are there and worth seeking out.

When Housman agreed to deposit some papers on English poets a friend hoped that Housman's piece on Swinburne, at least, might be published despite hearing

230 Housman, *A.E.H: Memoir*, p.90.
231 Carter: *Selected Prose*, p.176.

that the papers were to be destroyed after his death. The friend ventured to suggest that if Housman thought the piece in question was bad, he would surely have already destroyed it himself. 'I do not think it bad, I think it not good enough for me.'[232] It is indeed highly likely that Housman realised what a very good prose writer he was!

Fortunately, some of his prose does survive, principally, but not by any means exclusively, in the Prefaces to his classical works. Gow's efforts at retrieval and recording are a great help here. This is Housman: 'The firm strength and piercing edge and arrowy swiftness of his intellect, his matchless facility and adroitness and resource, were never so triumphant as where defeat seemed pure; and yet it is other virtues that one most admires and welcomes as one turns from the smoky fire of Scaliger's genius to the sky and air of Bentley's: his lucidity, his sanity, his just and simple straightforward fashion of thought.'[233]

And here he is again: 'Yet the virtues of his work are quenched and smothered by the multitude and monstrosity of its vices... [Friedrich Jacob] had no sense for grammar, no sense for coherency, no sense for sense, but being himself possessed by a passion for the clumsy hispid he imputed the disgusting taste for all authors whom he edited.'[234]

We could equally borrow from his prose appearing in *Classical Review*, the *Journal of Philology*, the *Classical*

232 Gow, *Sketch*, p.21.

233 Richard Bentley, 1662-1742, Master of Trinity College Cambridge, contemporary of Sir Isaac Newton with whom he corresponded. Brink, 'Reflections'.

234 *M. Manilii Astronomicon Liber Primus* (Reprinted) Cambridge University Press, 1937.

Quarterly and the *Cambridge Review* between 1890 and 1923. For example from the *Classical Review*: 'This edition gives proof of many virtues: common sense, alert perception, lucidity of thought, impatience of absurdity, a rational distrust of MS. tradition and a masculine taste in things poetical.'[235] Finally by way of example we have from the *Journal of Philology*: 'The treatise is written with admirable diligence, adequate learning and entire freedom from the spirit of faction: its faults spring from a deficiency, I will not say in critical faculty, but certainly in critical expression, partly, it seems, from the fact that though party spirit is absent preconceived opinion is not.'[236]

It is difficult today to appreciate Housman's achievements as a classicist and understand his standing in academia amongst his contemporaries. He was held in deep respect, but seen as an eccentric even for his time, odd, awkward, wooden as a lecturer but a legend to be admired, if not readily liked, and seen as special. Just a glimpse of the great man, a few words by him to a correspondent, and the latter would never be quite the same again.

235 *Classical Review* 1890, in Carter, *Selected Prose*, p.63.
236 *Journal of Philology*, 1892, p.103.

10. AS A HOMOSEXUAL

'I, a stranger and afraid.'

Was Housman homosexual? From that question follows a number of supplementary ones. If so, what is the evidence and if there is sufficient evidence, why do some not believe it? If he was homosexual what effect did that have on his life and in particular, for us, on his poetry? We should remember the times: as a generalisation, until the Wolfenden Report in 1957 brought the subject into the public domain most people generally neither thought about nor discussed homosexuality, yet it fascinated biographers of a certain age and era.

The case against him being homosexual can be summed up rather easily. He never confessed to being homosexual, neither to his family nor to his few close friends. There is no reference, no hint in his extant collection of letters, not even in those to his closest friends. There are, admittedly, a few letters that remain secret between Housman and Jackson but I suggest we don't hold our breath! Nor do his notebooks or any of his prose refer to homosexuality.

Some believe that Housman's use of certain words such as 'lads' are thinly disguised references to homosexuality, but 'the lads in their hundreds to Ludlow come in for the fair' could quite easily be arriving to enjoy the occasion – and it is difficult to believe that the Allied soldiers in two World Wars, and with the enemy, the Japanese, in the Second as well, going into battle with pocket editions of

ASL if the poems were obviously about homosexuality.

Housman's use of words in the context of his time can be rendered harmless.

> A single redcoat turns his head,
> He turns and looks at me
>
> (*ASL* XXII)

Kipling used similar language and he was never deemed to be homosexual. In his 'Ballad of East and West' he writes, 'They have looked each other between the eyes and there they found no fault.'

The poem by Housman which is often quoted as supposed evidence of homosexuality, *AP* XVIII, 'Oh who is that young sinner with the handcuffs on his wrists?' could be referring to Oscar Wilde's sentence for being a practising homosexual and all that Housman was doing was offering sympathy for what many people at the time also felt was a particularly harsh sentence and therefore nothing to do with empathy for a fellow homosexual, but rather a comment on the administering of justice.

Richards knew Housman well, and over a long time (Gow had a low opinion of him, describing him as 'a very unattractive man of the world, a bon-viveur, and a good-looking but unscrupulous ruffian.') Richards said he had asked Housman's Cambridge friends if he was homosexual: 'never has their response supported the accusation.'[237]

Richards expended plenty of energy in his biography

237 Richards, *Housman*, p.300.

of Housman refuting any homosexual accusations levelled at Housman, referring to them as 'calumny' of a kind that might 'sear virtue itself.' Richards argued that homosexuality was not a subject that should be reviewed in public, that it was a seedy subject and unworthy of Housman's reputation and achievements, saying 'this spying out of evil, this ugliness of surmise, was not a habit of English criticism or of English speech' and 'posterity should not have that bone to pick.'[238]

As Richards concedes, it was the publication of *MP* and *AP* posthumously, the ones Housman didn't allow to be published in his lifetime with their homosexual insinuations, and that of Laurence's *Memoir* in 1937 which meant that those who denied Housman's homosexuality had to act in order to counter the allegations; 'a sinister twist has been given to the facts.' A review of Laurence's memoir appeared in the *Church Times* on 3rd December 1937 which read 'it is surely a grave omission... to tell us nothing about the personal history behind one of the best known books of late Victorian poetry.' Richards didn't like it, tracked the author down and got the reply 'I can see that a study of Housman's character would have to deal obliquely with such problems; but they should be dealt with or left severely alone.' Richards was defensive – Housman merely suffered from 'home troubles and scholastic disaster' which were enough to 'warp the whole fibre of that sensitive brother's being, even apart from mental struggles which made him abandon his religious

238 Richards, *Housman*, p.295.

beliefs.'[239]

Richards admits that he had met Housman later in life and therefore after his passionate infatuation for Jackson which had resulted in 'the very great and real troubles of [his] early manhood' and when Housman had effectively confined the emotional turmoil of that period to his inner sanctum.[240]

Richards' attitude to Housman's sexuality is one of the more complicated and challenging to assess. On the one hand he almost ignores the evidence that was even available during Housman's lifetime and immediately after his death. It is interesting to note that Richards felt this outrageous criticism of Housman emanated from the posthumous publication of *MP* and *AP*: that is to say, the publication of the very poems that A.E. Housman did not want to see published in his lifetime. Even homosexual Laurence hesitated, but finally decided to publish. Richards is blinkered in his interpretation of what is surely evidence; for instance, when he arranged Housman's collection of modern books, not including therefore his classical ones, he found the collection creditable to a scholar 'whose interests were normal and widely spread' yet the collection included books on pornography.[241] Such conclusions reached by Richards are all the more strange considering how long and how intimately he knew Housman. Either this is a case of Richards refusing to accept what was surely a fact or thinking he was doing his friend a service

239 Richards, *Housman,* pp.295-6.
240 Richards, *Housman,* p.310.
241 Richards, *Housman*, p.301.

by covering it up and because of his closeness to Housman that his opinion would be respected.

When Jackson died Housman wrote, 'Now I can die myself: I could not have borne to leave him behind me in a world where anything might happen to him.'[242] But Housman wrote in a similar vein at the passing of others. On the deaths of his friend Sophie Becker and of the Wise sisters, he said to Withers 'how comfortably [he] could meet death now [his] three friends were at peace.'[243]

In later life he travelled to the Continent with paid male companions, but these relationships look harmless: they were merely companionship and practical – and by then Housman could afford to pay for such luxuries. In the early years of his French trips, Housman, if not accompanied by Richards, relied either on his own resources, if staying in Paris, or on an 'amiable... chauffeur' or on a proprietor of a garage who was a 'great connoisseur of the local scenery and delighted to take me by the best routes to the best spots.'[244] He wrote in 1933, 'I shall have with me a French companion, a nice young man, who regards me as a benefactor.'[245]

Admittedly, when in Paris, and without the need for a companion, Housman could disappear in the evenings. He wrote to Richards, 'If we are in Paris together I probably should not be free in the evenings but should be during

242 Burnett (ed.), *Letters*.
243 Sophie Becker, German governess to the Wise sisters, becoming a lifelong friend of Housman. When Housman's mother died, he stayed with his Godmother Elizabeth Wise at Woodchester.
244 Letter to Richards, 9 May, 1914. Letter to Withers, 18 January, 1920.
245 Burnett, Letters *II*, p. 371.

the day.'[246] Some conclude that was because Housman was taking up homosexual liaisons, but it could just as feasibly be because he had accepted invitations often for dinner and other engagements with those he knew from Cambridge or London visiting Paris: for example, one meeting was with L.M. Brandon who had collated his manuscripts. We know of another occasion when a young married couple were due to call on him and yet another when he needed to mention to others that he may not be able to make an evening commitment with them that was in his diary.

He wrote the following to Andrea, the Venetian gondolier, he met on holiday:

> Ho, everyone that thirsteth
> And has the price to give,
> Come to the stolen waters,
> Drink and your soul shall live.

And again in *MP* XLIV:

> Andrea, fare you well;
> Venice, farewell to thee.
> The tower that stood and fell
> Is not rebuilt in me.

There is a need to be cautious here, there is no concrete evidence of a relationship between Housman and Andrea. If the words in the poetry to a modern ear appear careless or dated, they do not imply homosexuality. Housman was

246 Letter Housman to Richards, 24 July 1923.

not a careless man, but he cannot be blamed for language dating!

Housman admittedly, on hearing of Andrea's 'final' illness, premature as it turned out, made a speedy journey across the Continent to be at his supposed deathbed. When Andrea died four years later Housman wrote, 'Now there is nobody in the world who respects me as much as Noble [the family dog] did.'[247] Typically Kate refuted the allegation in respect of Andrea, but we know she was an unreliable source when it came to her brother's sexuality. The rumours of any relationship with Andrea must have emerged early for Kate to have reacted in this way, and the rumours could have been circulating in Housman's lifetime. Housman had an affection for Andrea's family and he gave them financial support – but then he was a generous man by nature and Kate specifically went out of her way to refute this relationship with Andrea in the correspondence following her contribution to Richards' book which was published as an appendix.[248]

But there is another side to the debate. Moses Jackson was heterosexual and we don't know to what extent, if at all, he was ever aware of the infatuation Housman had for him, but Jackson was, nevertheless, the overwhelming reason for Housman's outpouring of poetry which initially saw the light of day in *ASL*. Richards, consistent with his denial of Housman's homosexuality, denies that there is any 'thread of devotion of fellow to fellow in

247 Letter Housman to Katharine E. Symons, 11 December, 1930.
248 Sotheby's *London Sale Catalogue*, 9 July 1968, p.161.

ASL or indeed in any of Housman's poetry.'[249] However, it is not especially in *ASL* where we should seek the evidence of his homosexuality, but in poems published late in Housman's life and amongst those published posthumously. Despite their later publication most were composed around the same time as the emotional turmoil created by the unrequited love for Jackson. Edgar Vincent, in his biography, comments that Housman 'lifted the veil' with some of the poems he wished to publish in *LP*.

Some of these poems were not included in *ASL* because they did not fit neatly into its dialogue, weak though that dialogue is, but it was mainly because they were poems which focused on and revealed Housman's sexual orientation. Another, with a similar sexual tone, this time included in *AP* would be:

Oh were he and I together,
Shipmates on the fleeted main,
Sailing through the summer weather
To the spoil of France or Spain.

Oh were he and I together,
Locking hands and taking leave,
Low upon the trampled heather
In the battle lost at eve.

(*AP* II)

This was published posthumously.

---

249 Richards, *Housman*, p.294.

> But if you come to a road where danger
> Or guilt or anguish or shames to share,
> Be good to the lad that loves you true
> And the soul that was born to die for you
> And whistle and I'll be there.

This poem was not published until included in the letters edited by Burnett. We know from his notebooks that it was composed at the time Jackson left in 1887 to join the Indian Civil Service to become Principal of the new Dayaram Jethmel Sind Science College in Karachi.

This departure has been described in some biographies as 'stiff' with Jackson even asking Housman to forget him. Jackson married in 1889 in London but didn't invite Housman to the wedding and Housman found out about the marriage only when Jackson had returned to India. He and Jackson re-established a degree of friendship with exchange of letters, a mere one or two a year, but that was about the extent of the subsequent relationship as far as Jackson was concerned.

Sir Tom Stoppard had no doubts about Housman's sexual orientation. He regarded the one-sided infatuation by Housman for Jackson as 'a high point of heroic absurdity, an unremitting, lopsided, lifelong, hopeless constancy to a decent chap who was in no need of it, temperamentally unfitted for it, and never for a moment inclined to call upon it.'[250] After Jackson's death Laurence

250 Sir Tom Stoppard b.1937, Czech born British playwright and screen-writer. He has written for television, radio, film and stage. Vice President Housman Society.

visited his brother at Trinity and on seeing a photo of a man over the fireplace asked who he was. 'In a strangely moved voice he answered, "That was my friend Jackson, the man who had more influence on my life than anyone else."'[251]

Housman concluded, as a result of his unrequited relationship with Jackson, that nobody can love truly and deeply more than once. If a person felt otherwise, then they 'had simply never really loved at all.' He reflected 'Pride, one of the seven deadly sins, is an efficient substitution for all the cardinal virtues.' Thankfully for Housman, he was able to compartmentalise his life, saying 'a great man is not also a great lover, because he can shake his life free from troubles of love.'[252] Or as he put it in verse.

> He would not stay for me; and who can wonder?
> He would not stay for me to stand and gaze.
> I shook his hand and tore my heart in sunder
> And went with half my life about my ways.
>
> (*AP* VII)

It is easy to feel sorry for Housman in respect of Jackson, but one should feel equally, and from a different perspective, sorry for Jackson too. It seems that Housman's declaration of love in 1885 was the reason for Housman's abrupt departure from their shared lodgings for a week. Housman's continued lifelong infatuation for Jackson

---

251 Parker, *Housman Country*.

252 P. Larkin, *Required Writing Miscellaneous Pieces 1955–1982,* Faber & Faber, 1983, pp.263–5.

followed Jackson to his deathbed. Jackson received a copy of *LP* with the inscription from Housman, 'I would much rather have followed you round the world and blackened your boots.'[253] Jackson replied 'I haven't your last letter here, but remember an extraordinary ebullition about blacking boots! My most presentable boots are brown, requiring no blacking.'[254] Housman had been trying throughout his life to impress Jackson and that that was the main motivation for all he achieved.

Housman failed his exams whereas Jackson succeeded, gaining a First, possibly adding to Housman's feeling of inferiority in respect of Jackson and enhancing his desire, over a lifetime, to impress him. Jackson's First was in Science. Andrew Jackson, the youngest son of Gerald and therefore the grandson of Moses, characterised his grandfather as 'typical of the Victorian English Gentleman scientist, believing strongly that science held the answers to the advancement of mankind, but that a sound knowledge of classics was required to shape a well-rounded individual.'[255]

Two contemporaries explained Housman's attraction to Jackson but without any reference to homosexuality. According to E. W. Watson, a contemporary at Oxford, Jackson was 'a vigorous rowing man, quite unliterary and outspoken in his want of any such interest', whereas Housman was retiring, quiet, interested in classics, not interested in sport – with only one thing in common, a

253 Letter Housman to Jackson, 19 October, 1922.
254 M.J. Jackson to Housman, 23 November, 1922.
255 A. Jackson, 'A Pivotal Friendship' *HSJ*, vol 36, 2010, p.48.

love of long country walks. Perhaps evidence of opposites attracting. Pollard thought so, at least noting that 'not even Moses Jackson could make Alfred babble but he was never reticent or stiff with me at Oxford', adding that he thought Housman was attracted to Jackson partly because the latter, unlike Housman, was often lively if never witty and that this, coupled with Jackson's simplicity and singlemindedness, made him attractive to Housman.

But Housman was confessing his homosexuality in ways appropriate for the times which would not result in trouble for him when practising homosexuality was still a crime.

> Ask me no more, for fear I should reply;
> Others have held their tongues, and so can I;
> Hundreds have died, and told no tale before:
> Ask me no more, for fear I should reply –
>
> How one was true and one was clean of stain
> And one was braver than the heavens are high,
> And one was fond of me: and all are slain.
> Ask me no more, for fear I should reply.
>
> (*AP* VI)

He also wrote a poem which included the lines:

> Because I liked you better
> Than suits a man to say,
>
> (*MP* XXXI)

It was partly because of his homosexuality, or that is the conventional view, that he felt he was an outsider both punished and rejected by God and he expressed it in verse. *LP* XII begins:

> The laws of God, the laws of man,
> He may keep that will and can;
> Not I: let God and man decree
> Laws for themselves and not for me;
> And if my ways are not as theirs
> Let them mind their own affairs.
> Their deeds I judge and much condemn,
> Yet when did I make laws for them?

And a few lines later he writes:

> I, a stranger and afraid
> In a world I never made.

Ending:

> Keep we must, if keep we can,
> These foreign laws of God and man.

A poem often quoted as evidence, *ASL* XLIV's 'Shot? so quick, so clean an ending?' is said to be a reference to a famous case at the time of a man whose homosexuality had been found out and it is claimed that this was Housman offering sympathy for the suffering of a fellow homosexual. The incident was of Henry Maclean, aged

19, a Woolwich cadet, who in 1895 shot himself as the only remedy for being homosexual. This was a mere two months after Oscar Wilde was jailed. In his papers Housman had inserted a newspaper cutting about the cadet adjacent to *ASL* XLIV.[256] Desmond Shawe-Taylor, writing in the *New Statesman*, is quite specific and bold in his assertions. 'Is it a coincidence that the greater part of *A Shropshire Lad* was written in the year, almost the month, of the Wilde trial... from Wenlock Edge he could see as far as Reading Gaol.'[257]

Colin Dexter was able to stand on the sidelines merely reflecting, almost in passing, 'I am conscious of only casual curiosity in the many rumours of his sodomitic susceptibilities and alleged cantankerousness.'[258] These are strong words, which although expressed only a few years ago, would now be deemed unacceptable. Alan Bennett once wrote that Housman was the one person to whom he could have confided the secret of his own sexuality.[259] (But that seems to be the very last thing that Housman would have wanted!)

Gow was a circumspect early biographer. He seemed to know a great deal about Jackson and what he meant to Housman and shrewdly implied that even in *ASL* there were hints of homosexuality. He further speculated that

256 Housman, *A.E.H: Memoir*, p.103.

257 *New Statesman,* 1 January, 1938.

258 C. Dexter 'The Housman Lecture, by Colin Dexter, Hay Festival', *HSJ,* vol.30, 2004, pp. 7-17.

259 A. Bennett, *Untold Stories*, London, Faber & Faber, 2006, p.140. Alan Bennett, 1934- , English actor, author, playwright, screenwriter, among many successes the play, *The History Boys*.

some of the poems published after Housman's death 'spoke of friendship in terms which evidently came from the heart', adding 'desire for friendship had been overborne by fear of what friendship might hold in store.'[260] Housman's sister, Kate, agreed with that sentiment by Gow, the nearest to her conceding that her brother was homosexual.[261]

Laurence was also homosexual – strangely Kate made no comment about that – and Housman appointed him his literary executor knowing full well that there were further poems to publish posthumously, ones that Housman could so easily have destroyed. Laurence was openly homosexual and for the time dangerously so. He did not regard homosexuality as a moral depravity and he openly consorted with a male lover, visited Oscar Wilde in Paris and tentatively supported the movement for homosexual law reform. We noted that *MP* was published by Laurence soon after Housman had died and many of these poems were especially homosexual in tone. Laurence even wrote after his brother's death that he had known for a very long time what Housman's 'tendency' was and that Housman knew that he knew as such.

Laurence and his brother took two summer touring holidays together and Laurence claims, perhaps with justification, that he grew closer to his brother in later years and that his brother opened up to him, 'maintaining his reserve over certain matters, he said, without my having asked "more I shall not tell you"'.[262] In 1942, six years after

260 Gow, *Sketch*, p.49.

261 M. Blocksidge, 'A.E. Housman's Early Biographers', *HSJ*, vol.42, 2016, p.41.

262 Housman, *A.E.H: Memoir*, p.95.

his brother's death, Laurence placed his brother's diaries in the British Museum under a 25 year embargo. Did he believe that homosexuality would be more liberally interpreted by then? Uncannily, it was exactly 25 years later that the practice of homosexuality was permitted in law.[263]

Included in that package was a 20-page manuscript titled *A.E. Housman's De Amicitia*. The author was Laurence, and according to Laurence it had two purposes: 'the more intelligent, the more charitable, the kindly of understanding... having fuller knowledge will be able to have more liking also for the man who in his own life-time could not let himself be better known.' The second purpose referred to his brother's homosexuality, a problem which had 'broken many heads and many hearts, and ruined many lives', hoping a more reasoned attitude would later prevail.

But was he a practising homosexual? E. M. Forster, a homosexual himself, had no doubts about Housman; writing about Housman he said 'Did he ever drink the stolen waters which he recommends so ardently to others?'[264] There is no evidence that he had a relationship with any of his undergraduates at either UCL or at Cambridge. Neither is there indisputable evidence anywhere at any

263 Sexual Offences Act 1967 legalised homosexual acts in England and Wales on the condition that they were consensual, in private and between two men who had attained the age of 21.

264 E.M Forster, *The Listener*, 11 November, 1936. It was somewhat brave of Forster to write in that vein, at that time. E.M. Forster, 1879-1970, OM, CH, English fiction writer, essayist, his novels often examine class differences and hypocrisy. Among his best-known novels are *A Room with a View, Howard's End, Maurice* and *A Passage to India*.

time. This still holds true despite the following. He enjoyed Continental holidays at a time when few took them. Was it a means of practising and not being detected? The much commented cards discovered as bookmarkers after his death record the restaurants in Paris he visited and some referred to meetings with 'boys'. Did the numbers stand for specific areas of Paris? *03910-9 arrondissement* was written on one of the cards, which happens to be where the Folies Bergère and also the Moulin Rouge are located. Another card refers to the area covering the Gare du Nord and the Gare du Midi, both well-known at the time as locations where boys gathered in order to meet male clients. Much time and energy has been focused on these cards, but they do not constitute conclusive evidence.[265]

Richard Perceval Graves claims that the numbers written in pencil in the second column were prices or indicators of quantity or quality, that words such as *boxeur*, *danceur*, *marin*, *naigre*, in the third column refer to male prostitutes.[266] H. Montgomery-Hyde told Graves that Housman's notes were very similar in tone to those made by Roger Casement in his homosexual diaries.[267] Maybe, but Housman was by then in his 63rd year! If Graves is right, then Housman's behaviour was not unique. John Maynard Keynes made similar visits to Paris at about the same time, and we know in his case, at least, it was for homosexual encounters.[268] Nor does the following constitute any

265 St John's College Library, Oxford. Housman Cabinet 1, row B, shelf 6.
266 Graves, *Scholar-Poet*.
267 H. Montgomery-Hyde, *The Trials of Oscar Wilde*, Dover, 1973.
268 John Maynard Keynes 1883-1946, one of the most original and brilliant economists who changed the theory and practice of macroeconomics,

evidence that he was a practising homosexual; on a visit to Constantinople he commented on 'the handsomest faces I ever saw… some of the Greeks make you rub your eyes, the features and complexions are more like pictures than realities.'[269] It is possible to admire without coveting, even if the language to a modern ear could be misinterpreted and therefore offer a different meaning.

The conventional take is that from the age of 30, when Jackson left for India, Housman suppressed all further sexual yearnings. That might not be entirely true. We will probably never know for sure, but what is true is that his homosexuality at a time when it was illegal contributed to his poetic output and was a fundamental, constituent part of his character. It is all too easy to search for evidence to substantiate a preconceived viewpoint on whether he was homosexual or not when trying to explain the character and behaviour of a man who in so many ways defies conventional definition.

> The word unsaid will stay unsaid
> Though there was much to say;
> Last month was time enough; he's dead,
> The news must keep for aye.
>
> (*MP* XLII)

Perhaps with that we should leave the subject – until Chapter 17.

---

influenced economic policy of successive British governments and argued strongly for a more lenient attitude towards defeated Germany after the First World War.

269 Burnett, *Letters I*, p.163.

11. SENSE OF HUMOUR

'A good raconteur of the pithy and caustic order.'

It is hard to believe that Housman's temperament would lend itself to a sense of humour; it did, and it was real, cutting, cruel and clever. He possessed an often academic prowess with a sense of the absurd, expressed in a variety of ways – in letters, prose and in nonsense verse (the last for the ears of his own family and for the Wise family in Woodchester) and, being Housman, his cutting refrains had a habit of making their point.

He admired wit – a quality he highlighted in others, listing it as amongst the qualities that made Dryden and Pope great men of letters; he enjoyed the wit in Ovid and even in Manilius. He hinted that the most distinguishing trait of a nation is its humour or lack of it.[270] He could be childish in his wit. When he and Jackson were staying at Pollard's house, all then middle-aged, Pollard noted 'when I retired to rest I found an apple-pie bed awaiting me and I think the Professor of Latin was a fellow victim, though I'm not quite sure he wasn't an aggressor. Anyway, we became very youthful and light hearted.'[271] When John Fothergill showed Housman around his garden Fothergill recalled 'I proceeded to point out all the plants with vile names... over there I have a Phallus Amorphus but it hasn't come up yet... "Perhaps modesty forbids" Housman conjectured.'

270 C. Clemens, 'An Evening with Cyril Clemens', *HSJ*, vol. 41, 2015, p.111.
271 Tree, 'Housman As Lyricist?'

At a dinner at Cambridge for 'Oxford migrants' he said he found Cambridge an asylum in both senses of the word. In verse Housman could write:

> But oh, good Lord, the verse you make
> It gives a chap the belly ache.
>
> (*ASL* LXII)

He enjoyed writing and reading limericks Laurence said that he and his brother 'exchanged naughty limericks' for which (when they were witty and not merely dirty) we both had a taste.' However, Housman could be dirty at least in the telling of jokes. 'Housman then told me one of the most obscene French stories I have ever heard in my life – not funny, only abominable.'[272]

Invariably, Housman refused to let his humorous poems be printed but one or two did make it into print. One, for example, was a skit on a poem by Frances Cornford (surely an underrated poet) which appeared in Rothenstein's *Men and Memories*, without Housman's permission.

Only one limerick by Housman seems to have survived despite him writing a fair amount and it is pretty ordinary:

> There was a young lady of Rhymss
> Who filled the cathedral with screamys
> And tore out her hair
> As she howled in despair
> 'I shall never be Countess of Wemyss.[273]

272 *The Diary of A.C. Benson Magdalen College Cambridge,* quoted in T.E.B. Howarth's, *Cambridge between Two Wars,* London, 1978, p.80.

273 California State University, East Bay, Special Collections, PR 4809. H15 AII, 1897.

On one occasion he was himself the subject of a limerick!

There was a Professor of Latin
Who honoured the Chair which he sat in,
In preparing a text
He was never perplexed,
When to strike this word out and put that in![274]

Not unexpectedly, being a textual critic, and a solver of puzzles, some of Housman's comic verse almost defies solution and in turn could be set as puzzles. It is no surprise that Colin Dexter used Housman's poetry to help solve a Morse mystery or two. Sometimes Housman used an impossible rhyme to complete a stanza, 'What was the date of Volcacius Sedigitus?' (The rhyme is 'fidget us'.)[275]

Whilst deprived of most of his limericks we are able to access and assess other forms of his light-hearted verse, penned rather incongruously as it is by an apparently dour, cloistered don. He was able to hint at the inherent absurdity in what is seriously intended – W. S. Gilbert was a master of that too as was Belloc in his *Cautionary Verses*. [276] Orwell said of Housman that, along with Lewis Carroll, he was a teacher who had 'done moving and delightful things.'[277]

274 UCLUM, 2.3. March 1907, p.93. quoted in P. G. Naiditch, *A.E. Housman at University College London*, Leiden, Brill, 1988, p.136.
275 N. Page, 'Housman as a comic writer', *HSJ*, vol.17, 1991, p.11.
276 Hilaire Belloc, 1870-1953, British-French writer, historian, orator, poet, satirist, writer of letters, soldier, MP 1906-1910, especially remembered for his *Cautionary Tales* aimed at children. Strong Catholic faith.
277 S.N. Behrman, *Portrait of Max,* New York, Random House, 1960, p.43.

There were a number of parallels between Carroll and Housman. Both could write nonsense verse, both were unmarried, both obsessive precisionists, especially over printers' punctuation – and both were clever and funny parodists.

Housman is known to have composed light verse whilst dressing in the morning; In a letter to Withers he begins:

> It is a fearful thing to be
> The Pope.
> That cross will not be laid on me,
> I hope.[278]

It was topical as well; the election of Pope Pius XI was then in progress. Housman liked to turn pomp into ridicule, rather as Jane Austen, an author he greatly admired, also did with effect.

Housman wrote a parody of the Salvation Army hymn:

> Hallelujah was the only observation
> That escaped Lieutenant Colonel Mary Jane,
> When she tumbled off the platform in the station,
> And was cut in little pieces by the train.
> Mary Jane, the train is through yer:
> Hallelujah, Hallelujah!
> We will gather up the fragments that remain.[279]

---

278 Withers, *Buried Life*, p.66.

279 Page, 'comic writer', p.11. Page reminds us that despite his melancholy, Housman could write light verse, for instance, *ASL* LXII 'say for what were hop-yards meant, or why was Burton built on Trent?'

When Professor at UCL, he returned an overdue book badly packed and incurred a fine. Housman defended himself; he had left the packing to a servant and servants were what God made them. When the Library Committee met – it was never well attended – and on this occasion only those present were the chairman, Housman and a librarian who had no vote, the chairman opened deliberations:

> The chairman said, 'I move that the fine be imposed.'
> There was silence.
> The chairman spoke again, 'I move that the fine be remitted.'
> 'I second that,' said Housman.
> 'Carried unanimously,' said the chairman.'[280]

Housman said if he could take only one book to a desert island it would be Sir Archibald Alison's *History of Europe* in ten volumes.[281] 'It was abominably written history, extremely prosy and diffuse... like so many inferior books, however, it had a charm and fascination all its own... Even today when I am obliged to go on a long railway journey, I always take one of Alison's volumes with me. I know that I shall never finish the one, much less the other nine.' He said to Clemens that if he were on that desert island 'if I did not want to show off, I would take Thomas' *Guide*

280 Naiditch, *Housman at UCL*, p.63.
281 Sir Archibald Alison, 1792-1867. Disraeli satirised him in *Coningsby* as Mr Wordy, yet the history proved to be a great commercial success. By 1848, 100,000 copies had been sold in the USA alone and it was translated into other languages. He wrote other lengthy, weighty tomes including on the criminal laws of Scotland.

to Practical Ship Building, so that I could get away from the island as quickly as possible.' He also told Clemens that he had introduced to England a hitherto obscure American author, Anita Loos. 'You see even a staid and sedate professor of Latin knows how to enjoy the lighter things of literature' and with a smile 'many years spent with Manilius, Lucan and Juvenal have perhaps quickened my English sense of humor [sic]'.[282]

Even in a lecture Housman could show humour of sorts – or was it simply cruelty whether intended or not? When a female undergraduate sat near the front making copious notes, which annoyed him, Housman said he would be in London, staying overnight, and that the next lecture would start a little later. Turning to the female undergraduate he added, 'Got that down?' and promptly left the hall. He could even be somewhat light-hearted in his reviews of learned works. He referred to one hapless scholar, Elias Stoeber, 'whose re-print of Bentley's text, with a commentary intended to confute it, saw the light in 1767 at Strasbourg, a city famous for its geese.'[283]

Wit was not in evidence in his lectures on textual criticism – hardly surprising considering the inherently dry subject matter. But he did offer engaging performances outside his curriculum courses where he also adopted a lighter approach to lecturing as we have noted – at Cambridge in 1911 for his inaugural lecture and in 1921 in his address to the Classical Association (despite the title 'The

282 Anita Loos quoted in *The International Mark Twain Society*, 1937, *Historical Series* 6.

283 Carter, *Selected Prose*.

Application of Thought to Textual Criticism'). Housman is being clever here – it is a snide comment that others treat as a purely dry, mechanical process, not requiring human agency through thought.) The other occasions were in the Leslie Stephen lecture and earlier when at UCL but again outside the curriculum.

On being Best Man, and in the presence of the bride's mother, he described the customs of an African tribe whose tradition it was to eat the mother-in-law at the wedding feast. Housman could understand a joke and quickly got into the mood. When Sir Stanley Leathes visited Trinity for a celebration, he was given rooms next to Housman's and told that if he wanted anything he merely had to knock on Housman's door, 'the very last thing I should think of doing.' But when he realised he had forgotten to pack his evening trousers he knocked reluctantly on that door. He said that a rapid survey of Housman's figure convinced him that the fit wouldn't be good and asked if he might split Housman's trousers down the back which Housman consented to with good grace. Leathes thought that it was the ridiculous nature of his request which appealed to Housman and that had he asked merely for a collar stud his reaction could have been very different.

As an after-dinner speaker at Trinity, Housman said, 'Cambridge has seen many strange sights. It has seen Wordsworth drunk and Porson sober. It is now destined to see a better scholar than Wordsworth and a better poet than Porson betwixt and between.'[284] (Indeed Lord Byron

284 Quoted from an account given by Professor R.W. Chambers referring to Housman's farewell dinner at UCL. Also quoted by G.K. Chesterton in his autobiography and quoted by others. Richard Porson, 1759-1808,

wrote in one letter about Porson, 'And I can never recollect him as such as drunk and brutal and generally both.') H. J. Chautor, Master of St. Catharine's College, Cambridge, who was present when Housman spoke at the Trinity dinner recalled 'he made the best speech that these dinners ever produced…'.[285]

He also had a reputation as a raconteur but, alas, it seems nobody recorded a single example, so they are lost forever; he had no Boswell to record for posterity. Housman could be witty in conversation. Norman Page recalls meeting an elderly Fellow of Jesus College, Cambridge, Dr L. Pars, who recalled in turn when Sir Arthur Quiller-Couch was a dinner guest and Housman had told a joke and Dr. Pars still remembered it fifty years later.[286]

Housman kept a notebook as we know – what Laurence called his 'stored ammunition' – and this was used to humorous effect. He called Kipling's *Jungle Book* a 'treat in Wolf's clothing' that 'any fool can write a sonnet, and most fools do' and 'my favourite work of fiction, the Latin dictionary.' (This latter quote rather echoes Wilde's comment referring to the *Peerage* 'the best thing in fiction the English have ever done.'[287]) It is a great pity that Housman wasn't alive in the 1950s and 1960s when

---

Regius Professor of Greek at Cambridge and Fellow at Trinity, a drinker of the first order.

285 H.J Chautor a letter dated 6 January, 1921 (Library of Congress USA). Sir Arthur Quiller-Couch, 1863-1944, British writer who published using the pseudonym Q. Prolific novelist, now mainly remembered for his *Oxford Book of English Verse 1250-1900* and for his literary criticism.

286 Page, 'Comic Writer', p.12.

287 Page, 'Comic Writer', pp.12-13.

there were television programmes such as 'What's My Line?' or was a member of the Brain's Trust. It is a fair bet that he would have excelled, becoming an unexpected, unconventional celebrity – via a medium appropriate to his character and talents.

The Times obituary refers to a laugh which betokened a great capacity for enjoyment and 'a good raconteur of the pithy and caustic order [...] by no means averse to gossip.' Laurence spoke of his brother's 'happy laugh' and sister Kate spoke of his ability to be 'quick to see humour in things about him, or to give grim things a humorous turn' adding that their father's increasingly dire financial affairs in their childhood, and the father's accompanying ill-health, meant that Housman's 'path to easy happiness became blocked.'[288]

Of course, humour can date, and dreadfully. Housman's humour is more in the cleverness emanating from a very clever man, sharp, brilliant, but sometimes an acquired taste. To many Housman and humour are not readily linked but a portrait of Housman without consideration of his humour would be incomplete.

288 K. Symons (ed.) *Alfred Edward Housman Recollections,* London, Bromsgrove School, 1936, p.22 & 30.

12. ON FOOD AND DRINK

'And malt does more than Milton can.'

Housman liked his food and drink. When asked by Richards if he was glad to be leaving London for Cambridge he replied, 'I am mostly satisfied because at Trinity, of which I shall be a fellow, I shall, I hope, be a member of the Wine and Garden Committees' (which he duly became) even if he was reluctant to leave his commendable landlady in Pinner. She seems to have had an almost maternal instinct for him as a competent cook and laundrymaid. At Trinity she said he would be 'taken out of himself, taken up, made to chatter like the rest of the world.'[289]

Reference to food appears liberally in his poetry and appreciation of good food and wine were about the only pleasures he allowed himself. Housman was a connoisseur of wine, but he seems to have often preferred a simple fare when it came to food if his comments in the Trinity suggestion books are a reliable guide. There are letters from Housman complaining of the menu and standard of cooking even during wartime. His comments in the suggestion books are regular and enjoyable to read, if you were not the college chef: 'Jugged hare without redcurrant jelly is not food!'; 'Spring onions are in season now, and we should have them sometimes with the cheese.' Nor is he shy to offer criticism: 'The sauce aux huître which we had last night with cod was not oyster sauce but Sauce Hollandaise into which an oyster or two had been dropped, combining

289 Richards, *Housman,* p.99.

no better than the Duke of Clarence with Malmsey.' (The said Duke was murdered in a vat of malmsey. [290])

One poem often quoted in this context is this one:

Say, for what were hop-yards meant,
Or why was Burton built on Trent?
Oh many a peer of England brews
Livelier liquor than the Muse,
And malt does more than Milton can
To justify God's ways to man.
Ale, man, ale's the stuff to drink
For fellows whom it hurts to think:
Look into the pewter pot
To see the world as the world's not.

(*ASL* LXII)

And again:

Could man be drunk for ever
With liquor, love, or fights,
Lief should I rouse at morning
And lief lie down of nights.

But men at whiles are sober
And think by fits and starts,
And if they think, they fasten
Their hands upon their hearts.

(*LP* X)

290 Powell, 'Recollections', p.29.

And finally:

> It shall not last for ever,
> No more than earth and skies;
> But he that drinks in season
> Shall live before he dies.
>
> (*MP* XXII)

Beer was little more than a welcome escape from rural toil which most of his lads in his poetry had to endure. Housman himself once said that he preferred beer to wine, and that there was before 1914, at least, a beer brewed on the border of Belgium and Germany which is 'the finest drink in the world.'[291]

Some of the village and hamlet locations in *ASL* would have brewed their own beer or would have done so in living memory. On Titterstone Clee Hill there was once a public house and it was there that Housman's Shropshire lad drank and met others.

> Oh turn not in from marching
> To taverns on the way.
> The drought and thirst and parching
> A little dust will lay,
> And take desire away.
>
> (*AP* XIII)

Housman might have enjoyed his pie and pint on Hampstead Heath and claim the occasions were a main

291 Richards, *Housman*, p.41.

source for the composing of *ASL*, but he hardly ever drank to excess, unlike his narrator, Terence. The narrator himself never advocates total abstinence. In *ASL* LXII:

> It should do good to heart and head
> When your soul is in my soul's stead;
> And I will friend you, if I may,
> In the dark and cloudy day.

Some of his drinking poems were never included in any of his collections, one being:

> Ned Lear and I were drunk last week,
> Oh, dripping drunk were Ned and I
> Too drunk to see, too drunk to speak,
> Too helpless drunk to reason why.
> You might have looked through Ludlow fair
> And never spied a tipsier pair.
>
> (*NF* XVIII)

Housman is making the point that the socialising process is made easier by the lubrication and freedom rendered by excess drinking and that there is a camaraderie generated.

However, Housman had odd views about certain foods. Joan Thomson recalls, 'bread and butter he abominated. He said it even distressed him to watch another person eat anything so unpalatable.'[292] When holidaying on the Continent and when in France or Italy, he would seek the best provincial cellars for the remains of great vintages. He

292 Thomson, 'Reminiscences'.

even had a dish named after him in a Paris restaurant and he introduced crème brûlée to the kitchen of Trinity.

He had a preference for Madeira. There was a limit to the price the Wine Committee would pay for Madeira and on one occasion that particular wine was above it. Housman made up the difference out of his own pocket. Although Richards, his companion on some of their trips, thought Housman was, on the whole, a man of moderation in drinking, he recalled a time when he and Housman together consumed two bottles of wine at lunch, and one at dinner followed by 'brandies of one sort or another.' Richards once called Housman 'a gourmand in don's clothing' and observed 'whatever else he denied himself, he saw no reason to deny the pleasure of eating and drinking', concluding that Housman's 'passion in life was, I should say, accuracy in Latin and in Greek, and he had also pleasure in architecture, but he liked his meals.'[293] Richards hints that Housman's love of food and wine was in part because of his 'having gone far to suppress other senses'. Richards added that he saw Housman a little worse for drink only on two occasions in over 40 years as his publisher and later as his friend.[294]

Richards reflected 'the phrase, to drink too much, is of course a relative term... Housman enjoyed his wine, drank it fastidiously, and carried it like a gentleman.' On one occasion staying overnight in Lyon and having consumed a bottle of Châteauneuf-du-Pape 1911, Housman slept

293 Richards, *Housman*, p.227 and p.38-43.

294 Richards also published books on travel and on food, including *The Gourmet's Guide to Europe*, 1903.

badly, complaining that he was kept awake by the collision of cars under his window.[295]

When Richards sent Housman a wine merchant's catalogue in 1927 Housman replied, 'I still have a fair amount of the pre-War vintages; and I am told that they do not now take proper care about making the wine, the War having greatly increased the demand among lower classes that used to drink it.'[296]

His sister Kate tried to link his interest in wine and gardening: 'He absorbed the look and scent of flowers with a vivid perception that visibly moved him. Maybe it was this sense that afterwards made him a connoisseur of wine.'[297]

Wilfred Scawen Blunt confided in his diary in 1911, '[Housman] does not smoke, drinks little, and would I think be quite silent if he were allowed to be.'[298] Housman said he thought that assessment of him by Blunt was a fair one! When Housman left UCL to go to Cambridge, he was presented with a silver loving cup with the inscription from his poetry – 'Malt does more than Milton can to justify God's way to man.' Housman amusingly described his predecessor at Cambridge, J.E.B. Mayor, as a man who drank like a fish, 'if drinking nothing but water be so described. When they see me come to Cambridge with this cup they will understand that things are going to be changed.'[299]

295 Richards, *Housman*, p.145 and p.235.

296 Letter Housman to Richards, February 1927.

297 'Alfred Edward Housman' supplement to the *Bromsgrovian*, p.24.

298 Blunt, *Diaries*.

299 Quoted by P. Sisley, 'Malt does more than Milton can', *HSJ*, vol.30,

Not many biographies need to include a reference to food and drink but we do in Housman's case. They were among his few luxuries and through his attitude towards them we get a glimpse into his character and even into his poetry. He might not have been good company at High Table for many, and on most occasions, but it seems that Housman enjoyed his meals even if those around enjoyed the food but not necessarily his company. He was a connoisseur of wine, and a person who appreciated decent cuisine – an indication of a cultured man.

2004, p.29. At least Housman admired Mayor regarding him as a 'venerable man' whose learning 'had no equal in England and no superior in Europe.' C. Ricks (ed.), *A. E. Housman Collected Poems and Selected Prose*, Allen Lane, 1998, pp.300-301.

13. HOLIDAYS AND TRAVEL

'Housman arrived... Housman went away.'

From an early stage, Housman enjoyed his Continental travels, and he was an observant traveller who packed in a great deal. 'I stayed in Paris a week, then went to Rome (two nights in the train) and stayed there three or four nights, then to Naples... At Naples I stayed about ten days and then came back by the same route, stopping four or five days at Rome and then at Paris.' He observed 'what most strikes me in Paris is the countless number of handsome streets, any five of which would constitute a fine town in England... Notre Dame is hardly equal to Westminster Abbey... The Bois de Boulogne is wilder and more picturesque than any of our parks.'[300]

There are many descriptive letters in his correspondence, again to his stepmother Lucy Housman. 'After you quit the lake [Lucerne]... the country is still interesting... the valleys are often surprisingly soft and pretty, full of smooth meadows and orchard trees and foaming streams of yellowish water; but many of the mountains would be better for having their tops taken off them.'[301]

He can slip in a lighter, but equally insightful point: 'I suppose Milan is the least Italian town in Italy; it considers itself the intellectual capital of the country and probably hopes to go to France when it dies.' He continues in respect of architecture: '[Milan] cathedral, though we

300 Letter Housman to Lucy Housman, 22 September, 1897.
301 Letter Housman to Lucy Housman, 27 September, 1900.

cannot call it good architecture if compared with French or English or even German or the best Italian Gothic is certainly impressive... except the west front, which has a mean effect and actually looks small thanks to the stupid Italian notion that the proper outline for a west front is the same as that for a dog-kennel.'[302]

Holidays with Richards, at least, were a combination of architectural delights, scenic treats and gastronomical fare. Richards wrote: 'I ask myself whether I shall go on with this vinous and gastronomic chronicle. I confess that I kept it rather for Housman's sake than for my own... You see, others have written of the churches, the architecture, of their enchanting towns, but no one else has eaten and drunk his way through them with such a companion.'[303]

Richards, in his book, seems to give their holidays together almost equal prominence to the coverage afforded to his friend's classical success and poetic output. He even names one chapter 'Eating and drinking our way to Dijon.' Richards implied that Housman showed insatiable curiosity and expected to be well briefed on the places he visited by the chauffeur 'who was supposed to know everything there was to know about Burgundy and any other district in which we might find ourselves' and Housman would choose routes to cover as much terrain of interest as possible; '[the chauffeur] found it rather difficult to adapt his mental processes to the requirements of his employer' who wanted to 'zigzag about the province in what [to the chauffeur] must have seemed an extraordinary

---

302 Letter, Housman to Lucy Housman, 27 September 1900.

303 Richards, *Housman*, p.224.

manner.'[304]

With Richards as his sole companion in France, Richards said he found Housman a delightful companion, 'equable in temper, seldom moody, a good talker, appreciative of attention, polite to those who smoothed his path and untiring. No one who has made his way down with me by wooded, rocky, uneven, tiring paths... has done it with more spirit and has shown more energy... And he loved the southern countryside with its views, its trees and its flowers.'[305] Quite clearly this was the formula for a holiday and companionship that Housman especially enjoyed.

Not wanting to change his routine, Housman visited the Riviera, Nice and Monte Carlo, in 1915. He wrote to Richards, 'Hitherto I have always refused to go to the Riviera, but now is my chance, when the worst classes who infest it are away.'[306] It seems an odd thing to do, visit the Riviera during the First World War. In fact, Housman seems to have had an unusual attitude towards that war. He didn't refer to it in any correspondence with Richards in 1914. Only once did he mention the war, in 1914, writing, 'I have three nephews being inoculated for typhoid and catching pneumonia on Salisbury Plain and performing other acts of war calculated to make the German Emperor realise that he is a very misguided man.'[307] He took a holiday in 1914, a mere three months before the outbreak of war. Having reeled off 12 locations he had visited, Housman

304 Richards, *Housman,* p.223.

305 Ibid, p.136.

306 Ibid, chapter 13.

307 Letter, Housman to Lily Thicknesse, 24 November, 1914.

writes, 'I was in Paris with the King, but he did me no harm, except rather keeping me waiting half an hour to cross the road.'[308]

Venice was also a favourite destination for Housman, no doubt because of the architecture and because of his friendship towards Andrea and his family. His regular visits to Paris satisfied a number of needs: architectural, as a gourmet and as a possible location for homosexual activity.

Housman might not have visited Shropshire on a regular basis, but he did holiday in Britain, for example, in Scotland and with Richards in Cornwall. He was not always the perfect guest. In 1931 Housman stayed in the 75 room house, built in 1888-92 at the head of Loch Aline in Argyllshire. His host, Owen Smith, knew Housman at Trinity where he was an undergraduate. The host noted in his diary, 'Thursday 20th August, I caught a 12lb salmon... Somehow or other he got the gut round his gills and turned up on his side after about five minutes. Housman arrived.'[309] He was one of 17 mainly distinguished guests, not ideal company for the shy Housman, and he seems to have spent most of his stay walking alone. After the diary note of the 20th August on his arrival, there is no further mention of Housman in his host's diary until his departure

308 Letter, Housman to Richards, 2 May, 1914. Housman invited Richards to dinner at Trinity in 1915 and therefore in wartime, 'do not be surprised if a sentry tries to keep you out with a bayonet, as this is now a barracks, sparsely inhabited by four Fellows of Trinity. We do not dress for dinner.' He could have added that there were 500 soldiers billeted at Trinity at the time. Letter Housman to Richards, 17 February, 1915.
309 Quoted in *Country Life*, October, 1973.

eight days later when Smith merely noted, 'Friday 28th August... very hot again: did very little. Housman went away.'[310] His visits to closer friends seem to have been somewhat more successful, particularly those spent with Richards and his family at their own home and on holiday.

Housman took to air travel enthusiastically. He was a keen flier in the pioneering days when that mode of transport was highly unsafe. In 1920, he flew to Paris for a holiday at a time when few did. This was a mere 11 years after Blériot had flown across the English Channel for the very first time. On landing he sent a postcard saying 'Alright. A. E. Housman.'[311] Nor did he bother to take precautions – no stuffing of ears to reduce the incessant noise, nor did he wear his flying suit, another precaution. He admitted to having one but said he bought it in the coal strike and used it merely to keep himself warm. A month before the 1920 flight, which was his first flight, he wrote to Richards 'My inclination to go by Air Express is confirmed by the crash they had yesterday, which will make them careful in the immediate future.'[312]

Housman was perfectly aware of the dangers. He wrote to Kate in 1929, 'I am not flying, as I am taking great care of my life till the book I am now engaged on is finished.'[313] This was the final volume of *Manilius*. His attitude towards flying also gives us a hint of his sense of humour. In one letter dated 17th June 1932, now at

310 N. Goodison, 'A Poet's Argyllshire Holiday,' *HSJ,* vol.36, 2010, pp.54-57.

311 J. Bourne, 'Housman in the Air', *HSJ*, vol.23, 1997 p.42.

312 Letter from Housman to Richards, 15 August 1920.

313 Letter to Kate, 16 August 1929.

Trinity, Housman observes 'pilots have become much more clever and accomplished, and can fly above clouds and even through them without losing their way so that one is not in constant danger of hitting trees and knocking off tall people's hats.'[314] It was even reputed that he was more proud of having travelled so frequently by plane in those early days of air travel than he was of being Kennedy Professor or of having written *ASL*. He wrote to Kate, 'My chief trouble is that what I want is no longer a motor and a chauffeur but an aeroplane and a safe pilot, which I suppose are more expensive.'[315]

He was equally blasé about the dangers of travel by boat. In March 1916, *SS Sussex* went down in the English Channel and Richards had mentioned to Housman that he and his wife might be on it. Housman replies, 'I am assuming that you either were not on the *Sussex* or are one of the rescued' and then goes on promptly to add, 'I enclose a list... to whom I wish copies of *Manilius III* to be sent... The sinking of the Sussex is no deterrent to me; quite the reverse. I argue thus: only a certain number of steamers are destined to sink; one of that number has sunk already without me on board; and that diminishes by one the number of my chances of destruction.'[316]

There is something endearing in Housman's almost youthful enthusiasm for travel and at a time when driving on the Continent was still in its infancy, and for flying

314 D. Butterfield, 'Your affectionate but inefficient godfather' The letters of A.E. Housman to G.C.A. Jackson, *HSJ,* vol.42, 2016.

315 Richards, *Housman,* p.179. Letter Housman to Kate, 3 October, 1920.

316 Letter, Housman to Richards, 28 March, 1916.

when flying was still an unnecessary danger. He relished the sights, the history, the food and wine with carefully selected companions. It must have been exhausting for the chauffeur and sometimes even for his companion but also often fun and unmissable.

14. WOMEN AND CHILDREN

'Women cannot reason.'

'Better if [no] children were there to spoil the fun.'

As with food and drink, we need to touch on other varied topics in order to understand more fully this fascinating and enigmatic man. We can continue with women.

Any fleeting references to women by Housman are emotional, not physical. Joan Thomson thought Housman possessed 'emotion terrifying in its strength' and R. W. Chambers noted the reserved, chivalrous friendliness which marked his relationship with the women of the men he really loved.[317] But it doesn't add up to much and the assumption is surely that whilst some individual women registered and played a part in his life – sister Kate and Joan Thomson are almost, in fact, the sum total. Also in that select group were the wives of Withers and Richards; Withers also identified Sophie Becker, who helped to nurture him after his mother's death and with whom he corresponded for fifty years.

We do need to be careful, on occasion, when trying to interpret Housman's attitude towards women. Although reputed to be sensitive to the wishes of women when on those rare occasions he entertained them to a meal, it might seem that he preferred their exclusion. When Richards said that he, his wife and step-daughter were to be in Paris when Housman would be holidaying there,

317 Thomson, 'Reminiscences'. R. W. Chambers, 1874-1942, British literary scholar, author, academic, at UCL. James Tait Memorial Prize.

Housman wrote 'of course I should be pleased to entertain Mrs Richards and Hélène too but I would rather see you alone.'[318] He explained further that he had suggested their exclusion because he wanted the opportunity to persuade Richards to change his plans and join him for a motoring holiday for two weeks! So far so good, but Housman rather inopportunely added, 'I'd ask Mrs Richards and Hélène to come with us but you know my views about ladies; they are very well, but not for a holiday in a car, an architectural, gastronomic holiday.' To make amends Housman did at least invite Richards and the two ladies to a meal on another occasion.

In a letter to Richards giving 'Miss or Mrs Jewell permission to set and publish [the poems] to her heart's content' he added that she displayed 'an honourable scrupulousness which is doubly remarkable inasmuch as it makes its appearance in a woman and an American.' Wisely he suggests that Richards and not he himself should convey that opinion to her.[319] In another letter Housman writes, 'Women cannot reason, so I suppose your designs are knocked on the head.'[320]

Both Laurence and their sister Clemence were keen and active participants in the suffragette movement, but they got little support from their brother. Housman refused to add his name to the list of authors who in turn had lent their names and support for women's suffrage, on the grounds 'I don't think writers as a class are particularly

318 Letter, Housman to Richards, August 22, 1927.

319 Richards, *Housman,* p.86.

320 Letter, Housman to Richards, 28 March, 1916.

qualified to give advice on the question, and moreover it is signed by Galsworthy and Hewlett and everyone that I can't abide.'[321] Whilst some can agree with the first part of this statement, the second is rather ungenerous.

We get a further insight in his reply to a letter sent to him by Lily Thicknesse, in 1909. She was a legal luminary, supporter of the vote for women. She sent Housman a copy of her husband's pamphlet *The Wrongs of Women.* The pamphlet stated that women cannot serve in the army or navy to which Housman writes 'cruel, cruel!' She cannot be ordained a priest or deacon – Housman adds, 'nor become a Freemason.' She cannot be a member of the Royal Society – and he adds 'nor of the Amateur Boxing Association.' Housman concludes, 'your unhappy sex seems to have nothing to look forward to, except contracting a valid marriage as soon as they are 12 years old; and that must soon pall.'[322] Sarcasm, yet Housman is also saying that the world is full of unfairnesses, injustices, inequality and imperfections. In the end, though, he cast his vote in favour of women's suffrage.[323] However, on one occasion Housman became impatient with a request for *LP* to be included in an anthology, refusing permission to any of the National Federation of Women's Institutes and Richards hypothesized that the refusal was prompted by Housman's lack of sympathy for the Feminist Movement.[324]

321 S. Hopkins, 'Housman and Votes for Women,' *HSJ*, vol.26, 2000, pp.62-72.

322 The Thicknesse Letters. From a file belonging to Housman's nephew N.V.H. Symons.

323 K. Jebb, *A.E. Housman*, Bridgend, Seren, 1992, pp.54-55, 121.

324 Richards, *Housman,* p.282.

Much time has been devoted to the study of Housman's relationships with other men – the undisputed love of his life, Jackson, his brother Laurence, his friends such as Richards and Withers. Housman was the typical confirmed bachelor. He confessed to Withers that death and marriage were raging through Trinity and he was grateful to have escaped both. Laurence stated that his brother was a born bachelor and had chosen the habit of life that suited him best.

We have a glimpse of Housman's character developing from childhood. Whilst never conceding that her brother was anything other than a gifted poet and classicist, whose temperament deserved respect and sensitive interpretation, Kate said of their childhood spent at Fockbury: 'Our gatherings were generally hilarious; yet in looking back it is in these doings that we can now see that [Housman] had an emotional nature, subject to gloom that spread in spite of his efforts to subdue it.' Kate's Housman was an adult before his time, sometimes taciturn, already adopting in adolescence the habits of later years. 'Punctuality, industry, fixed routine, daily walking, love of flowers and trees, woods and hills,' she noted as the defining parameters of his life.[325]

Being the eldest of seven, understandably, Housman took the leading role amongst the siblings. Typical examples are recorded by Laurence in his autobiography. For instance, his reference to acting plays as children which were of their 'own composing, unwritten and impromptu.' Housman would announce 'we are going to do a play

325 Symons, *Recollections*, p.17 & p.29.

to-night... and there and then he would tell us the plot and assign to us our parts... and without any rehearsal... the play was performed less to their entertainment, I imagine than ours.' He added, 'I don't think we acted well; and I don't remember that we ever got praised for our performances.'[326]

Laurence interestingly mentions the attitude adopted by their stepmother with her Puritan streaks: 'and it was only gradually that we escaped into the larger airs of our own choosing... the blend of so many and so opposite qualities [in our family] made membership of it a liberal, if not an easy education.'[327] He refers to their intellectual games, often with a literary persuasion – nonsensical verse, the writing of short poems containing a collection of nouns, with each member of the company supplying one.

Laurence also recalls the time when Housman joined him up a tree and told him that he must write a sonnet, even though he was too young to understand what a sonnet was, let alone write one. Housman had written a poem which he didn't think good enough for himself but he didn't want it to be lost and so he decided he would 'stuff it down my throat' so that the rejected poem would be passed off as that of his younger sibling.[328]

Housman was still in this bullying mode many years later: 'I had far, far, rather have my poems mistaken for yours, than your poems mistaken for mine.'[329] Did he,

326 Housman, *Unexpected Years,* p.77.

327 Ibid, p.97.

328 Ibid, p.20.

329 Ibid, p.20.

therefore, on occasion, think that some of his poetry was not good enough and that might be a contributory reason why he declined the Poet Laureateship? Pure speculation! Despite not liking the idea of any of his poems being mistaken for Laurence's he still appointed Laurence as his literary executor.

There are few references in respect of the adult Housman to children other than reflections by a nephew and a passing reference by Richards. 'That February visit was to destroy in my mind, once and for all, the idea that Housman did not like children, had no interest in them, no sympathy with them... as we [Housman and I] walked up through the garden a whoop of angry defiance and one of my infants... dashed into view... Having been warned that they were neither to be seen nor heard by the visitor... being very obedient children they pulled themselves up in confusion at the sight of the ogre whom they supposed him to be. [Housman] was friendly; he talked to them; he adapted himself for a few minutes to the high spirits... He took pains to learn their names. He won their hearts and thereafter in all his visits would wish to see them; and he continued to interest himself in their progress.'[330] Presumably Housman had a reputation for disliking children, otherwise Richards would not have forewarned his own children or bother to record it in his memoir. He declined an invitation to share Richards' birthday when he knew there would be other company: 'I do rather think that the birthday etc. might go off better if no irrelevant visitor were there to spoil the fun; and so, in spite of my

330 Richards, *Housman,* pp.92-93.

affection for children, I should like to postpone my visit.'[331]

When Housman accepted an invitation to join Richards and his family on a holiday in Cornwall in a 'small and ancient cottage' filled with five children Richards commented 'if it were true that Housman did not take kindly to the society of women, did not like children, and had no affection for animals, he would have shown signs of discomfort.' And there was no 'discomfort' recorded. Richards did add, however, that his guest left on the appointed date and merely in order to pursue his usual life and interests – his books, his own desk, the attractions of near solitude, of architecture and of well-balanced meals.[332]

Housman's attitude to Laurence in childhood, even taking into account every normal aspect of conventional sibling rivalry, was unusual. It was fortunate that Laurence, and Kate to a lesser extent, forgave their brother, excusing his behaviour and even making light of it. Housman was also awkward towards women and probably little more than tolerant of children.

---

331 Letter, Housman to Richards, 16 October, 1907.

332 Richards, *Housman,* pp.151-3.

Sir Henry Lamb, portrait sketch of A.E. Housman, 1909
reproduced by kind permission of Trinity College, Cambridge

15. HIS CHARACTER

'My books are more interesting than the man.'

When delivering his Gray lectures on Housman in 1946, Garrod confessed, 'I have lost myself – which of his contemporaries has not? – in the enigma of the man.' With Housman there is evidence of kindness, humour, generosity, genuine modesty, coupled with an acute inability to relate to people. Yet he was often crusty, unable to express concern, show enthusiasm, offer encouragement or accept accolades, adulation and appreciation from grateful fellow scholars or from non-academics.

The Times in its lengthy obituary referred to his 'rhetorical emphasis and gesture' but also to being so 'unapproachable as to diffuse a frost, and shroud himself in impenetrable reserve... [He] was most reticent about himself and his experiences... impatient of conventions and stupidities... [He] held back from intimate relations, and [preferred] isolation to giving himself away... [He] matured and mellowed much at Cambridge... but... his scathing tone of criticism, the restraint of his poetry, his irony in talk, and his tenacious reserve were defences deliberately adopted by a sensitive nature against the courser and ruder incursions of the world upon his privacy. He preferred to go his way unchallenged, unpitied, and alone.'[333]

Richard Middleton compared him to 'an undertaker's mule' in his monologues in 1913.[334] Stanley Baldwin, the

333 *The Times* obituary, May, 1936.

334 Richard Middleton, 1882-1911, English poet and author chiefly remem-

Prime Minister, found him a 'most unclubbable man.'[335] Augustus John, the artist, recording his first meeting with Housman, summed it up as 'not auspicious... Housman looked like a solicitor but didn't behave like one.'[336] William Plomer described Housman as 'unsociable and decidedly sour' in the *Listener* in 1951.[337] But Housman's bedmaker at Trinity said to Laurence, 'I loved your brother. When I first began to do for him, I used to be afraid to go into the room; but it was all right when I got to know him.'[338] The matron at the nursing home where he died echoed similar sentiments.

Housman was known to be a dry and unapproachable scholar. There is no known recording of Housman's voice but the general impression of him as a lecturer was that he possessed an impassive voice, spoke without enthusiasm, was erect, punctual (if a student was late, he would pause until the student had reached their place), allowed a certain sparseness to accompany his delivery, used a precision of phrase and was always austere in manner.[339] There is nothing particularly unusual in a scholar of Housman's stature and time being dry in presentation. His delivery was pedestrian, not helped by reading his lectures word

---

bered today for his short ghost stories, in particular *The Ghost Ship*.

335 A remark made on an occasion when sitting next to Housman at a Cambridge dinner in 1933.

336 A. John, *Chiaroscuro*, London, Cape, 1952, p.76.

337 William Plomer was a contemporary of Housman's, a novelist, poet and literary editor.

338 Housman, *Memoir*, p.120.

339 Only Fothergill, who called his an 'attractive, thin mandarin voice,' and Thomson are known to have commented favourably on his voice; most made no comment or were marginally disparaging.

for word, never looking up to see what impression, if any, he was making, his face expressionless, with its heavy overhanging moustache, his bald cranium, a middle-aged man. Indeed, Housman could be intimidating and controlling at the same time but with it came great insights and wisdom. One former undergraduate called his lectures 'impressive, but repellent.'[340]

His students were aware of being in the presence of an extraordinary mind – they knew they couldn't fail to learn from these 'athletic exercises.' He was in complete control of his lecture room. No undergraduate would dare to misbehave or mock him, and they knew that his words were infallibly correct. With difficult passages he was known to spend an hour covering seven or eight lines. The audience were left feeling that they had received the moral enlargement of a great sermon. For Housman textual criticism was the exercise of moral self-discipline: rigorous, logical but rather dull, devoid of passion. Could there be a greater contrast to his poetry? Housman won praise in his lectures for his critical rigour, but few could fully understand the lectures. Geoffrey Gorer, a student and later an anthropologist, stated 'with the possible exception of his old friend A.E. Housman, [J.G. Frazer] was the worst lecturer I ever sat under.'[341]

He could upset his students, reducing female undergraduates to tears and a week later he would have forgotten the occasion or wouldn't be able to remember

340 UCL MS. Add 6877.2

341 J.G. Eayrs, *Greenpeace and her enemies*, Toronto, Anansi Press, 1973, p120.

which undergraduate he had upset. No undergraduate would dare to approach this odd intellect in his worn gown, with traces of splatter made rusty with time.[342] He hardly ever made eye contact even when proceeding to the rostrum, a habit broken in his penultimate lecture course in 1936, an occasion when there was also recorded a vague resemblance of a smile.

Housman was not averse to being less than complimentary about the lecturing style of others. In 1926, a student was advised by his supervisor, J.T. Sheppard, to attend Housman's lectures on Horace's *Epodes* and thereby learn how textual criticism should be tackled and this recommendation was despite Housman saying, 'I hear your lectures are very well attended so I know they must be bad.'[343]

This 'mental machine of great power and precision', added Powell, 'could be excused the severity of his presentation as it was not of passionlessness but of suppressed passion, passion for true poetry and passion for truthfulness.' He was unaware of Powell's idol worshipping. Powell never spoke to Housman until he was himself a Fellow at Trinity or on the occasions when he sat beside him at High Table. But conversation then was limited to food and wine. Housman never initiated the conversation: 'I have to confess that the correct use

342 Miraculously it seems that all his lecture notes survive constituting 29 volumes but unfortunately there is little record of how they were received; they are in University Library, Cambridge.

343 Reminiscences of L.P. Wilkson, from a paper read at Durham University to the Northumberland and Durham Branch of the Classical Association, 27 February, 1973.

of red pepper was the only actual piece of learning I ever imbibed from him in personal intercourse.'[344]

To the poet Wilfred Scawen Blunt, Housman was 'a typical Cambridge don, prim in his manner, learned, accurate, and well-informed.' Blunt goes on to say what others often did, that he had a 'disconcerting way of refusing to smile.' Blunt, whilst commenting on Housman being silent and rather shy, did manage to 'have much pleasant talk all day and sat up again till twelve at night telling ghost stories. He takes an interest in these.'[345] Housman told Gow that Blunt's description of the visit was correct but that 'so far as [he] could remember there was little to drink.'[346]

George Lyttelton, father of the jazz musician, Humphrey Lyttelton, also held strong views about Housman. 'Housman [...] was absurdly donnish, aloof and prim, except when slightly tight, when he revealed a Rabelaisian vein and even broke into silvery laughter. He was easily the most affable man I have ever met, but I imagine he was all a tangle with complexes and inhibitions and what not.'[347]

Housman was a perfectionist, obsessed with plainness

344 Powell, 'Recollections', pp.28-29.

345 Blunt, *Diaries,* Part II, p.287.

346 Gow, *Sketch,* p.47.

347 Humphrey Lyttelton, 1921-2008, English jazz musician and broadcaster. George Lyttelton, 1863-1962, member of the aristocratic Lyttelton family, inspiring teacher of classics and literature at Eton, avid sportsman. The publication of his letters gave him posthumous success. Not such a competent musician as his son Humphrey, 'when... he [practises] the cello all the cats in the district converge upon his rooms in the belief that one of their members is in distress.'

of speech, saying that accuracy is a duty not a virtue. He wrote, 'I have spent most of my time in finding faults, because finding faults, if they are real and not imaginary, is the most useful sort of criticism' adding 'a vague and conventional laudation which is distributed at large, like the rain of heaven by reviewers who do not know the truth and consequently cannot tell it' is quite pointless.[348] He also said 'it is the critic's chief duty, and should be his chief pleasure, to commend what is good.'[349] He praised the scholar Herbert Richards, saying there are too few severe and thorough scholars of his sort. He once said that 'the faintest of all human passions is the love of truth' and he had a very low opinion of most fellow scholars, borrowing a sentence from Swift: they are 'as little qualified for thinking as for flying.'[350] He expressed his views on knowledge thus: 'A scholar who means to build himself a monument must spend much of his time in acquiring knowledge which for its own sake is not worth having and in reading books which do not in themselves deserve to be read.'[351]

Housman could be unreasonable and disingenuous. We have noted some of his comments about fellow classicists. Robinson Ellis, Professor of Latin at Oxford, gave him a reference for the chair at UCL, an act of faith and considerable foresight considering that Housman had failed his Greats and had only recently passed by

348 *Classical Review,* 1900, p.469.
349 *Classical Review,* 1890, p.106.
350 Quoted in Garrod's Grays lecture.
351 A. Platt, *Nine Essays With a Preface by Housman*, Cambridge, Cambridge University Press, 1926, p.xi.

studying in the evenings.[352] He described Robinson Ellis as someone whose readers were 'in perpetual contact with the intellect of an idiot child.' Yet Robinson Ellis thought kindly of Housman, saying he always found him amicable and modest. Housman was lucky in the circumstances to secure no less than 14 distinguished classical scholars from around the world as his referees. One was a former tutor T.C. Snow who went about 'with collar occasionally fastened by string.'[353] Despite his eccentricity Snow was perceptive, referring to Housman's 'brilliancy, learning, and sound common sense.'[354]

Housman's apparent unreasonableness can perhaps be seen when he shared a landing with Ludwig Wittgenstein.[355] Housman had his own lavatory, Wittgenstein did not; and when the latter was taken short one day and asked Housman if he could use it, Housman refused, on the grounds that he disagreed with Wittgenstein's philosophical theories. This might be apocryphal and we will never know for certain. There are also variations of this alleged incident. If true it is at moments such as this that I have to remind myself – as literally smelling salts – that this same man could also write such lines as 'Farewell to barn and stack and tree;' 'On moonlight heath and lonesome bank;' 'On

352 Carter, *Selected Prose*. Robinson Ellis, 1834-1913, Corpus Professor of Latin, Oxford, formerly Professor of Latin at UCL.
353 D. Wilson, *Gilbert Murray OM 1866-1957*, Oxford, Oxford University Press, 1987, p18.
354 Naiditch, *Housman at UCL*, p.20.
355 Ludwig Wittgenstein, 1889-1951, Austrian-British philosopher; worked mainly in logic, the philosophy of mathematics, of the mind and of language.

Wenlock Edge the woods in trouble;' 'From far, from eve and morning;' 'On the idle hill of summer;' 'In midnights of November;' 'When I would muse in boyhood;' 'Tell me not here, it needs not saying.' Alan Bennett, in his address at the unveiling of the memorial panel to Housman in Poets' Corner in Westminster Abbey, recalled that Wittgenstein's most famous aphorism was, 'whereof one cannot speak, thereof one must be silent', reflecting such a philosophy was surely common ground between Housman and Wittgenstein.

A conventional take on Housman is that he was a modest man. In response to a request in 1921 for some biographical details to accompany an article on him to be published in America, Housman replied, 'Some men are more interesting than their books but my books are more interesting than the man.'[356] Furthermore, he declined certain honours such as the Poet Laureateship and the Order of Merit, in fact all professional honours other than an Hon. Fellowship of St John's College Oxford, because, as he put it, he had a contempt for his passion for distinction. *The Times,* in its obituary, observed 'his haughty spirit despised notoriety.'

However, it is also possible he felt inadequate, that he could not live up to the expectations of being a great national poet that the Laureateship would have conferred upon him. It was strange to have been offered the Poet Laureateship at all, or at least then. He was never a prolific poet, as we know, and he had published at the time (he had written more) only about 100 poems and most of those were

356 Letter, Housman to Richards, September 1921.

less than 50 lines long. It is a reminder of the high regard the Establishment had for Housman at the time. If one of the main requirements for being a success as Poet Laureate was to compose verse to order, then he might have found that either tedious or a challenge. When Richards asked him to seek out an appropriate phrase from a Greek or Latin author on Herbert Richards' tombstone, Housman failed to find one despite consulting 'a good many pages' and '[having] thought about the matter from time to time' and nor did he volunteer to pen a line or two of poetry for that occasion.'[357] Nor, as we noted, did he compose one on the death of his nephew. There is record of only one occasion when he did anything like this, namely on the death of his brother Herbert.

Gow commended his decision to decline the OM, saying that Housman in so doing belonged to the more exclusive group who had rejected one. Richards records that when asked about the OM, Housman expressed anger.[358] Others have also declined the Laureateship; Kipling did, for example, wanting to be regarded as the poet of the British Empire, not just of England. Housman declined to stand for the Public Oratorship of Cambridge University: 'not if the stipend were £150,000, instead of £150, would I be Public Orator.'[359]

We have noted that Scawen Blunt, amongst others, considered Housman to be a shy man, which may also have contributed to his aversion to accepting accolades and

357 Richards, *Housman,* p.157.

358 Ibid, p.159.

359 Maas, *Letters*, p.170. letter dated 3 January, 1920.

honours. This shyness may go a long way to explaining the constant references throughout his life to his proverbial silences. Withers wrote 'it was questioning alone which positively assured his talking' adding that the comments were worth the wait as Housman's phrases were like 'a burnished rapier, a steel forthrightness.'[360] Withers found Housman's silences frustrating yet the friendship of each to the other was mutually regarded as their most valued. Gow was alert to Housman's less attractive traits, to his unsociability on many occasions, agreeing that Housman could prove 'exhausting' as a dining companion, and that 'to the end of his life he remained, in ordinary society, a little difficult by reason of his silence.'[361] Aldington said 'he was hopelessly and helplessly shy and sensitive, as well as proud and exacting.'[362]

Joan Thomson said when Housman opened up 'to talk with Housman was to realise what great beauty and force is in the English language' and that he 'would give of his very best in conversation with someone who cared for him.'[363] Powell cared for him, so did Barrie, as did many others, but they were usually consigned to an interminable ordeal at High Table. When Barrie and Housman, two literary giants, met as guests when Barrie was staying at Jesus College, the two men sat in total silence, side by side, throughout the meal. Barrie wrote: 'When dinner was over I was dying to ask him up to my rooms for a smoke

360 Withers, *Buried Life*, pp.23-25.
361 Gow, *Sketch*, p.48.
362 Aldington, *Housman and Yeats*, p.7.
363 Thomson, 'Reminiscences'.

and a chat – but I couldn't. So I sat down and wrote him a letter.

> Dear Professor Houseman
> You must have found me very incommunicative in hall tonight. But I am a strangely silent man.'

The reply was pure Housman:

> Dear Sir James
> You must have found me very incommunicative in the hall the other night: I, too, am a strangely silent man. By the way, you spell my name wrong.[364]

Barrie, however, always retained an admiration for Housman, regretting that he never got to know him better. It didn't make the slightest difference to Housman that by then Barrie was famous for *Peter Pan* and knighted.

To Max Beerbohm he was 'like an absconding cashier. We certainly wished he would abscond – sitting silent and saying only "there is a bit of a nip in the air, don't you think?"'[365] Beerbohm wrote a quatrain about Housman and Hardy, believing that the two literary greats shared much in character:

> How compare either of these grim two?
> Each has his equal knack
> Hardy supplies the pill that's blue,

364 Anderson, *Memories*.

365 D. Cecil, *Max: A Biography*, Boston, Houghton Mifflin, 1965, p.262.

Housman the draught that's black.[366]

Despite all, Housman enjoyed Beerbohm's caricatures. On a visit to Withers' home 'he spent most of one day voluntarily with the several volumes of Max Beerbohm's caricatures in visible and audible enjoyment.'[367]

Yet J. J. Thomson, Master of Trinity in Housman's time, found Housman to be always good company and hence he was pleased to have the chance to sit next to him. George Macauley Trevelyan, the eminent historian, commented 'he was always very kind to me and I delighted in talk with him'.[368] Housman was a regular participant at The Family, a dining club at Cambridge of 12 members each of whom took it in turns to entertain the rest, and in whose company he would expand and relax with flashes of wit and anecdotes. However, it should be added that on one occasion when Stanley Baldwin was a guest in 1930, Baldwin said afterwards that he regretted that he hadn't had the courage to speak to Housman![369] By then Baldwin had served as Prime Minister twice and was the current Chancellor of Cambridge University. On another occasion with Laurence, he visited Mary Anderson de Navarro – they had invited themselves to lunch at her home. During the meal Housman was in a talkative mood, complimenting the good food and the well-

366 J.G. Reiwald (ed.), *Rhymes and Parodies of Max Beerbohm*, Stephen Greene Press, 1963.

367 P. Withers, *New Statesman*, 1936.

368 C. Clemens, *Mark Twain Society*.

369 S. C. Roberts, *The Family: The History Of A Dining Club*, printed for the club, Cambridge, 1963, p.23.

selected wine. They then adjourned to the garden where Housman showed how knowledgeable he was on flowers. Later Laurence said to his brother that it was time to go. Housman merely commented 'I am being hurried away, and I would like to stay here for hours.'[370]

Housman seems to have been disciplined and self-contained throughout his life. As an undergraduate at Oxford, he gave the impression of being a 'well-behaved young man, studious and orderly, and anything but the commoner type of drinking, hunting and whoring rowdy. In fact he passed through Oxford without getting into trouble or debt.'[371]

Housman was a person who had intense likes and dislikes. We have noted that his reactions could be both odd and unconventional in respect of certain foods. Just as he confided in Joan Thomson about bread and butter being abominations, she noted that 'he was apt to take a strong antipathy to a person at first sight, merely if it happened that he disliked the shape of the individual's nose or his complexion. So strong might this antipathy be that Housman would find it almost impossible to look at the person concerned, far less to associate with him.'[372] To Joan Thomson again he said how much he loved nature, the countryside, flowers, especially brilliant colours, how he admired scarlet anemones and how he preferred the scent of violets. She noted also that he appreciated ecclesiastical architecture; similar comments were made

370 M. Anderson de Navarro, *Memories*.

371 Maas, pp.10-11.

372 Thomson, 'Reminiscences'.

by Kate, Richards and Kidd.[373]

Housman was reluctant to have his portrait done. When Rothenstein asked if he could do a second portrait Housman replied 'I also do not want to sit (the more so because I have suffered enough from his pencil for one lifetime)... Rothenstein cannot draw a likeness' – yet he was one of the most preeminent portrait painters of his day.[374] His reputation was endorsed by Edmund Gosse who described one portrait of Housman by Rothenstein as 'superlatively good.'[375] Rothenstein presented the sitter with one of the portraits but that didn't stop Housman in response to Rothenstein seeking permission to reproduce one of them to note 'no doubt [he chose] the more repulsive.'[376] Sitting for a portrait for Henry Lamb was no more appealing, Housman writing, 'I have noted the day and hour at which I am to go and have my teeth taken out by Lamb.'[377]

Generally, he seemed to be reticent to have any depiction of himself whether in a portrait or a photograph. When the *Bookman* took a photograph of him he quipped, 'O damn the Bookman... I thought that my reply had chilled him off. I have not been photographed, I think, since 1894...

373 Beresford James Kidd, 1864-1948, Anglican priest and Church historian, Warden of Keble College, Oxford, 1920-1939.

374 Letter Housman to J.M Barrie, 28 February, 1928.

375 Sir Edmund Gosse CB, 1849-1928, English poet, author and critic. His account of his childhood brought up strictly by the Plymouth Brethren is generally regarded as the first psychological biography.

376 Letter Housman to Richards, 24 September, 1913.

377 Richards, *Housman*, p.88. Henry Lamb, 1883-1960, Australian born British painter, follower of Augustus John, founder member of the Camden Town Group in 1911 and the London Group in 1913.

As to Rothenstein, the one he shows in exhibitions, is a venomous libel, to which he adds fresh strokes whenever he feels nasty.'[378] He showed more willingness when a request came in 1922 to be photographed, a photograph which became the basis for a medallion of Housman which he accepted later that year and presumably found the depiction acceptable.

Housman had a generous streak – he helped the family of the gondolier Andrea as we know. Soon after leaving Oxford with no degree and with poor prospects and engaged in a modest role at the Patent Office, he deposited £200 from a relatively small inheritance from his aunt to help pay the mortgage interest on Perry Hall, his family home, not an example repeated by his siblings despite their inheritance.[379] When his nephew, N. V. Housman Symons, lost an arm in action in 1917, he wrote 'my poor dear fellow' and wanted him to have the best possible artificial arm and promising that he would pay for it.

He was generous towards his godson, Gerald Jackson. Writing to him in 1931 whilst Gerald was studying in Canada, he said 'if in these times you find yourself at all in straits... I hope you will apply to me. Unless we have a Labour government, in which case I should be unable to do anything for anyone.'[380] And when later Gerald returned to Imperial College after a term at Cambridge, Housman paid the previous term's bill. Further offers of financial help were made later. Housman made it clear to

378 Letter, Housman to Richards, 28 September, 1920.

379 Kate Symons introduction to Richards, *Housman*.

380 Butterfield, 'Your affectionate godfather', pp.89-10.

Gerald why he was so generous: 'if you could have any idea of what my feeling for your father was and still is you would not grudge me the pleasure.'[381]

He was also adamant that he should never make money out of his poems, insisting that they be published in cheap editions and so made available to all. For over 20 years Housman expected Richards to apply royalties from *ASL* towards reducing the price of the book, although later he accepted royalties from *ASL* and indeed from *LP*. Nor did he wish to make money out of the musical compositions, whether from the composer or the music publisher. In one letter he states, 'I have not exacted fees from other people who have set other pieces, so I don't want to begin now. Vanity, not avarice, is my ruling passion... So long as young men... would rather part with their hair than their copy of my book, I do not feel the need of food and drink.'[382]

Housman was especially generous – and frequently so – towards Richards. Richards had been swindling Housman out of monies from the American edition of *ASL* but Housman forgave him. At least Richards tried to repay some of the debt. He had published four of George Bernard Shaw's plays which Shaw had subsequently inscribed and they were valued in 1926 at £250 (about £3000 today). Richards wanted to sell them and give the proceeds to Housman. Richards was an inept businessman and went bankrupt in 1905. In 1920 when he went bankrupt for the second time, Housman lent him £500, transferring

381 Quoted by Edgar Vincent in 'With affection,' *TLS*, 30 September 2016, pp.16-17.
382 Letter Housman to H.H. Ettrich, 22 June, 1903.

the loan into a gift the following year, and advanced him a further £250. When Richards failed again in 1926, there was no letter of anger from Housman for the unpaid royalties; Housman merely took the necessary legal action in order to try and protect his interests. He was never a wealthy man, but one detects that he could live well but frugally as a result of his relatively low daily expenses, being a Fellow at Trinity and living in cloistered academia for the majority of his adult life.

Witter Bynner managed to get permission in 1903 to reprint some of Housman's poems – and duly sent Housman a cheque, though he was not obliged to do so by copyright. Housman returned it. The two men never met. However, they corresponded between 1903 and 1935 and Bynner said the correspondence was characterised by 'a reserved friendliness.'[383]

N. V. Housman Symons recalled how his uncle was a 'most generous tipper. During our boyhood he was not famous except in classical circles and as far as we boys were concerned he was a quiet and pleasant visitor.' When Housman Symons stayed at Trinity 'for a few days' he said Housman 'did me proud.' Lunch always 'included a large bottle of Trinity Audit Ale and at dinner at High Table two or three cut glass decanters of vintage port.' Furthermore, 'every door was open to him without question and he was treated everywhere with the greatest

383 Witter Bynner in James Craft (ed), *Selected Letters*, New York, 1981. Witter Bynner, 1881 - 1968, American poet, playwright, translator from the Chinese, a literary hoaxer and long-time promoter of Housman's works, poetry editor of *McClure's Magazine* in which he printed 13 poems of *ASL*.

deference and respect.'[384] He did add, however, that he thought he might have been the only person ever to have been Housman's guest at Trinity for more than one dinner, bed and breakfast.

Later in life Housman made two reasonably generous gifts to H. M. Treasury for the war effort and again during the financial crisis in 1931 'he came to the rescue so far as his means allowed.'[385]

We know that Housman regarded himself as an outsider, born an outcast according to the 'laws of God' (largely in his view because of his homosexuality). He was sympathetic to others who were deemed outsiders, judged for the colour of their hair (*AP* XVIII). In his poems he even had sympathy for the criminal, often a murderer, although we are not always told what crime had been committed by the luckless lad.

He realised that he could not escape this earth, even though as an outsider he might, on occasion, have wished to do so:

> And since, my soul, we cannot fly,
> To Saturn nor to Mercury,
> Keep we must, if keep we can,
> These foreign laws of God and man.
>
> (*LP* XII)

Philip Larkin understood this 'inner agony' which appears

384 N.V. Housman Symons, 'Some Recollections of the Victorian Housmans', *HSJ*, vol.7, 1981, pp.5-15.
385 Richards, *Housman*, p.125.

to be so central to the soul of Housman. Indeed, there is a parallel in his and Housman's lives; both felt a deep loneliness, both had university careers, careers outside university, both were successful poets and both went to St. John's College, Oxford. Larkin reflected, as only a kindred spirit who is also a poet was able to do, Housman's 'sorrow required its own mythology, the haunting, half-realised legend of ploughing, enlisting, betrothals and betrayals and hangings, and always behind them summertime on Bredon, and the wind on Wenlock Edge, and nettles blowing on graves.' Larkin wrote 'one's first impression is that Housman's life was, if not happy, then remarkably successful and well organised... To be more unhappy than fortunate suggests some jamming of the emotions.'[386]

Just as Larkin could relate to Housman, Housman in turn could relate to T. E. Lawrence, Lawrence of Arabia; when Lawrence wrote, 'There was my craving to be liked... The terror of failure in an effort so important made me shrink from trying'.[387] In his own copy, in the margin, Housman wrote 'This is me.' His brother Laurence reiterated this by saying 'Alfred's craving to be liked was also a craving to be understood.'[388]

We also know that Housman denied that he was a pessimist. He claimed that he was on the whole a happy man even if he held that the world was not. We have seen

386 Larkin, *Required Writing*, p.262-265. Interestingly in Larkin's *Twentieth-Century English Verse* Housman gets 8 poems, the same as Masefield and de la Mare, one fewer that Eliot and Edward Thomas and one more that Wilfred Owen.

387 T.E. Lawrence, *Seven Pillars of Wisdom*, 1922.

388 Housman, *De Amicitia*.

that Housman frequently preferred his own company, for example when a guest at Loch Aline. We should remember though that many dons in the nineteenth and early twentieth centuries – along with schoolmasters of public schools – were eccentric compared to their 21st century counterparts. Housman's desire for solitude was not uncommon in his day.

Kate thought that it was the surprising exam failure in Greats which 'permanently influenced his attitude towards the outside world' and that 'poetry seems to have acted as a safety valve to his mental sufferings' especially whilst living in London.[389]

Laurence shared many of Kate's views on their brother and this made his task, as Housman's literary executor, all the more difficult if he was to honour his brother's character, respect his sensitivities and protect his reputation. In fact, Laurence was better qualified to be the literary executor than both Kate and others might have thought despite his shortcomings; he understood being homosexual himself the deep anguish and suffering Housman endured.

It was easy to misunderstand Housman and some never got a second chance to improve on their first impressions. Gow remarked, 'Our first encounter however was not very productive for Housman spoke little and said nothing memorable.'[390] A typical reaction. We commented earlier on Richards' first meeting with Housman, of him being polite, precise but not especially congenial. Writing 40 years later Richards records that he had thought Housman

389 Symons, *Recollections*, p.30.

390 Gow, *Trinity Review* Lent Term, 1967, p.13-14.

was 'an enigma' and that he 'carries no surface secrets... and I have no reason to write otherwise today, although I am not now quite sure what a "surface secret is!"'[391]

Housman corresponded with a wide range of people other than his close friends and family – including T. S. Eliot, Sir Arthur Quiller-Couch, John Masefield and J. B. Priestley.[392] For a man who lived a rather cloistered existence, the letters are surprisingly wide ranging, but Henry Maas concluded on editing Housman's letters that his subject's life was not adventurous. Via them we can see a generous and kindly Housman, even if often crusty and irascible, but in that mix was some humour, and hardly any pomposity. Maas concluded 'I found myself liking him despite myself.'[393]

Archie Burnett published a further collection of Housman's letters, filling 1296 pages, and he reached a similar conclusion to Maas, finding him to be 'an even greater, more amicable, more sociable, more generous, more painstaking, and altogether more complex person that his biographers and the previous edition of the letters led me to believe.'[394] William Semple, who, incidentally, constitutes the only known instance of Housman supervising anyone for a Doctorate, wrote 'to [Housman's] direction and criticism and support I owe more than I could

391 Richards, *Housman,* p.31.

392 John Masefield, 1878-1967, OM, English poet, Poet Laureate 1930-1967, amongst his best known works are his children's novels *The Mid-night Folk* and *The Box of Delights* and the poems 'The Everlasting Mercy' and 'Sea-Fever'.

393 Preface to Maas, *Letters.*

394 Burnett, *Letters*, vol. 1.

ever express.'[395] And being Housman, it is very unlikely that any of the letters were written with a wider audience in mind or for posterity. It would not be in his character to write a letter hoping that it would be found on some distant shore and attract a wider audience.

When the grandson of Semple discovered a further cache of 30 letters in 2020 from Housman to his grandfather he too commented that Housman appeared a warmer personality than he had hitherto understood him to be. The discovery of these letters so recently could mean, of course, that there are other letters somewhere still to be discovered. Only a decade ago there was a consensus that Burnett's *Collected Letters* was a complete and as comprehensive a collection as we could reasonably expect. Then a large collection of letters of Gerald Jackson appeared, showing again the human side of Housman in a way that we had not seen previously.

This human side can be seen in a letter from John Maycock, a colleague of Housman's at the Patent Office, who wrote to Housman, 'I like you better than any man I ever knew. There is as far as I could ever discover, absolutely no flaw in your character as a man, and no one would ever hope for a better friend'. He goes on to say how much he admired the way Housman can 'stick to a friend like you have to Jackson.'[396]

Some of the letters are a mere single word, 'refuse',

395 Letter Semple to Richards, May 1936. William Semple, 1900-1981, Hulme Professor of Latin at Manchester University 1937-1967, maintained friendly correspondence with Housman until the latter's death.
396 Maas, *Letters,* p.28.

while others are more fulsome. We quoted earlier that Housman wrote 'vanity, not avarice' was his 'ruling passion.' Housman is being light-hearted; if he had to choose a Deadly Sin he is not bothered about becoming rich, though pretends that vanity appeals to him, assuming that his reader will take this as a self-effacing comment. Many are about detail, print runs, proofreading, copyright, but these can also reveal part of his character, that of the pedantic perfectionist, and his humour. 'Mr Thomas thanks me for a poem, but prints two: which is the poem he doesn't thank me for?'[397]

With such a contradictory character, it is no wonder that Housman has been parodied – but then so have others including Dylan Thomas; indeed, there are whole books of them, for instance, *The Faber Book of Parodies*. In fact, Housman also features in this anthology as a parodist with *Fragment of a Greek Tragedy*. One example, by Hugh Kingsmill, a contemporary and a writer and journalist, composed one on Housman which was based loosely on *ASL* XLIV: 'Shot? so quick, so clean an ending?'[398] His version goes:

> What, still alive at twenty-two,
> A clean upstanding chap like you?
> Sure, if your throat 'twas hard to slit,
> Slit your girl's and swing for it.[399]

---

397 Letter Housman to Richards, 29 June, 1907.
398 Hugh Kingsmill, 1889-1949, British writer and journalist, science fiction and crime as well as non-fiction for periodicals, parodies and humour, biographies.
399 M. Holroyd, *The Best of Hugh Kingsmill: Selections from his Writings*, 1970.

Housman admired this effort. Kingsmill's pastiche captures the apparent cruelness in some of Housman's verse. It has an appearance of brutality, and this is what appealed to Housman about Kingmill's few lines. Housman was certainly not a cruel man per se, but he did want his verse to be on occasion an emphatic statement of the nineteenth century's apparent disregard for young life.

John Masefield, who corresponded with Housman and for whom he had a high regard, cleverly encapsulated Housman's verse:

> Too many lads of pith and relish
> Who put their all in pledge,
> Find love a hell and living hellish
> Twixt Clun and Wenlock Edge.
> Cureless and broken hearts and breaking,
> They ache; but here was one
> Who made a music of the aching
> Twixt Wenlock Edge and Clun.[400]

A mere three years after Housman's death, the young audacious Auden, as previously quoted, wrote,

> No one, not even Cambridge was to blame
> (Blame, if you like, the human situation):
> Heart-injured in North London, he became
> The Latin Scholar of his generation.

400 Correspondence between Housman and Masefield began at least as early as 1910. Burnett, *Letters I,* p.256.

If that was not sufficient Auden further wrote:

> Deliberately he chose the dry-as-dust,
> Kept tears like dirty postcards in a drawer;
> Food was his public love, his private lust
> Something to do with violence and the poor.[401]

However, Auden, like others, could praise Housman, more, in Auden's case, for his classical scholarship, which he probably didn't understand, than for his poetry.

There were even legends attached to Housman in his lifetime and most were probably unfounded, but it is interesting why they came into being in the first place – for example, that he kept a record of the dogs he kicked on his afternoon walks. Others appear to have a ring of truth about them. Rothenstein said that when Housman lived in Highgate and was travelling by train to Gower Street, someone tried to get into conversation with Housman, 'upon which he moved to Pinner.' Whilst often repeated at the time and could have been true, it was not. He moved to Pinner simply because his landlady, who looked after him so well, had moved herself to Pinner. True or untrue such stories illustrate Housman's difficult character.

It is no coincidence that Withers' book on Housman was given the title *A Buried Life,* implying unfathomed psychological depths which even he, a long established and trusted friend, found impossible to fully penetrate. Indeed, despite their intimacy, Withers felt that he

401 Printed in *New Writing*, 1939.

had never 'the smallest assurance that I had got an inch nearer to Housman himself'. He had 'a buried life that he determined to keep buried.' One can imagine Withers as the faithful, observant friend, no classicist, merely one who with great affection could reflect on the 'charming and ready smile [which] had something of sadness in it and how quickly the smile passed, and the face relapsed into sadness as though that were its native element.' Reference again to the smile or lack of one! Withers also talked of Housman's 'sardonic quips, his biting satire, his easy retort to mockery and scoffing' but, on the other hand, he rightly commented that emotionally there beat in Housman 'as warm and generous a heart, as willing for self-sacrifice as I have ever known.'[402]

On reading *A Buried Life* Richards said he had never seen signs of agony or torment in Housman. However, as we know, Gow deemed Richards an unreliable source, describing him as a 'ruffian.' But then Gow didn't seem to think much of *A Buried Life*, regarding it as not a bad picture but also not very edifying for those who knew Housman well.[403]

Housman could open up to Gow too, a fellow classicist, a very different character to Withers, but both were members of Housman's small inner circle. Despite noting his silences, Gow recalled that Housman 'would greet the contributions of others with bursts of silvery laughter which retained to the end of his life something boyish and

402 Withers, *Buried Life*.

403 Letter, 14 June, 1941.

infectious.'[404] Gow referred to Housman's 'grim censorious manner, acerbity of wit and tartness of speech' to which Housman said, 'no one could have a better friend than I have in Gow.'[405]

The Times Literary Supplement in the year Housman died said he was a strange and solitary man, difficult to know, difficult to understand, difficult to portray. Housman himself said of another 'what most eludes description is not the excellence of his gifts but the singularity of his essential being, his utter unlikeness to any other creature in the world.'[406] This could equally apply to Housman himself.

In Housman we find a very rich and long list of characteristics, some contradictory and some apparently difficult to explain. He was rude, generous, an introvert, often an embarrassment, unhelpful; but a fine critic, a plain speaker, a perfectionist, apparently sufficiently self-disciplined to decline top honours, awe-inspiring to his disciples, more attractive on knowing if he allowed greater familiarity, a confirmed bachelor, a risk taker, a homosexual, an outsider – a life aimed principally at impressing Moses Jackson. Despite all, his life was perhaps not an inherently unhappy one, just very different from most.

404 Blocksidge, 'Early Biographers', p.50.
405 Withers, *Buried Life*.
406 *The Times*, May, 1936.

16. HIS BIOGRAPHERS

'At present Who's Who gives all the external facts.'

Housman said, 'there is no biography of Matthew Arnold so there certainly need be none of me.'[407] Yet the speed in which the biographies came so soon after his death would almost certainly have surprised him. All the early biographers, even though they had the advantage of knowing Housman, at least as well as Housman would allow, admitted that their versions were incomplete. All concealed Housman's sexual orientation, some knew of it, including Gow and Laurence, others denied it, including Kate and Richards.

Housman stated, 'I expressly desire and wish my desire to be made as widely known as possible that none of my writings which have appeared in periodical publications shall be collected and reprinted in any shape or form.'[408] The reason for this is mainly because the writings covered a long period of his life and understandably he changed some of those opinions. But we should remember also that some were occasional papers often brief and illustrating a particular point, whilst at the same time being deeply knowledgeable.

Many of the biographies relied rather heavily on the answers that Housman gave to the young French Scholar, Maurice Pollet, who sent him a questionnaire via Richards in 1933. It was surprising that he replied at all and

407 Maas, *Letters,* p.xi.
408 A. E. Housman's will.

even more so that he answered expansively but Housman said he did so 'for the sake of posterity'.[409] Although his answers might have acted as the backbone to subsequent biographies, Housman remained typically circumspect. When Pollet asked if Housman would object to an English translation of his subsequent essay appearing in an English paper he replied '[Pollet's] essay... is certainly complimentary, and is not silly, and I should not raise objections... though I... have no wish that he should succeed.'[410] It is uncertain whether it ever appeared in an English newspaper but it did appear in a French one in 1937.

Within a year of his death on 30th April 1936, the first biographies on Housman had been published – A.S.F. Gow's *A. E. Housman: A Sketch,* and Kate's edited *Alfred Edward Housman: Recollections*, a series of essays to which Kate contributed one, other contributors including Pollard, Laurence, Gow and Sparrow.[411] Kate courted the idea of writing a full biography, even calling it provisionally *A Housman Patchwork* but it was incomplete at the time of her death in 1945. Laurence assembled the unpublished poems for the two collections *More Poems* and *Additional Poems* and had also started writing his book on his brother *AEH: A Personal Memoir*, which appeared in 1937. This, in turn, was followed by the publication of his own autobiography *The Unexpected Years* which inevitably included plenty of thoughts on his brother and is especially insightful into

409 Burnett, *Letters*, p.330.

410 Letter Housman to Richards 28 September, 1933.

411 J. Sparrow, (ed.), *A.E. Housman Collected Poems*, Penguin Poets, 1956. J. Sparrow & J. Carter (eds.), *A. E. Housman, an Annotated Handlist,* London, Rupert Hart-Davis, 1952. Warden of All Souls College, Oxford.

Housman's earlier years.

Brother and sister didn't see eye to eye over Laurence's book on Housman, Kate dismissing it as 'spatchcocked stuff' and preferring Gow's 'gentle version'.[412] Gow quickly became the repository of confidences from both Kate and Laurence – not an enviable or easy role. 'I drank in gratefully all you said towards the end about the tenderer inner-man that he possessed,' said Kate.[413] Typical of her; soon after her brother's death she adopted a defensive approach to her brother's reputation. In her appendix to Richards' book she didn't even mention Moses Jackson. We noted that both Kate and Richards tried to defend Housman's reputation when it came to likely innuendos or assumptions associated with Jackson – Kate was in denial and Richards merely recorded what he saw. Laurence says, however, that Kate knew; she was 'quite well aware of the HS problem, and has guessed it in regard to AEH.'[414]

It became clear that there was a sibling rivalry developing between Kate and Laurence over the image each wished to leave of their brother to posterity, Laurence claiming that he was the legitimate custodian of his brother's reputation having been appointed his literary executor. Kate and Laurence had their differences over the format of the funeral and their differences emerged in the biographical sketches both penned so soon after their brother's death. Kate became particularly vehement. She said to Gow that she never rated Laurence's writings per se: 'They really

412 Trinity College Cambridge MS Add 71-32.
413 Trinity College Cambridge MS Add 71-97.
414 Trinity College Cambridge MS Add 71-139.

seemed to me to be so superficial,' she wrote, adding dramatically, 'Alfred lies dead with his brother's knife in his side.'[415]

Although out of fashion today, Laurence also made a reputation in his own lifetime and in a number of ways. He was a book designer ('long years ago I warned Laurence that if ever I wrote a book I would never let him decorate it'[416]), artist, illustrator, poet, journalist, novelist, dramatist, critic, lecturer, campaigner, feminist, suffragist, a socialist, a pacifist, a rebel, a mystic, a Quaker, an Internationalist and a Humanitarian. According to their nephew, N.V. Housman Symons, Laurence was also the opposite of Alfred – he was a 'warm and forthcoming extrovert.'[417] Despite Housman's comment, Richards as his publisher rated Laurence's ability more highly as an illustrator: 'he designed the spine decorations for my World's Classics, for the Winchester Edition of Jane Austen and for the Elizabethan Classics.'[418]

Laurence recorded some of the conversation between the dying Housman and his doctor, R.S. Woods. Kate disapproved of these conversations in the circumstances. Kate regarded Gow as a more worthy repository of her brother's austere, Victorian outward image. Gow appeared more reliable because of what he didn't write in his biography. The full title of Gow's biography was *A.E. Housman a sketch together with a list of his writings and indexes to his classical papers*.

415 Trinity College Cambridge MS Add 71-75.

416 Letter Housman to Richards, 6 June, 1908.

417 Symons, 'Recollections', p.10.

418 Richards, *Housman,* p.82.

However, Gow did take the time and make the effort to consult those who had known Housman at Oxford and UCL and even at least one person from his Patent Office days. He was a fellow classicist concentrating on Housman the classicist rather than on Housman the man. The words 'sketch', 'list', and 'index' are a true reflection of the book – sketches run to 54 pages and the list and indexes to 77! He seems to have disguised some of his conclusions and reflections; on Housman's homosexuality he writes, 'some of the poems published after [Housman's] death spoke of friendships... [They are] unambiguous as to the warmth of the friendship between Housman and Jackson.'[419]

And there was disapproval by the academic, classicist, close friend Gow, of the efforts of the non-academic and non-classicists Withers and Richards who he felt were ill qualified to understand and penetrate the inner sanctum of Housman's true worth. Yet all three knew Housman for much of his adult life and Housman showed great affection and reliance in different ways towards all three. Each had an advantage over the other and each, as a result, offered an extra ingredient to the story.

Withers was a dear friend and Housman could readily open up to him as far as he was able or prepared to do; Richards was a business colleague who over 40 years became a friend and whose company whether in England or on the Continent Housman cherished and enjoyed. Gow had the advantage of being a fellow academic and an eminent classicist, but he was also rather cantankerous, particularly in later life, and one can detect a desire by him to

419 Gow, *Sketch*, p.49.

seek reflected glory from his long association with a fellow classicist of Housman's standing – he wasn't going to share, if he could avoid it, with a sometime GP like Withers or a failed businessman like Richards. However, both Withers and Richards produced very readable accounts of Housman.

Included in these early offerings comes the kindly and often perceptive deliberations of Joan Thomson in her biographical 'Reminiscences' included in Richards' biography, which she wrote three years after Housman's death, responding to a 'sudden longing.' There is some evidence, however, that this was prompted by her reading of Laurence's autobiography *The Unexpected Years*. Her final passage in the 'Reminiscences' is tender, loyal, perceptive and endearing. She ended her biographical 'Reminiscences' originally with the words 'it might be said that life had given him everything – fame, adequate means, and congenial occupation – but he lacked what was to himself the most important thing of all.' Richards thought that ending was not quite sufficient, so she redrafted and wrote 'he had the divine gift of charity, the power of love, in full measure, and he paid for it to the last farthing with his unsatisfied need of being loved himself.'[420]

The biographies kept coming. In 1940 we have Withers' *A Buried Life*. Withers' book, whilst not ignoring Housman's frustrating silences, was perhaps the best at conveying what it was like to be in Housman's company. He would rather wait for Housman to open up – often a frustrating wait – than ask questions himself. Kate thanked

420 Thomson, 'Reminiscences'.

Withers for his refusal 'to be repelled by his forbidding aspects.'[421] In 1941 Richards published *Housman 1897–1936*. Richards' account is based on an equally long association and friendship. When Richards married for the second time, Housman wrote 'whatever your other faults may be, there can be few ladies who have a more good-tempered husband.'[422] He was no academic despite being the son and nephew of Oxford dons, but he captured a side of Housman's personality and life, his love of food and wine and of foreign travel, and he attempted to make Housman seem as conventional as possible. Kate endorsed Richards' book generally. She thanked him for giving a 'new picture of [Alfred] to those who imagine him to have been only a curmudgeonly recluse.'[423] But she did not endorse the book when it referred to Housman's personal life – typically of Kate as we know as she attempted to be the self-appointed custodian of that part of her brother's legacy, '[t]he fullest possible knowledge [of which did] not belong to Mr Richards' but to herself.[424]

A virtual floodgate had opened. Some biographers clearly disliked Housman, including George Watson.[425] Others were too uncritical or inaccurate such as Maude Hawkins.[426] Classical and English literary influences on

421 Sommerville, Withers Collection, Box 15, Letter dated 25 August, 1940.

422 Housman to Richards, 3 October, 1915.

423 Trinity College Cambridge MS 71-74.

424 N. Page *A. E. Housman: A Critical Biography*, Palgrave Macmillan, 1996, p.12.

425 G. Watson, *A.E. Housman; A Divided Life,* Rupert Hart-Davis, 1957.

426 M. Hawkins, *A.E. Housman: Man behind a Mask,* Chicago, 1958. 'I was quite dismayed when I came to a chapter in which I am mentioned.

Housman's poetry were covered in a thorough way in *A.E. Housman, Scholar and Poet* by Norman Marlow. Others still focused on one aspect and contributed handsomely to our knowledge; Burns Haber on the notebooks (although he has his critics), for instance, and regularly over the years there have been weighty, suitably learned insights from the *Housman Society Journal*.[427] By the 1960s there was focus on his techniques and the meaning of his notebooks and an appreciation of Housman's individual style and his mastery of the English language – to an even greater degree. Particularly worthy of note, covering both Housman's personality and his poetry, is F.L. Lucas' chapter on Housman entitled 'Fool's-errand to the Grave' (itself a line of Housman's poetry). In the 1970s greater attention was given to the Housman family from its earliest times thanks to John Pugh and Richard Perceval Graves.[428] In 1983 came the shrewd analysis by Norman Page, *A.E. Housman: A Critical Biography*.[429] Housman as the classical scholar was given worthy treatment in *English Classical Scholarship* by C.O. Brink, whilst in the same decade we saw a work which offered much valued comment on Housman's lectures, his reviews, the classical editions and classical papers edited by Sir Christopher Ricks, *A.E. Housman: Collected Poems and Selected Prose*.[430]

Not only Mrs Hawkins told the small anecdotes incorrectly...' Thomson, 'Reminiscences', 1940.

427 Burns Haber, *Manuscript Poems of A.E. Housman*.

428 J. Pugh, *Bromsgrove and the Housmans,* Housman Society, 1974.

429 N. Page, *A. E. Housman: A Critical Biography* first published 1983.

430 C.O. Brink, 'Historical Reflections on Bentley, Porson and Housman', *English Classical Scholarship,* 1986. C. Ricks (ed.), *A. E. Housman Collected*

In the 1990s John Bayley gave further insights into the poems and thanks to Jane Allsopp's *The Land of Lost Content* we can visit the landscape of Housman country and not get lost, except perhaps in the sheer enjoyment of the locations associated with his poetry.[431] Robin Shaw's *Housman's Places* was another worthy edition.[432] Housman said, 'I did not apprehend that the faithful would be making pilgrimages to these places.'[433]

A short gem is the *Westerly Wanderer* by Jeremy Bourne and more recently Peter Parker's *Housman Country* in which the literature, landscape, music and emotion of the period in which Housman lived all play their part in painting the portrait of the scholar poet.[434] Parker, however, did not escape the critics – 74 pages out of 389 were on homosexuality and nothing on what Housman called 'the day job' – the classics.

Then Edgar Vincent's *A.E. Housman: Hero of the Hidden Life* was especially effective in adding additional insight into well-known aspects of Housman's life by further analysing Housman's correspondence.[435]

In his lifetime Housman discouraged any thought of would-be biographers. When Douglas Goldring visited Housman in 1923 with a view to writing a biography, Gol-

---

Poems and Selected Prose, Allen Lane, 1998.

431 J. Allsop, *The Land of Lost Content*, Shropshire Books, 1995.

432 R. Shaw, *Housman's Places,* Housman Society, 1995.

433 Letter in response to Laurence accusing Housman of romantic falsification in giving Hughley church a spire.

434 P. Parker, *Housman Country*, Little, Brown, 2016.

435 J. Bourne, *Westerly Wanderer*, Housman Society, 1996. E. Vincent, *A. E. Housman: Hero of the Hidden Life*, Boydell & Brewer, 2018.

dring recalls a 'flush of annoyance... gave me my answer before he opened his mouth.'[436] Housman 'considered that kind of writing most impertinent' adding that a man should be judged by the value of his work. He said that when he is dead he didn't think that more than one person in a thousand would appreciate the real achievement of his life – his work on Manilius!

Goldring did his best to get on the right side of Housman, but it was a difficult task. He opened the conversation on what he thought might be safe ground, with references to Oxford and to a public school education, suggesting that such 'a liberal education equipped a man to be profitably idle.' This got a parable for an answer: 'A tallow chandler in Bromsgrove sold his business, with the stipulation that he be allowed to call at the shop and spend a day there when the tallow was melting – thereby ensuring one day's joy a week.' Ten years later another request from Goldring was also declined but by then Housman had mellowed. 'I am naturally flattered... but neither you nor anyone else could possibly write one, and I certainly would give no assistance.'[437]

Clemens corresponded with Housman but Housman had a low opinion of his literary prowess and of the man. Housman had corresponded with Clemens since 1927 and he was his guest at High Table in 1930, but Housman described him as 'a very vacuous young man... [who] stayed

436 Douglas Goldring, 1887-1960, English writer and journalist, early influence in establishing the Georgian Society, increasingly left wing later in life.

437 D. Goldring, *The Nineteen-Twenties,* Nicolson & Watson, 1945, chapter 6.

here for some time trying to improve his mind.' When Clemens submitted a draft of an article which he hoped one day might constitute a chapter for a future biography, Housman replied that he had 'corrected or marked the most inaccurate of your inaccuracies', having already told Clemens, 'At present Who's Who gives all the external facts.'[438] Clemens quickly squandered any inherent goodwill felt by Laurence and Kate by his incompetence and inaccuracies. When Clemens asked for assistance from Laurence and Kate for the likely biography, Laurence told him he was not 'competent to do what he has undertaken.'[439] By 1937 Clemens had, as far as Laurence was concerned, become a 'damned nuisance.' What has survived of Clemens' early draft justifies these hostile reactions. Despite all discouragement Clemens seemed to be utterly undeterred, continuing to admire everything and every person associated with Housman. He dedicated copies of his *Mark Twain's Quarterly* to specific people – 'to Mrs E.W. Symons, admirable chronicler of A.E.H.'s youth' – even electing Gow to an Honorary Membership of his society.

In the final weeks of his life, Housman's resistance was weakening further. To Houston Martin, a young American admirer, he wrote, 'I hope that if you can restrain your indecent ardour for a little I shall be properly dead and your proposed work will not be by its nature unbecoming.' The correspondence showed warmth on Housman's part, possibly because he knew they would never meet. In

438 Burnett, Letters *II,* pp. 227-284.

439 Trinity College Cambridge AD MAS 71-2001. Kate described Clemens' work as a 'deplorable hash', Trinity AD MAS 71-60.

fact Housman once said 'it is almost always disappointing to actually meet anyone.'[440] He added that he did not understand why Americans were so fond of writing about personal matters, and concluded that it was a national characteristic of theirs and 'it makes me unwilling to meet them, though they are always so kindly and friendly.'[441] He seems to have strange views about the Americans. At the time of the publication of *LP* and in response to a request to publish it in America, Housman wrote 'Mr Vickers can have what he wants, and any of his countrymen. I am told that Americans are human beings though appearances are against them.'[442] Similarly, in a response to a request to have a description of himself to accompany an article, Housman regarded such a request as low, unworthy, and American.[443]

Despite the general reluctance of Housman to cooperate with those who wished to capture his achievements and character, and despite relatively few being close friends or associates and fewer still understanding his 'day job' – that of a classicist – the combined efforts of many have pieced together a vivid and fascinating portrait.

440 Thomson 'Reminiscences', p.448.

441 Burnett, *Letters II*, p.284.

442 Letter, Housman to Richards, 30 November, 1922.

443 Letter, Housman to Richards, 27 September, 1921.

17. HOUSMAN AS AUTISTIC: A NEW INTERPRETATION

When pared down to all but the essentials we find in Housman a person who manifests many of the principal characteristics of autism spectrum disorder (ASD), something not mentioned in other biographies.[444] It is important at the outset to state that autism is more common that many realise and that to be autistic doesn't mean that the person will tick all the boxes of recognised autistic behaviours. Even where autistic behaviour is evident there are levels of severity. Furthermore, autism is not an illness, it is a 'different way of communicating and interacting with the world.'[445] In fact, society generally has gained considerably from the achievements of autistic people in many walks of life. Finally, there is nothing inherently disloyal in advocating that many of Housman's behavioural patterns place him on the autism spectrum. This assertion simply helps us to understand him better.

There have been meaningful advances in recent years in our understanding of the condition with indicators grouped under three headings: social communication, social interaction and restricted and repetitive behaviours including sensory differences.[446] Some of the main characteristics of the first include struggling to talk about

444 American Psychiatric Association, Diagnostic & Statistical Manual (DSM-5), 2013.

445 National Autistic Society 2020.

446 The ADD-vance ADHD and Autism Trust.

one's own feelings, misunderstanding a tone of voice or body language; of the second appearing aloof, insensitive or rude; and in the third becoming fixated with detail, as well as experiencing synaesthesia where different senses feel connected.

Housman is in good company, and there is a growing list of those from the past who are suspected now to have been on the autism spectrum. In the literary domain from the past these may include Jane Austen, Lewis Carroll, Emily Brontë, James Joyce, Mark Twain, Hans Christian Andersen and George Orwell.[447]

In Housman's day, he wouldn't have been aware of the condition, only of its consequences, and he would have been surrounded by those who were equally unaware. However, on occasion, a contemporary got very close to the truth. Auden, for instance, wrote 'this enigmatic figure, lonely, irresponsive, setting us so many questions and answering none of them, crediting none of us with truth and intelligence but allowing us to make what we can of the fire and ice which contend in his nature.'[448] The title of Withers' book, *A Buried Life,* is also a fair attempt to describe the confusing enigma of his close friend. Such reflections are typical of Housman's contemporaries in the absence of the fuller understanding of autism that we now have. When we examine the diagnostic criteria we can see how they go some way to explaining the apparent contradictions of the man.

447 M. Fitzgerald, *The Genesis of Artistic Creativity: Asperger's Syndrome and the Arts,* Jessica Kingsley, 2005.

448 H.W. Garrod, 'Mr. A.E. Housman', *HSJ,* vol. 40. 2014, p.116.

Firstly, 'deficits in social communication and social interaction' were obvious in many contexts. People on the autism spectrum struggle to communicate because they often misinterpret tone of voice and body language, as well as taking a very literal interpretation of words. Cleverly or conveniently Housman expressed his inner thoughts via his poetry; 'poetry's aim and nature was one of communication not of thought but of emotion.' This means of communication gave him plenty of time to express himself comfortably and appropriately rather than be put on the spot. Add to this the difficulties associated with using the 'unwritten rules' of social interaction (the ones we learn early in life via social intercourse) in different contexts and we can see why Housman often struggled to develop, maintain and understand relationships.

He was blunt and rarely showed remorse or sensed disapproval; first meetings were often a disaster. On first meeting Housman, Richards thought he was an enigma; his bedmaker commented, 'when I first began to do for him I used to be afraid to go into his room.' The matron at the nursing home at the end of his life expressed a similar thought, as did a Fellow at Trinity: 'our first encounter was not very productive, for Housman spoke little and said nothing memorable'. To Baldwin he was unclubbable and to Barrie he said nothing all evening.

Both Laurence and Kate understood, as siblings, their brother's character. Laurence especially was always forgiving of Housman's apparent rudeness to him. Laurence recalls the occasion when visiting a friend in

Cambridge he announced that he was going round to see his brother. His friend was amazed: 'I thought you were not on speaking terms.' Laurence protested that this was not the case and discovered the root of this false interpretation of the brothers' relationship was a conversation that his friend had had at High Table with Housman. The friend had said 'I have the pleasure of knowing your brother Mr Laurence Housman;' Housman stiffly replied 'knowing my brother is no introduction to *me*.' Laurence shrugged this off and laughed saying this was characteristic of his brother: 'it only meant that the poor man didn't want to have the trouble of talking to you; or else, possibly, he disliked you at first sight, and chose that as the most direct way of avoiding conversation.'[449]

Housman was honest, open and forthright in his views – not peculiar to autism, but nevertheless autistic traits. Few were spared; not the academic referee, nor composers and would-be biographers, nor fellow classicists and not even dead poets. Neither could he differentiate between a prime minister and the person who tidied his rooms at Trinity. When Baldwin visited him at Trinity, by then a former Prime Minister, Baldwin said he was 'not made very welcome.' Someone on the autistic spectrum might display a similar difficulty in adapting to different social contexts, such as the visit of a former Prime Minister. He treated everyone the same, as do autistic people.

Housman took umbrage with the shortcomings of others. Clemens was careless, Housman shot back leaving

449 Housman, *Unexpected Years,* p.364.

Clemens in no doubt about how careless Housman thought he was. Clemens, however, continued to admire him. Housman would have been unaware of how rude he had been and also unaware of the continuing admiration shown by Clemens, a typical autistic response. When Housman caused offence, as he did with the female undergraduate who made prolific notes, he wasn't aware how blunt he had been and soon forgot the incident.

Because of his rudeness it was assumed that he wouldn't secure the Kennedy Chair despite being the strongest candidate. Herbert Richards said of Housman 'he's been too rude to the men he didn't like'. Doing Housman a favour was no protection. Both Rothenstein and Snow could vouch for that. He was unhelpful and rude to would-be biographers and composers – Richards was surprised that Housman replied to Pollet; Vaughan Williams was constantly discouraged. He was no more encouraging towards the enthusiastic correspondence from the struggling E.M. Forster and Powell's eagerness to access his classical learning was acknowledged merely with a brief note.

Housman had to intellectualise responses to a world he couldn't understand in a conventional way. He found it exhausting and where possible something to be avoided. He had to make constant assumptions. The fact that he appeared arrogant, cold or both was probably due to the fact that he had assumed wrongly. He may have struggled to read facial expressions accurately and it is likely that he failed to convey this to others adding to the general confusion on both sides. We noted what Housman wrote against T.E. Lawrence's 'There was my craving to be liked... The terror of failure in an effort so important made me shrink from trying', noting in the margin 'This is me.'[450]

As an autistic person, Housman would have been using his intellect rather than instinct in order to work out what people around him were thinking and feeling. In Housman's case, as is typical, this led to misunderstandings. A kind gesture might be perceived as a hostile intrusion; when Withers played a composition by Vaughan Williams of Housman's poetry, intended as a compliment, to the great surprise of Mrs Withers seated nearby, Housman thought that Withers was being deliberately unkind. He couldn't understand his motive – an example of what on the autism spectrum is termed 'mindblindness', which often leads to abnormal responses in social situations.[451]

Housman's annoyance at the continued misprinting of his works, whilst entirely understandable, was nevertheless expressed abruptly. Housman was rude to and about Rothenstein, an eminent artist who would not wish to offer a substandard work, least of all to the sitter. Even if Housman had reason to be disappointed in the portrait, the usual behaviour, and in particular from someone who is also creative and who would know, therefore, the effort needed to create a work of art, would not be to express their true feelings so bluntly and so repeatedly.

---

450 T.E Lawrence in Gow, *Sketch*, pp.53-54.

451 https://thepsychologist.bps.org.uk/volume-21/edition-2/theories-autistic-mind

Most of us learn how to do this early, instinctively, inevitably, and then navigate our social world accordingly with relative ease, as we are able to predict how others will behave. Autistic people struggle to assess this accurately and consequently find people's behaviour confusing, unpredictable, even frightening. As a result they show a preference for predictable routines and rituals. They may become anxious and distressed by even small unexpected changes.

Many autistic people describe the constant intellectualising of social interaction as exhausting. Underneath an often placid façade there would be a churning of strong and confused emotions leading, on occasion, to meltdowns (external outbursts) or shutdowns (withdrawal). There is some evidence that Housman suffered emotional shutdowns when things didn't go to plan. Kate commented that he was 'sensitive and easily wounded, but wounds he bore in silence'; it was wise to tread carefully in order not to upset him unintentionally.[452] His abrupt departure from the house he shared in London with Jackson was possibly another example.

Autistic people are often more sensitive to particular sensory stimuli – in Housman's case, the beauty of flowers. As his sister Kate said, 'he absorbed the look and scent of flowers with a vivid perception that visibly moved him.' We need look no further than *ASL* XXIX: 'And there's the windflower chilling | With all the winds at play,' or *ASL* XLII: 'Once in the wind of morning | I ranged the

452 Quoted by R.P Graves in his Ludlow Lecture, 30 April 2008.

thymy wold; | The world-wide air was azure | And all the brooks ran gold.'

Housman needed to intellectualise a hostile environment, a classic example of synaesthesia, a mixing of sensory input, seeing people in special and unusual ways, associating someone or something with characteristics which are capricious and fantastic to most of us. The subject of such reactions can be legion. Housman associated bread with a repulsion, a person's physique could be an instant turn-off: 'he was apt to take a strong antipathy to a person at first sight,' commented Joan Thomson, a matter of hyper- or hypo-reactivity to sensory input, to use the rather ugly but technical terminology. Nor would Housman change his mind; it was impossible for someone to reason with him – he was invariably right.

Latest research into autism describes the need for autistic people to adopt an 'energy accounting' model in order to cope with emotional overload or 'autistic fatigue'. Housman was 'successfully autistic'.[453] He managed to create a predictable bubble for himself which played to his strengths. Kate noticed from childhood that he preferred a well-established routine, noting his 'punctuality, industry, fixed routine'.

Later on, academic life provided the structure and routine which enabled him to learn appropriate responses to familiar scenarios, thereby reducing the stress of everyday social interactions. Richards commented on the reason why Housman decided to return from the holiday in

453 L. Eisenberg and L. Kanner, *Childhood schizophrenia; symposium*, 1955. VI. Early infantile autism, 1943-5.

Cornwall, admittedly on the agreed date, but only in order to return to the structured routine of meals, preparation of lectures and the comfort of his books. Trinity was the ideal environment; punctuality and the precise timing of his lectures were examples of his ritualised behaviours, an attempt to keep his day predictable and therefore managed. It allowed for intense periods of focused work during term time, followed by long holidays to recuperate from 'autistic fatigue.'[454]

High Table constituted a regular challenge, the only downside of the routine college life provided for him, putting him on the spot; he would all too easily and frequently conclude that his companion was there to criticise or to challenge, hence he remained unusually aloof, even to those who wanted to compliment or seize the opportunity afforded to understand a little more about the great scholar-poet. Insistence on sameness and an inflexible adherence to routines is evident at all levels of the autism spectrum. Even in wartime, Housman expected no disruption to the Trinity cuisine.

Housman's lonely walks on Hampstead Heath when at UCL were a set routine – he took the same route on a daily basis. Later, at Loch Aline where there were other guests, most of whom were strangers, he walked alone in order to remove himself from a group he didn't know perhaps to process and recharge his 'social battery'. His walks generally could be long; Gow commented on meeting Housman miles from Cambridge and added that Housman

454 'Autistic Fatigue' https://www.autism.org.uk/advice-and-guidance/topics/mental-health/autistic-fatigue/autistic-adults#H2_2

would pass a person by 'with a visibly abstracted air and often failed to notice one as he passed.' Kate said 'it was alone that he liked to tramp.'

Housman couldn't see when a person was an admirer. All Powell got from sitting beside his idol at High Table was advice on the proper use of red pepper, despite Housman knowing that Powell was a classical scholar. Barrie, despite his own literary fame, was rewarded with total silence. Navarro-Anderson was advised not to mention *ASL* despite being Housman's most celebrated collection of poetry: a case of not being prepared to share interests which is a symptom of autism. Each of these people were construed as unwelcome. It did not matter whether they were fellow writers, fellow classicist, composers, or even, on occasion, a friend.[455]

With our greater understanding today of autism, we know the best way to attempt to engage with a person such as Housman at High Table would have been to be direct whereas his contemporaries were, on the contrary, often deferential. Withers stumbled upon this truth: 'it was questioning alone which positively assured his talking.'[456] In order to engage, Housman liked literal brevity (although

455 Tony Attwood suggests that individuals with ASD, especially those with superior intellectual abilities, may overcompensate for feelings of inadequacy in social situations by becoming 'arrogant and egocentric' and they may 'have considerable difficulty acknowledging that they have made a mistake... can be hypersensitive to any suggestion of criticism, yet overly critical of others, including teachers, parents or authority figures.' T. Attwood, *The Complete Guide to Asperger's Syndrome,* Jessica Kinsley Publishers, London and Philadelphia, 2007, pp.20-21.
456 Withers, *Buried Life*, pp.23-25.

his excellent prose is anything but concise, even if every word chosen is appropriate). T.S. Eliot, despite his own literary skills, said everyone would write like Housman if they could and E.H. Carr strongly echoed that sentiment. Housman used Selden's *Table-Talk,* the epitome then of the correct expression in prose, 'as a corrective, both of slipshod and flummery', Housman again rectifying, in his mind, an injustice. He only relaxed with those he knew well, such as Withers, Gow, Richards, Thomson and the Fellows. His recorded easy going manner when walking with friends from the Patent Office fits within the confines of familiarity and with the comfort afforded by a small, close knit group. In childhood he was relaxed with the Wise family and with Sophie Becker, because of their early central role in his life

Many autistic people turn 'a lack of ability in social play with peers... [into] behaviors to achieve dominance and control.'[457] Laurence in his memoir does not give many instances of Housman at play; when he does he shows how his brother both dominated and controlled, for example in a less than collaborative approach to putting on a play, and demonstrated classic 'mind-blindness' in trying to force a young child to write a sonnet up a tree.

Aided by drink, well-practised anecdotes and a clear understanding of social expectations, the autistic person can be the centre of a gathering and enjoy the role. Housman liked his drinks, both wine and beer, and was sufficiently lubricated within the safe fraternity of the Fellows. Gow noted how Housman could, in the right

457 Attwood, *Aspergers,* p.26.

company, be 'as vivacious as any member of the party... an admirable raconteur.'[458] His notebooks of anecdotes and jokes were his armoury. It is no surprise that the Master of St Catharine's College regarded Housman's speech at a gathering as the best he had heard. Housman was addressing a familiar audience and would have had plenty of time to prepare and to draw on his notebooks. His cutting wit, sometimes cruel, was a manifestation of an autistic person's grasp of language, of wordplay, as too was his interest in puzzles, whether conventional or in complicated verse.

Housman would have been at home in the known surroundings of the UCL Council and as Treasurer of UCL Professors' Dining Club, positions chosen by him, and so familiar and acceptable to him.

Housman's lack of interface with undergraduates, entering the room, reading the script then leaving with no eye contact, discouraging questions, is pure autism. As a professor he didn't interpret his remit as requiring tutorial supervision thereby avoiding eye contact and social intrusion, displaying by this avoidance what the autism spectrum terms abnormalities of eye contact and of discouraging questions. Housman could teach at Bromsgrove, his former school, as he had time to prepare for each class, in an environment he knew well and with holidays to recoup.

Surprisingly, perhaps, some with autism not only choose teaching as a profession but excel in it, despite

---

458 Gow, *Sketch,* p.50.

the challenges. A teacher who is willing to meet these challenges can turn them often to advantage, offering focus, greater research and variety of educational approaches, mixing teaching styles to make a classroom lively, a session of fun. Recent developments with online learning can make teaching and learning easier for the autistic teacher and pupil alike. The persistent downside for the autistic teacher is the challenge of networking and of attending academic conferences because of social difficulties. An autistic teacher can sometimes concentrate too much on one topic to the disadvantage of the pupils. Housman was known to devote an hour to the analysis of a few lines of classical text. This is not unknown in classical studies and not evidence of autism in isolation. In one of his occasional papers he devoted five pages to discussing a single word on Sophocles!

His famous failure in his Finals was possibly little more than Housman adopting a fall-back situation, when expectations create a challenge perceived as being too great. Even entering the exam room with others may have disorientated him; there could have been too much distracting sensory stimuli. Today, with our greater understanding, many autistic students are given a separate, familiar room under supervision. It is possible that studying in the evening and under less pressure, suited him; this is certainly at least how he eventually passed his exams. He passed his Mods two years earlier and with a First, but he failed his Finals unexpectedly and spectacularly.

Another contributory factor is likely to have been the

fact that he wanted to write about what he was interested in rather than what was on the syllabus, and this attitude is a classic case of 'mind-blindness'. He may have assumed they would be impressed even if he didn't answer the questions they wanted answered. He said he had no respect for his tutor and purposely studied subjects which were not part of the curriculum and on which he would not be tested. No wonder he failed his Finals!

Finally, we must not forget that the sad news days before his Finals concerning his father's declining health must have affected him, but by then he should have prepared thoroughly and he never refers to his father's health as a reason for that failure. As an autistic person, it is unlikely he would have been able to articulate or muster the emotional reaction common and natural to others.

Housman self-analysed his perception of being an outsider as being due to his homosexuality and to the accompanying condemnation by God. It is common for high-functioning autistic people to perceive themselves as outsiders. Perhaps Housman's poem *LP XII*, 'And since my soul we cannot fly, | To Saturn nor to Mercury' is an example from Housman of an autistic person feeling like an alien on the wrong planet. Feeling an outsider was the likely reason why Housman declined the Poet Laureateship and the OM (and not, therefore, because of 'contempt for my passion for distinction'), why he didn't put his name forward for the Public Oratorship and why he didn't take the initiative in applying to Cambridge from UCL. These honours and positions were acknowledged accolades of a conventional society; autistic people may avoid such recognition, perhaps due to fear of failure.

Housman's obsession with Manilius, 27 years expended on an unworthy subject, was because he became obsessed with a project, becoming focused and determined to see it completed to a satisfactory conclusion, in order, as Gow said, to 'build himself a monument' or, in autistic terms, a preoccupation with unusual objects, excessively circumscribed. Likewise, his study of over 170 ancient Greek and Roman writers. His obsession with textual criticism and condemnation of the work of other classicists is more of the same. To Housman he was rectifying an injustice; what had been accepted hitherto, should no longer be allowed. His criticism of eighteenth-century poets is of the same ilk, all evidence of weak central coherence often noted in those on the autism spectrum.

His desire to fly, unnecessary and dangerous, was a way of viewing the world as a fatalist, avoiding emotion, seeming thereby to welcome danger. This is evidence of the autistic person's one-track mind, with its narrow focus on what is regarded as important thereby finding ways to justify such risks. He even regarded his flying as a greater achievement than both his poetry and classical reputation. Today this is termed under social interaction as a strong attachment to a preoccupation or perseverative interest – an unattractive phrase but a clinical description nevertheless. Housman's total disregard for the dangers of sea travel during the First World War and his comments following the sinking of *SS Sussex* – only so many ships can be sunk – underlines this.

He was showing a total indifference to danger. His wish to be driven on the Continent in the early 1920s – when car travel was in its infancy and his choice to visit the Riviera in wartime – equalled danger and the opportunity to visit in the absence of others.

Relative and comfortable isolation were reasons why he arranged Continental holidays either alone or with a trusted friend or a with paid companion despite his genuine interest in architecture. He devised unreasonable or demanding itineraries without necessarily considering others, whether Richards or his chauffeur, and wouldn't be deflected. When driving through northern France he would have heard the sound of the guns on the Western Front – he was showing he was different, that he could do special things, unusual things, something that autistic people seek. He didn't reference the war in correspondence to Richards in 1914; he was ignoring events around him; his focus was on his own agenda.

Housman's need for a select few to be central in his life – to help him navigate unpredictable social situations and unfamiliar places – is a routine strategy of an autistic person. First his mother, not unique, but especially unfortunate for the young Housman to lose her on his twelfth birthday, then the Woodchester family and Sophie Becker – he clung emotionally to the latter for half a century via correspondence; he couldn't let go. Perhaps he felt understood and supported by her? She was probably more straightforward and less confusing in her manner than were many others. Withers wrote that when Housman referred to her death his 'voice faltered, his whole frame seemed shaken as he told the brief story [of Sophie's death].[459] At Oxford, Pollard and Jackson (in Jackson's case an obsession not merely a navigator) played a similar role and later still Gow, Withers, Richards and Thomson. Intellectually able autistic people often mask their difficulties by 'modelling' themselves on somebody they admire in order to try and 'fit in' with the world around them. This connection and interest with someone they admire may be misconstrued as romantic love. Poor Jackson; Housman wanted to impress him, largely the reason why he wrote the poetry and why after an absence of 20-plus years he agreed to publish *LP* as Jackson was dying, with a dedication to him. He wrote to Jackson 'I would much rather have followed you', thereby emphasising that his attachment to Jackson was worth more to him than all his success as both a poet and as a classicist. Each in his circle offered different navigational roles, first and foremost as friends; Withers as a listening, patient friend, Gow as a fellow classicist, Richards as his publisher. Housman was so dependent on Richards emotionally that he forgave him his many indiscretions; he couldn't afford to lose that friendship.

His infatuation for Jackson was a teenage idolisation, a stage most grow out of, but Housman couldn't move on; he had not developed the emotional tools. Understandably, Jackson was surprised that Housman retained this constant desire for closeness, despite infrequent meetings and no encouragement from him. Even after Jackson's death Housman clung to that relationship, confessing to Gerald

459 Withers, *Buried Life*, p.129.

that the reason for his generosity, as a godfather, was his undiminished affection for his father, Moses. It begs the question, however, why Moses invited Housman to be godfather to his son when Housman had been 'stalking' him for half a lifetime and across half the globe. It was going to be misconstrued by Housman as encouragement and add to the latter's emotional turmoil. Housman said 'one can truly only love one person'; not the case for most of us but can be the case for the autistic person. This is another example of 'restricted and repetitive behaviours.' Housman's obsession with the distant Jackson mirrors his academic obsession for the long dead Manilius.

Without the autistic interpretation of this continued infatuation we are left with ingenious but wrong reasoning given by others in their endeavours to find answers. 'I believe it is apposite to turn back to those medieval concepts of friendship... it is essential that we should transcend those limited and uninformative notions of a physical determinism that merely equates love or friendship with sexuality.'[460] A good try! Kate also attempted in an amateurish way to find an explanation. She referred to her brother's inner sufferings, believing that poetry acted as a cathartic, even quoting an article by Aldous Huxley: 'excessive repression of the sexual impulses tends, by some obscure mechanism of compensation, to produce an excessive development of pride and ambition.'[461]

460 S. Hopkins, '*A.E Housman's "De Amicitia"*', *HSJ*, vol. 26, 2000, p.41.

461 Richards, *Housman,* p.42. A. Huxley, 1894-1963, English writer and philosopher, wrote nearly 50 books, both novels and non-fiction as well as wide ranging essays, narratives and poems. Born into the prominent Huxley family.

Others again defensively argue that what Housman had to endure was enough to explain why he acted and reacted as he so often did. Cited among those reasons are a difficult circumcision, his mother's death, his agonising over his loss of faith, his realisation that he was homosexual in an unforgiving age, the reaction of a successful grammar schoolboy being confronted at Oxford by those who appeared more socially reassured, the failure in his Finals, the hopelessness of his infatuation for Jackson.

Sometimes Housman's reactions were inexplicable per se. His vehement dislike for Galsworthy, for instance, and his less vehement dislike for de la Mare and Henley was odd to say the least. What did any of them do to upset him so? There was bound to be something minuscule which he disliked from a sensory point of view. His odd reactions to people eating bread and a person's physique are surely in the same category.

Autism is a spectrum and a surprising number of people show the tell-tale characteristics. In the 1940s, autism pioneers like Kanner believed the condition was very rare, just 1 in 10,000, and was always accompanied by intellectual disability. However, thanks to better methods of identification, the number with a degree of autism is now estimated to be between 1-2%. We also understand that autism is independent of IQ and that some autistic people may be incredibly intelligent. Indeed, they may unwittingly use their intellect to compensate for autistic differences and therefore mask social, emotional and sensory difficulties. Not only does autism explain some of the contradictions evident in Housman, it also helps perhaps to explain why he was such an extraordinary talent. Roughly 10% of autistic people excel in one or more ways; Housman did in classics and as a poet. And fortunately, society is just starting to realise the benefits of neurodiverse thinking to solve some of the world's biggest problems.[462]

There are sets of behaviour prevalent amongst those on the spectrum which are to be admired or which at least give the person an advantage in life over others and these were evident in Housman's life. They include a steely determination, attention to detail, seeking of perfection, enjoying solitude, having special skills and pursing special interests and possessing exceptional loyalty.

Each example of apparent autism can be countered in isolation by being the typical behaviour of those who are certainly not autistic, but it is the combining of a number of these traits in one person which helps to define Housman as somebody on the autistic spectrum.

Housman showed many autistic traits; if we were able to assess him by today's criteria, surely he would be diagnosed. Though this different way of thinking undoubtedly led to moments of extreme discomfort and heartache during his life, it is also the very core of what made him so special. Housman and autism could prove a rich vein for future academic research.

462 https://hbr.org/2017/05/neurodiversity-as-a-competitive-advantage

18. ON RELIGION AND DEATH

'Whatever brute and blackguard made the world.'

'In all the endless roads you tread,
There's nothing but the night.'

In a letter to Kate, Housman summed up his journey from faith to apparent atheism, 'a deist at 13, a theist at 21', defining himself later as a 'high Church atheist' and remarking that 'the only form of Christianity that I profess is anti-Protestantism.' Housman said he read Lemprières *Classical Dictionary* when aged eight and that the experience had inclined him towards paganism! Although willing to allow his poems to be set to music with conditions, he refused one request – from Rev. H.S. Allen – and Richards concluded 'I have forgotten the reason but it may well have been anti-clericalism.'[463]

But that is not the complete picture.[464] He was known to slip quietly into the organ loft of Trinity Chapel in later life in order to hear a good preacher, and as we know his knowledge of the Bible was deep and he used it as a source for ideas and inspiration for his poems. In his lecture 'The Name and Nature of Poetry' Housman quoted from Proverbs: 'He that sinneth against me wrongeth his own soul: all they that hate me, love death', adding 'that is to me poetry because of the words in which the idea is clothed.' He went on to quote Psalm 49: 'But no man may deliver his brother nor make agreement unto God for

463 Richards, *Housman,* p.114.

464 Housman's reply to M. Pollet's questionnaire, 30 January 1933.

him,' saying those words were 'to me poetry so moving that I can hardly keep my voice steady in reading it.'

One poem was even called 'The Carpenter's Son' (*ASL* XLVII) and has:

> 'Here hang I, and right and left
> Two poor fellows hang for theft...

A neat summary in verse of the crucifixion of Christ with thieves on either side.

There is a hint that Housman was rejecting the concept of an authoritarian God rather than a more fatherly, kindly, accepting Being. The former might have been the prevalent interpretation in late Victorian England, but Housman seems to have retained a curiosity for a more accommodating God. Against the couplet written by Kipling, 'The God of Things as They Are', Housman wrote, 'The God of Things as They Are is never the God for me, | For He is the God of Things as They did Not Ought To Be.'[465]

There are just as many Biblical references in Housman's poems as there are military ones:

> When Adam walked in Eden young,
> Happy, 'tis writ, was he,
> While high the fruit of knowledge hung
> Unbitten on the tree.
>
> (*AP* III)

465 William White, 'A. E. Housman on Blunt and Kipling', *N&Q*, CLXXXI, chapter 22, 29 November 1941, p.301.

When Israel out of Egypt came
Safe in the sea they trod;
By day in cloud, by night in flame,
Went on before them God.

(*MP* II)

But if, the grave rent and the stone rolled by,
At the right hand of majesty on high
You sit, and sitting so remember yet
Your tears, your agony and bloody sweat,
Your cross and passion and the life you gave,
Bow hither out of heaven and see and save.

(*MP* I)

He even entitled this one 'Easter Hymn'.

In a lecture to the Cambridge Classical Society entitled 'The Application of thought to Textual Criticism' Housman reflected, 'It may be that a scribe who makes changes accidently, because he is sleepy or illiterate or drunk is guilty of none; but that is a question which will be determined by competent authority on the Day of Judgement and is no concern of ours.' He hinted at further knowledge of the Bible when commentating on the Latin phrase 'in diem vivere' – to live for the day, to take no thought for the morrow 'as the gospel bids us.'

Housman's crumbling faith echoed his time – it was a moment of exceptional debate fomented by the works of Darwin (Housman was born in the same year as the publication of the *Origin of Species*), Huxley, Tyndale and Spencer.[466] He alluded to their influences in his inaugural lecture as Professor of Latin at UCL. 'Man stands today in the position of one who has been reared from his cradle as the child of a noble race and the heir to great possessions, and who finds at his coming of age that he has been deceived alike as to his origin and exceptions.'[467] It is hard for many today, brought up in a largely secular society, to fully comprehend the effect these debates had on Housman's generation. Indeed, his generation was the first to bear the full brunt of the debate that raged against the hitherto – for many at least – certain and accepted Christian beliefs.

There were additional reasons for his declining faith – the early death of his beloved mother and the realisation that he was homosexual at a time when the Church condemned it. Housman, of course, felt rejected by God and regarded himself as an outsider. Having grandparents on both sides as ministers of the Church seemed to have made no difference. He concluded that God might exist but moved in very mysterious ways and that he, Housman, had been cast out – yet for what purpose? He expressed his doubts in poetry:

---

466 William Tyndale, 1494-1536, English scholar, leading figure in the Protestant Reformation, translator of the Bible into English, influenced by Erasmus and Luther. Executed 1536. Edmund Spencer, 1552/3?-1599, English poet, author of *The Faerie Queene,* one of the main poets of early English verse.

467 Introductory Lecture, UCL, 1892.

From far, from eve and morning
And yon twelve-winded sky,
The stuff of life to knit me
Blew hither: here am I.
(*ASL* XXXII)

He revisits this theme in 'For My Funeral', one of the few titled poems outside *ASL* and with a hint of a residual Christian faith:

O thou that from thy mansion,
Through time and place to roam,
Dost send abroad thy children,
And then dost call them home,

That men and tribes and nations
And all thy hand hath made
May shelter them from sunshine
In thine eternal shade:

We now to peace and darkness
And earth and thee restore
Thy creature that thou madest
And wilt cast forth no more.
(*MP* XLVII)

This was sung at his funeral in Trinity College Chapel on 4th May 1936.

Into the void left by a receding or lost religious faith,

Housman pursued his long-held fascination for astronomy, a fascination since reading a book on the subject in childhood. He called a poem, included later as *LP* XVII, 'Astronomy', and one verse goes:

> And now he does not even see
> Signs of the nadir roll
> At night over the ground where he
> Is buried with the pole.

As children, the three brothers played a game with an astronomical theme – with Laurence as the sun, Alfred the moon and Herbert the earth.

We get an idea of his knowledge of astronomy from an analysis of Shelley's 'To a Skylark':

> Keen as are the arrows
> Of that silver sphere
> Whose intense lamp narrows
> In the white dawn clear
> Until we hardly see,
> We feel that it is there.

Housman says 'in the stanza... the silver sphere is the Morning Star, the planet Venus; and Shelley is giving a true description of her disappearance and using an apt comparison. The moon, when her intense lamp narrows in the white dawn clear, is not a sphere but a sickle; when she is a sphere at sunrise she is near the western horizon, visible in broad daylight and disappearing only when she set; so that, nothing could be less like the vanishing of a skylark.'[468] Another example of Housman never allowing a perceived mistake to pass him by.

Later, as he grappled with the central themes of life and death, he added the classical world's interpretation of death to the Christian interpretation and included the astronomical where the souls of the dead, whether good or evil, are escorted by Mercury to the realm of Pluto, there to be judged, remaining in the Elysian Fields for eternity. He expressed these images in *MP* XXIII:

> Crossing alone the nighted ferry
> With the one coin for fee,
> Whom, on the wharf of Lethe waiting,
> Count you to find? Not me.

Stoppard used this theme to great effect in his sensitive portrayal of Housman in his play *The Invention of Love*.

Parallel to his loss of faith Housman turned to nature's indifference to the human condition, that we are mortals stripped of the prospect of Christian redemption. *ASL* itself is a depiction of a flawed Arcadia. In his struggle to combine Christianity and the classics and thereby hopefully find a substitute for his lost Christian faith, he concluded that classical interpretation was both a deception and trickery and that Christian superstition was a farce. But the intellectual turmoil continued for the rest of his life. As he mellowed he opened his inner thoughts to a select

468 Housman in *TLS,* 20 December, 1928.

few. When John Sparrow wrote a paper entitled 'Echoes in the Poetry of A. E. Housman' and sent Housman a copy, Housman replied, 'I see that you are not such a student of the Bible as I am.'[469]

He was certainly a student of the Scriptures. In 'Epitaph On An Army Of Mercenaries' is the phrase 'earth's foundations.' The 'Foundations of the earth' is found in the books of Job, Isaiah and Hebrews. The same poem has a shared DNA with Psalms, Romans and the book of Revelation. The full meaning of 'If it chance your eye offend you' can only be found if one knows the words of Christ in the Gospels. No wonder Withers commented that Housman had 'a vast store of hymnology' and could quote whole stanzas by heart.[470]

In his memorial poem to Robert Louis Stevenson, 'Home is the sailor, home from the sea', he writes:

> Home is the hunter from the hill:
> Fast in the boundless snare
> All flesh lies taken at his will
> And every fowl of air.
>
> (*AP* XXII)

This is lifted from 2 Timothy 2.26, 'That they may recover themselves out of the snare of the devil, who are taken captive by him at his will.'

His two-verse poem 'Parta Quies', which he wrote when he was only 22 and which is read each year by the

469 Maas, *Letters*, p.356.
470 Withers, *Buried Life*, p.12.

Housman Society beside his final resting place, is a mature piece with Christian understanding running through it. It was written after his supposed loss of faith. It was also excluded from *ASL*. Why? Perhaps partly because he felt he had lost his faith or because he didn't choose to let what was left of it be part of his public image.

Housman even wrote a hymn – although he never referred to it as such – appearing later as *MP* XLVII, which, as we know, was written for his own funeral. It is a fine hymn, or would be if it had been included in a collection of hymns. It was considered as part of the *Book of Common Praise* but did not make the cut, not because it wasn't deemed good enough – it was excellent – but because by then Housman was known publicly as an atheist, writing verse which included:

> Whatever brute and blackguard made the world
> (*LP* IX)

> Who made the world I cannot tell,
> 'Tis made, and here am I in hell,
> (*MP* XIX)

Not the sort of material expected from the pen of a hymn writer! It might also have been excluded because, whilst the words might be addressed to God, they needn't necessarily be a direct invocation, and he probably intended that ambiguity. Interestingly, Laurence succeeded where his brother failed; Hymn 71 in the *Book of Common Praise* is by him.

Housman accepted the invitation from Jackson to become godfather to his fourth and youngest son, Gerald, but this is not evidence of a residual faith, but rather accepted as a favour to Jackson. He was, however, a conscientious godfather, as we saw and he addressed Gerald warmly in the extant correspondence – 'My dear Gerald' and closing with 'Your affectionate godfather' – a very warm opening and closing for Housman. On one occasion he wrote to Gerald and, after hoping that he would 'not fall out of your aeroplane onto geological objects, however attractive', he adds 'my godfather is now 88, so it is not an unhealthy profession.'[471]

Housman's attitude to death was defined by his attitude to religion, to his declining faith, to his efforts to combine Christianity and the interpretation of death as portrayed in the classics in order to find a meaningful code by which to live. He never said the lot offered to him was unfair; he merely drew down the curtain early in life to contain his emotions. We are the lucky recipients of that experience because we can enjoy his way of expressing his feelings in his poetry. That poetic output was like a volcano which needed on occasion to erupt and with the eruption there was an outflow of poetry of which we are the recipients. But the process was painful to him even if the eruptions were brief and resulted only in infrequent bursts of composition.

When Housman focused in his poems on the dead, they are a restless lot – not much of the 'darkness and

471 Part of the cache of unpublished Housman letters acquired by Trinity College in 2016.

silence and slumber' for them. The dead seem to find it unnaturally hard to relinquish their connections to the world they have left or to the living. Such a paradox in the hands of another would degenerate into the absurd, but Housman pulls it off. Poems such as 'The True Lover' (*ASL* LIII) and 'Is my team ploughing' (*ASL* XXVII) consist of a dialogue between a ghost and a living person. Ghosts in dialogue with the living is a common theme in Scottish Border ballads and we know Housman was influenced by them. Other principal influences were the classics, Heine's – if stoic – poems and Shakespeare.

His image of eternity is hardly an optimistic one; it constitutes sleep, endless sleep. In 'By shores and woods and steeples' (*MP* XXXVIII) the poem ends:

> Now who sees night for ever,
> He sees no happier sight:
> Night and no moon and never
> A star upon the night.

and in *ASL* LX:

> Now hollow fires burn out to black,
> And lights are guttering low:
> Square your shoulders, lift your pack,
> And leave your friends and go.
>
> Oh never fear, man, nought's to dread,
> Look not left nor right:

In all the endless road you tread
There's nothing but the night.

He states that those who are born and those who are dead are equally unfortunate in 'Be still, my soul, be still' (*ASL* XLVIII), which ends:

Ay, look: high heaven and earth ail from the prime foundation;
All thoughts to rive the heart are here, and all are vain:
Horror and scorn and hate and fear and indignation –
Oh why did I awake? when shall I sleep again?

In *ASL* XVI he hints at the continued link between the living and the dead – and in simple words:

The nettle nods, the wind blows over,
The man, he does not move,
The lover of the grave, the lover
That hanged himself for love.

Housman can express the same sentiment in different ways, following his own philosophy that poetry is not the thing said, but the way of saying it. Under Housman's spell the above stanza is reimagined:

The sigh that heaves the grasses
Whence thou wilt never rise
Is of the air that passes
And knows not if it sighs.

(*LP* XXVII)

Being an outsider and with his frequent focus on death, Housman touches on the state of mind which can lead to suicide, playing on the pressures for social conformity and the penalties imposed by society on those who defy these pressures and norms. He expressed this in the two poems 'The Laws of God, the laws of man' (*LP* XII) and 'Oh who is that young sinner' (*AP* XVII), but he never, contrary to the views of some, endorsed suicide as an act; rather he sympathised in the plight which can end that way.

A lad that lives and has his will
Is worth a dozen dead.

(*ASL* XXV)

W. Rothenstein, portrait sketch of A.E. Housman, 1906.

19. APPROACHING THE END

'My life is bearable, but I do not want it to continue.'

In 1934 he said to Withers 'my life is bearable, but I do not want it to continue, and I wish it had ended a year and a half ago.'[472] A few days later he wrote to his sister in a similar vein 'I can bear my life but I do not at all want it to go on, and it is a great mistake that it did not come to an end a year and a half ago.'[473] In these final years, Housman used to 'go up the steps (of Whewell's Court at Trinity to his rooms) two at a time, hoping to drop dead at the top.'[474] But he later paid to have a lift installed for access to a less distant room, no doubt at considerable cost considering the nature of the building. The lift is still in operation and the current occupant of Housman's rooms uses it once a week with his shopping to ensure that it remains in good working order!

Gow was a kind and thoughtful friend to Housman in these final weeks. He masterminded the move from Whewell's Court including Housman's large library to his new ground floor accommodation. Kate expressed her gratitude to him.

As the end drew near, a colleague visited him and tried to cheer him up by telling him about a judge affecting ignorance in order to enlighten the jury when the expres-

472 Letter from Housman to Withers, 24 November, 1934.

473 Letter from Housman to Kate, 3 December, 1934.

474 Letter from Housman to Laurence, 9 June, 1935. The letter was characteristically precise, giving the number of stairs as 44.

sion 'platinum blond' arose in Court. The judge said: 'Am I to understand by "platinum blond" a precious metal or a common one?' Housman breathed feebly and uttered 'That is indeed very good. I shall have to repeat that on the Golden Floor!'[475] And apparently with that he died. It was April 30th, which adds poignancy to his lines:

> The sumless tale of sorrow
> Is all unrolled in vain:
> May comes tomorrow
> And Ludlow Fair again.
>
> (*LP* XXXIV)

May did come tomorrow but it was the first dawn after his death which he failed to see.

Although Richards was surprised how many did not recognise the name of Housman at the time of his death, news of it was treated as more than of literary or academic interest. In Germany and central Europe it was as a scholar that he was remembered; in Britain and America more as the poet. *The Times* had a leading article and the obituary was two columns, rather poetically reminding its readers that Housman had died in cherry blossom time: 'while his favourite tree is in perfect beauty, the poet has closed his eyes on that and all other earthly loveliness.'

After the cremation at Golders Green, the funeral service took place in Trinity College Chapel. The original

---

475 Letter from R.S. Woods and recorded by P.G. Naiditch in 'Problems in the life and writings of A.E. Housman', *HSJ*, 12, 1987, p.32.

tune chosen by Housman, 'When the Time Came', was deemed 'rather a common place one' and the tune by Melchior Vulpus, harmonised by Bach, was suggested and Housman had accepted it.[476]

The occasion inspired a poem:

> Now from the hills that he had known
> His way lies dark and long;
> It is as though a bird had flown,
> But left behind his song.[477]

Laurence and Kate fell out over the funeral arrangements, Laurence claiming that the service wanted by Kate was 'rather too Christian' for their brother and there was even debate over where the ashes should rest.[478] The final depositing of them was beside the north wall of the lovely church of St. Laurence in Ludlow. Only relatives were present. The casket was decorated with Shropshire heather and bloom, scattered with fragrant herbs and flowers and the soil came from Housman's Worcestershire homes, mingled with the ashes. It had been collected from under the garden trees at the Clock House, Fockbury and from Perry Hall. At the conclusion of the service a chaplet of laurel and bay, with rosemary and ivy was placed below the memorial tablet.

---

476 Richards, *Housman,* p.248.

477 Richards, *Housman,* p.293. The poem was by Lord Dunsany, 1878-1957, Anglo-Irish writer and dramatist, mostly fantasy genre, prolific writer with more than 90 books to his name.

478 Trinity College Cambridge MS Add 71-111.

> Now, of my threescore years and ten,
> Twenty will not come again.
>
> (*ASL* II)

He exceeded that, dying aged 77.[479]

The last word could go to Rt. Rev. Mervyn Charles-Edwards: 'Ever since 1929 when I bought my first car... part of its essential equipment (and the same applied to all the cars I owned) was a pocket edition of A. E. Housman's *A Shropshire Lad*; and still today, 52 years after, amid the maps, the Highway Code and the car handbook, a copy of the poems has its place.'[480]

And by my bedside is always a copy of his *Complete Poems*.

---

479 Typically, the notice in *The Times* announcing his death quoted incorrectly: that he died aged 76. A final misprint and the last opportunity to do so.

480 Mervyn Charles-Edwards, 1902-1983, Bishop of Worcester, an Honorary Chaplain to the King. Quoted in *HSJ* vol.8. p1.

SELECTED POEMS BY A.E. HOUSMAN

From *A Shropshire Lad*

I

1887

From Clee to heaven the beacon burns,
  The shires have seen it plain,
From north and south the sign returns
  And beacons burn again.

Look left, look right, the hills are bright,
  The dales are light between,
Because 'tis fifty years to-night
  That God has saved the Queen.

Now, when the flame they watch not towers
  About the soil they trod,
Lads, we'll remember friends of ours
  Who shared the work with God.

To skies that knit their heartstrings right,
  To fields that bred them brave,
The saviours come not home to-night:
  Themselves they could not save.

It dawns in Asia, tombstones show
  And Shropshire names are read;

And the Nile spills his overflow
  Beside the Severn's dead.

We pledge in peace by farm and town
  The Queen they served in war,
And fire the beacons up and down
  The land they perished for.

'God save the Queen' we living sing,
  From height to height 'tis heard;
And with the rest your voices ring,
  Lads of the Fifty-third.

Oh, God will save her, fear you not:
  Be you the men you've been,
Get you the sons your fathers got,
  And God will save the Queen.

II

Loveliest of trees, the cherry now
Is hung with bloom along the bough,
And stands about the woodland ride
Wearing white for Eastertide.

Now, of my threescore years and ten,
Twenty will not come again,

And take from seventy springs a score,
It only leaves me fifty more.

And since to look at things in bloom
Fifty springs are little room,
About the woodlands I will go
To see the cherry hung with snow.

III

THE RECRUIT

Leave your home behind, lad,
  And reach your friends your hand,
And go, and luck go with you
  While Ludlow tower shall stand.

Oh, come you home of Sunday
  When Ludlow streets are still
And Ludlow bells are calling
  To farm and lane and mill,

Or come you home of Monday
  When Ludlow market hums
And Ludlow chimes are playing
  'The conquering hero comes',

Come you home a hero,
  Or come not home at all,
The lads you leave will mind you
  Till Ludlow tower shall fall.

And you will list the bugle
  That blows in lands of morn,
And make the foes of England
  Be sorry you were born.

And you till trump of doomsday
  On lands of morn may lie,
And make the hearts of comrades
  Be heavy where you die.

Leave your home behind you,
  Your friends by field and town:
Oh, town and field will mind you
  Till Ludlow tower is down.

VII

When smoke stood up from Ludlow,
  And mist blew off from Teme,
And blithe afield to ploughing
  Against the morning beam
  I strode beside my team,

The blackbird in the coppice
  Looked out to see me stride,
And hearkened as I whistled
  The trampling team beside,
  And fluted and replied:

'Lie down, lie down, young yeoman;
  What use to rise and rise?
Rise man a thousand mornings
  Yet down at last he lies,
  And then the man is wise.'

I heard the tune he sang me,
  And spied his yellow bill;
I picked a stone and aimed it
  And threw it with a will:
  Then the bird was still.

Then my soul within me
  Took up the blackbird's strain,
And still beside the horses
  Along the dewy lane
  It sang the song again:

'Lie down, lie down, young yeoman;
  The sun moves always west;
The road one treads to labour
  Will lead one home to rest,
  And that will be the best.'

Agnes Miller Parker, illustration to *VII* in *A Shropshire Lad*, 1940.
A Shropshire Lad, George G. Harrop & Co Ltd , London , First Edition, 1940.

IX

On moonlit heath and lonesome bank
  The sheep beside me graze;
And yon the gallows used to clank
  Fast by the four cross ways.

A careless shepherd once would keep
  The flocks by moonlight there,
And high amongst the glimmering sheep
  The dead man stood on air.

They hang us now in Shrewsbury jail:
  The whistles blow forlorn,
And trains all night groan on the rail
  To men that die at morn.

There sleeps in Shrewsbury jail to-night,
  Or wakes, as may betide,
A better lad, if things went right,
  Than most that sleep outside.

And naked to the hangman's noose
  The morning clocks will ring
A neck God made for other use
  Than strangling in a string.

And sharp the link of life will snap,
  And dead on air will stand

Heels that held up as straight a chap
  As treads upon the land.

So here I'll watch the night and wait
  To see the morning shine,
When he will hear the stroke of eight
  And not the stroke of nine;

And wish my friend as sound a sleep
  As lads I did not know,
That shepherded the moonlit sheep
  A hundred years ago.

XVI

It nods and curtseys and recovers
  When the wind blows above,
The nettle on the graves of lovers
  That hanged themselves for love.

The nettle nods, the wind blows over,
  The man, he does not move,
The lover of the grave, the lover
  That hanged himself for love.

XIX

TO AN ATHLETE DYING YOUNG

The time you won your town the race
We chaired you through the market-place;
Man and boy stood cheering by,
And home we brought you shoulder-high.

To-day, the road all runners come,
Shoulder-high we bring you home,
And set you at your threshold down,
Townsman of a stiller town.

Smart lad, to slip betimes away
From fields where glory does not stay
And early though the laurel grows
It withers quicker than the rose.

Eyes the shady night has shut
Cannot see the record cut,
And silence sounds no worse than cheers
After earth has stopped the ears:

Now you will not swell the rout
Of lads that wore their honours out,
Runners whom renown outran
And the name died before the man.

So set, before its echoes fade,
The fleet foot on the sill of shade,
And hold to the low lintel up
The still-defended challenge-cup.

And round that early-laurelled head
Will flock to gaze the strengthless dead,
And find unwithered on its curls
The garland briefer than a girl's.

XX

Oh fair enough are sky and plain,
  But I know fairer far:
Those are as beautiful again
  That in the water are;

The pools and rivers wash so clean
  The trees and clouds and air,
The like on earth was never seen,
  And oh that I were there.

These are the thoughts I often think
  As I stand gazing down
In act upon the cressy brink
  To strip and dive and drown;

But in the golden-sanded brooks
  And azure meres I spy
A silly lad that longs and looks
  And wishes he were I.

XXI

BREDON[1] HILL

In summertime on Bredon
  The bells they sound so clear;
Round both the shires they ring them
  In steeples far and near,
  A happy noise to hear.

Here of a Sunday morning
  My love and I would lie,
And see the coloured counties,
  And hear the larks so high
  About us in the sky.

The bells would ring to call her
  In valleys miles away:
'Come all to church, good people;
  Good people, come and pray.'
  But here my love would stay.

1 Pronounced Breedon.

And I would turn and answer
  Among the springing thyme,
'Oh, peal upon our wedding,
  And we will hear the chime,
  And come to church in time.'

But when the snows at Christmas
  On Bredon top were strown,
My love rose up so early
  And stole out unbeknown
  And went to church alone.

They tolled the one bell only,
  Groom there was none to see,
The mourners followed after,
  And so to church went she,
  And would not wait for me.

The bells they sound on Bredon,
  And still the steeples hum.
'Come all to church, good people,' –
  Oh, noisy bells, be dumb;
  I hear you, I will come.

Agnes Miller Parker, illustration to *XXII* in *A Shropshire Lad*, 1940.

Agnes Miller Parker, illustration to *XXIII* in *A Shropshire Lad*, 1940.

XXII

The street sounds to the soldiers' tread,
  And out we troop to see:
A single redcoat turns his head,
  He turns and looks at me.

My man, from sky to sky's so far,
  We never crossed before;
Such leagues apart the world's ends are,
  We're like to meet no more;

What thoughts at heart have you and I
  We cannot stop to tell;
But dead or living, drunk or dry,
  Soldier, I wish you well.

XXV

This time of year a twelvemonth past,
  When Fred and I would meet,
We needs must jangle, till at last
  We fought and I was beat.

So then the summer fields about,
  Till rainy days began,
Rose Harland on her Sundays out
  Walked with the better man.

The better man she walks with still,
  Though now 'tis not with Fred:
A lad that lives and has his will
  Is worth a dozen dead.

Fred keeps the house all kinds of weather,
  And clay's the house he keeps;
When Rose and I walk out together
  Stock-still lies Fred and sleeps.

XXVI

  Along the field as we came by
A year ago, my love and I,
The aspen over stile and stone
Was talking to itself alone.
'Oh who are these that kiss and pass?
A country lover and his lass;
Two lovers looking to be wed;
And time shall put them both to bed,
But she shall lie with earth above,
And he beside another love.'

And sure enough beneath the tree
There walks another love with me,
And overhead the aspen heaves
Its rainy-sounding silver leaves;
And I spell nothing in their stir,
But now perhaps they speak to her,
And plain for her to understand
They talk about a time at hand
When I shall sleep with clover clad,
And she beside another lad.

XXVII

'Is my team ploughing,
  That I was used to drive
And hear the harness jingle
  When I was man alive?'

Ay, the horses trample,
  The harness jingles now;
No change though you lie under
  The land you used to plough.

'Is football playing
  Along the river shore,
With lads to chase the leather,
  Now I stand up no more?'

Ay, the ball is flying,
  The lads play heart and soul;
The goal stands up, the keeper
  Stands up to keep the goal.

'Is my girl happy,
  That I thought hard to leave,
And has she tired of weeping
  As she lies down at eve?'

Ay, she lies down lightly,
  She lies not down to weep:
Your girl is well contented.
  Be still, my lad, and sleep.

'Is my friend hearty,
  Now I am thin and pine,
And has he found to sleep in
  A better bed than mine?'

Yes, lad, I lie easy,
  I lie as lads would choose;
I cheer a dead man's sweetheart,
  Never ask me whose.

XXVIII

THE WELSH MARCHES

High the vanes of Shrewsbury gleam
Islanded in Severn stream;
The bridges from the steepled crest
Cross the water east and west.

The flag of morn in conqueror's state
Enters at the English gate:
The vanquished eve, as night prevails,
Bleeds upon the road to Wales.

Ages since the vanquished bled
Round my mother's marriage-bed;
There the ravens feasted far
About the open house of war:

When Severn down to Buildwas ran
Coloured with the death of man,
Couched upon her brother's grave
The Saxon got me on the slave.

The sound of fight is silent long
That began the ancient wrong;
Long the voice of tears is still
That wept of old the endless ill.

In my heart it has not died,
The war that sleeps on Severn side;
They cease not fighting, east and west,
On the marches of my breast.

Here the truceless armies yet
Trample, rolled in blood and sweat;
They kill and kill and never die;
And I think that each is I.

None will part us, none undo
The knot that makes one flesh of two,
Sick with hatred, sick with pain,
Strangling – When shall we be slain?

When shall I be dead and rid
Of the wrong my father did?
How long, how long, till spade and hearse
Put to sleep my mother's curse?

XXIX

THE LENT LILY

'Tis spring; come out to ramble
  The hilly brakes around,
For under thorn and bramble
  About the hollow ground
  The primroses are found.

And there's the windflower chilly
  With all the winds at play,
And there's the Lenten lily
  That has not long to stay
  And dies on Easter day.

And since till girls go maying
  You find the primrose still,
And find the windflower playing
  With every wind at will,
  But not the daffodil,

Bring baskets now, and sally
  Upon the spring's array,
And bear from hill and valley
  The daffodil away
  That dies on Easter day.

XXXI

On Wenlock Edge the wood's in trouble;
  His forest fleece the Wrekin heaves;
The gale, it plies the saplings double,
  And thick on Severn snow the leaves.

'Twould blow like this through holt and hanger
  When Uricon the city stood:

'Tis the old wind in the old anger,
  But then it threshed another wood.

Then, 'twas before my time, the Roman
  At yonder heaving hill would stare:
The blood that warms an English yeoman,
  The thoughts that hurt him, they were there.

There, like the wind through woods in riot,
  Through him the gale of life blew high;
The tree of man was never quiet:
  Then 'twas the Roman, now 'tis I.

The gale, it plies the saplings double,
  It blows so hard, 'twill soon be gone:
To-day the Roman and his trouble
  Are ashes under Uricon.

XXXII

From far, from eve and morning
  And yon twelve-winded sky,
The stuff of life to knit me
  Blew hither: here am I.

Now – for a breath I tarry
  Nor yet disperse apart –

Take my hand quick and tell me,
  What have you in your heart.

Speak now, and I will answer;
  How shall I help you, say;
Ere to the wind's twelve quarters
  I take my endless way.

XXXIII

If truth in hearts that perish
  Could move the powers on high,
I think the love I bear you
  Should make you not to die.

Sure, sure, if steadfast meaning,
  If single thought could save,
The world might end to-morrow,
  You should not see the grave.

This long and sure-set liking,
  This boundless will to please,
– Oh, you should live for ever
  If there were help in these.

But now, since all is idle,
  To this lost heart be kind,

Ere to a town you journey
  Where friends are ill to find.

XXXV

On the idle hill of summer,
  Sleepy with the flow of streams,
Far I hear the steady drummer
  Drumming like a noise in dreams.

Far and near and low and louder
  On the roads of earth go by,
Dear to friends and food for powder,
  Soldiers marching, all to die.

East and west on fields forgotten
  Bleach the bones of comrades slain,
Lovely lads and dead and rotten;
  None that go return again.

Far the calling bugles hollo,
  High the screaming fife replies,
Gay the files of scarlet follow:
  Woman bore me, I will rise.

XXXVII

As through the wild green hills of Wyre
The train ran, changing sky and shire,
And far behind, a fading crest,
Low in the forsaken west
Sank the high-reared head of Clee,
My hand lay empty on my knee.
Aching on my knee it lay:
That morning half a shire away
So many an honest fellow's fist
Had well-nigh wrung it from the wrist.
Hand, said I, since now we part
From fields and men we know by heart,
For strangers' faces, strangers' lands, -
Hand, you have held true fellows' hands.
Be clean then; rot before you do
A thing they'd not believe of you.
You and I must keep from shame
In London streets the Shropshire name;
On banks of Thames they must not say
Severn breeds worse men than they;
And friends abroad must bear in mind
Friends at home they leave behind.
Oh, I shall be stiff and cold
When I forget you, hearts of gold;
The land where I shall mind you not
Is the land where all's forgot.
And if my foot returns no more

To Teme nor Corve nor Severn shore,
Luck, my lads, be with you still
By falling stream and standing hill,
By chiming tower and whispering tree,
Men that made a man of me.
About your work in town and farm
Still you'll keep my head from harm,
Still you'll help me, hands that gave
A grasp to friend me to the grave.

XXXIX

'Tis time, I think, by Wenlock town
  The golden bloom should blow;
The hawthorn sprinkled up and down
  Should charge the land with snow.

Spring will not wait the loiterer's time
  Who keeps so long away;
So others wear the broom and climb
  The hedgerows heaped with may.

Oh tarnish late on Wenlock Edge,
  Gold that I never see;
Lie long, high snowdrifts in the hedge
  That will not shower on me.

XL

Into my heart an air that kills
  From yon far country blows:
What are those blue remembered hills,
  What spires, what farms are those?

That is the land of lost content,
  I see it shining plain,
The happy highways where I went
  And cannot come again.

XLI

  In my own shire, if I was sad,
Homely comforters I had:
The earth, because my heart was sore,
Sorrowed for the son she bore;
And standing hills, long to remain,
Shared their short-lived comrade's pain.
And bound for the same bourn as I,
On every road I wandered by,
Trod beside me, close and dear,

The beautiful and death-struck year:
Whether in the woodland brown
I heard the beechnut rustle down,

And saw the purple crocus pale
Flower about the autumn dale;
Or littering far the fields of May
Lady-smocks a-bleaching lay,
And like a skylit water stood
The bluebells in the azured wood.

Yonder, lightening other loads,
The seasons range the country roads,
But here in London streets I ken
No such helpmates, only men;
And these are not in plight to bear,
If they would, another's care.
They have enough as 'tis: I see
In many an eye that measures me
The mortal sickness of a mind
Too unhappy to be kind.
Undone with misery, all they can
Is to hate their fellow man;
And till they drop they needs must still
Look at you and wish you ill.

XLII

THE MERRY GUIDE

Once in the wind of morning
  I ranged the thymy wold;
The world-wide air was azure
  And all the brooks ran gold.

There through the dews beside me
  Behold a youth that trod,
With feathered cap on forehead,
  And poised a golden rod.

With mien to match the morning
  And gay delightful guise
And friendly brows and laughter
  He looked me in the eyes.

Oh whence, I asked, and whither?
  He smiled and would not say,
And looked at me and beckoned
  And laughed and led the way.

And with kind looks and laughter
  And nought to say beside
We two went on together,
  I and my happy guide.

Across the glittering pastures
  And empty upland still
And solitude of shepherds
  High in the folded hill,

By hanging woods and hamlets
  That gaze through orchards down
On many a windmill turning
  And far-discovered town,

With gay regards of promise
  And sure unslackened stride
And smiles and nothing spoken
  Led on my merry guide.

By blowing realms of woodland
  With sunstruck vanes afield
And cloud-led shadows sailing
  About the windy weald,

By valley-guarded granges
  And silver waters wide,
Content at heart I followed
  With my delightful guide.

And like the cloudy shadows
  Across the country blown
We two fare on for ever,
  But not we two alone.

With the great gale we journey
  That breathes from gardens thinned,
Borne in the drift of blossoms
  Whose petals throng the wind;

Buoyed on the heaven-heard whisper
  Of dancing leaflets whirled
From all the woods that autumn
  Bereaves in all the world.

And midst the fluttering legion
  Of all that ever died
I follow, and before us
  Goes the delightful guide,

With lips that brim with laughter
  But never once respond,
And feet that fly on feathers,
  And serpent-circled wand.

XLIII

THE IMMORTAL PART

When I meet the morning beam,
Or lay me down at night to dream,
I hear my bones within me say,
'Another night, another day.

'When shall this slough of sense be cast,
This dust of thoughts be laid at last,
The man of flesh and soul be slain
And the man of bone remain?

'This tongue that talks, these lungs that shout,
These thews that hustle us about,
This brain that fills the skull with schemes,
And its humming hive of dreams, –

'These to-day are proud in power
And lord it in their little hour:
The immortal bones obey control
Of dying flesh and dying soul.

''Tis long till eve and morn are gone:
Slow the endless night comes on,
And late to fulness grows the birth
That shall last as long as earth.

'Wanderers eastward, wanderers west,
Know you why you cannot rest?
'Tis that every mother's son
Travails with a skeleton.

'Lie down in the bed of dust;
Bear the fruit that bear you must;
Bring the eternal seed to light,
And morn is all the same as night.

'Rest you so from trouble sore,
Fear the heat o' the sun no more,
Nor the snowing winter wild,
Now you labour not with child.

'Empty vessel, garment cast,
We that wore you long shall last.
– Another night, another day.'
So my bones within me say.

Therefore they shall do my will
To-day while I am master still,
And flesh and soul, now both are strong,
Shall hale the sullen slaves along,

Before this fire of sense decay,
This smoke of thought blow clean away,
And leave with ancient night alone
The steadfast and enduring bone.

XLIV

Shot? so quick, so clean an ending?
  Oh that was right, lad, that was brave:
Yours was not an ill for mending,
  'Twas best to take it to the grave.

Oh you had forethought, you could reason,
  And saw your road and where it led,
And early wise and brave in season
  Put the pistol to your head.

Oh soon, and better so than later
  After long disgrace and scorn,
You shot dead the household traitor,
  The soul that should not have been born.

Right you guessed the rising morrow
  And scorned to tread the mire you must:
Dust's your wages, son of sorrow,
  But men may come to worse than dust.

Souls undone, undoing others, –
  Long time since the tale began.
You would not live to wrong your brothers:
  Oh lad, you died as fits a man.

Now to your grave shall friend and stranger
  With ruth and some with envy come:
Undishonoured, clear of danger,
  Clean of guilt, pass hence and home.

Turn safe to rest, no dreams, no waking;
  And here, man, here's the wreath I've made:
'Tis not a gift that's worth the taking,
  But wear it and it will not fade.

XLVII

THE CARPENTER'S SON

'Here the hangman stops his cart:
Now the best of friends must part.
Fare you well, for ill fare I:
Live, lads, and I will die.

'Oh, at home had I but stayed
'Prenticed to my father's trade,
Had I stuck to plane and adze,
I had not been lost, my lads.

'Then I might have built perhaps
Gallows-trees for other chaps,
Never dangled on my own,
Had I but left ill alone.

'Now, you see, they hang me high,
And the people passing by
Stop to shake their fists and curse;
So 'tis come from ill to worse.

'Here hang I, and right and left
Two poor fellows hang for theft:
All the same's the luck we prove,
Though the midmost hangs for love.

'Comrades all, that stand and gaze,
Walk henceforth in other ways;
See my neck and save your own:
Comrades all, leave ill alone.

'Make some day a decent end,
Shrewder fellows than your friend.
Fare you well, for ill fare I:
Live, lads, and I will die.'

XLVIII

Be still, my soul, be still; the arms you bear are brittle,
  Earth and high heaven are fixt of old and founded strong.
Think rather, – call to thought, if now you grieve a little,
  The days when we had rest, O soul, for they were long.

Men loved unkindness then, but lightless in the quarry
  I slept and saw not; tears fell down, I did not mourn;
Sweat ran and blood sprang out and I was never sorry:
  Then it was well with me, in days ere I was born.

Now, and I muse for why and never find the reason,
  I pace the earth, and drink the air, and feel the sun.
Be still, be still, my soul; it is but for a season:
  Let us endure an hour and see injustice done.

Ay, look: high heaven and earth ail from the prime foundation;
  All thoughts to rive the heart are here, and all are vain:
Horror and scorn and hate and fear and indignation –
  Oh why did I awake? when shall I sleep again?

L

Clunton and Clunbury,
        Clungunford and Clun,
Are the quietest places
        Under the sun.

In valleys of springs of rivers,
  By Ony and Teme and Clun,
The country for easy livers,
  The quietest under the sun,

We still had sorrows to lighten,
  One could not be always glad,
And lads knew trouble at Knighton
  When I was a Knighton lad.

By bridges that Thames runs under
  In London, the town built ill,
'Tis sure small matter for wonder
  If sorrow is with one still.
And if as a lad grows older

The troubles he bears are more,
He carries his griefs on a shoulder
That handselled them long before.

Where shall one halt to deliver
This luggage I'd lief set down?
Not Thames, not Teme is the river,
Nor London nor Knighton the town:

'Tis a long way further than Knighton,
A quieter place than Clun,
Where doomsday may thunder and lighten
And little 'twill matter to one.

LII

Far in a western brookland
That bred me long ago
The poplars stand and tremble
By pools I used to know.

There, in the windless night-time,
The wanderer, marvelling why,
Halts on the bridge to hearken
How soft the poplars sigh.

He hears: no more remembered
  In fields where I was known,
Here I lie down in London
  And turn to rest alone.

There, by the starlit fences,
  The wanderer halts and hears
My soul that lingers sighing
  About the glimmering weirs.

LIII

THE TRUE LOVER

The lad came to the door at night,
  When lovers crown their vows,
And whistled soft and out of sight
  In shadow of the boughs.

'I shall not vex you with my face
  Henceforth, my love, for aye;
So take me in your arms a space
  Before the east is grey.

'When I from hence away am past
  I shall not find a bride,
And you shall be the first and last

I ever lay beside.'
She heard and went and knew not why;
Her heart to his she laid;
Light was the air beneath the sky
But dark under the shade.

'Oh do you breathe, lad, that your breast
Seems not to rise and fall,
And here upon my bosom prest
There beats no heart at all?'

'Oh loud, my girl, it once would knock,
You should have felt it then;
But since for you I stopped the clock
It never goes again.'

'Oh lad, what is it, lad, that drips
Wet from your neck on mine?
What is it falling on my lips,
My lad, that tastes of brine?'

'Oh like enough 'tis blood, my dear,
For when the knife has slit
The throat across from ear to ear
'Twill bleed because of it.'

Under the stars the air was light
But dark below the boughs,
The still air of the speechless night,
When lovers crown their vows.

LIV

With rue my heart is laden
  For golden friends I had,
For many a rose-lipt maiden
  And many a lightfoot lad.

By brooks too broad for leaping
  The lightfoot boys are laid;
The rose-lipt girls are sleeping
  In fields where roses fade.

LV

Westward on the high-hilled plains
  Where for me the world began,
Still, I think, in newer veins
  Frets the changeless blood of man.

Now that other lads than I
  Strip to bathe on Severn shore,
They, no help, for all they try,
  Tread the mill I trod before.

There, when hueless is the west
  And the darkness hushes wide,
Where the lad lies down to rest
  Stands the troubled dream beside.

There, on thoughts that once were mine,
  Day looks down the eastern steep,
And the youth at morning shine
  Makes the vow he will not keep.

LVI

THE DAY OF BATTLE

'Far I hear the bugle blow
To call me where I would not go,
And the guns begin the song,
"Soldier, fly or stay for long."

'Comrade, if to turn and fly
Made a soldier never die,
Fly I would, for who would not?
'Tis sure no pleasure to be shot.

'But since the man that runs away
Lives to die another day,
And cowards' funerals, when they come,
Are not wept so well at home,

'Therefore, though the best is bad,
Stand and do the best, my lad;
Stand and fight and see your slain,
And take the bullet in your brain.'

LX

Now hollow fires burn out to black,
  And lights are guttering low:
Square your shoulders, lift your pack,
  And leave your friends and go.

Oh never fear, man, nought's to dread,
  Look not left nor right:
In all the endless road you tread
  There's nothing but the night.

LXI

HUGHLEY STEEPLE

The vane on Hughley steeple
  Veers bright, a far-known sign,
And there lie Hughley people,
  And there lie friends of mine.
Tall in their midst the tower
  Divides the shade and sun,
And the clock strikes the hour
  And tells the time to none.

To south the headstones cluster,
  The sunny mounds lie thick;
The dead are more in muster

  At Hughley than the quick.
North, for a soon-told number,
  Chill graves the sexton delves,
And steeple-shadowed slumber
  The slayers of themselves.

To north, to south, lie parted,
  With Hughley tower above,
The kind, the single-hearted,
  The lads I used to love.
And, south or north, 'tis only
  A choice of friends one knows,
And I shall ne'er be lonely
  Asleep with these or those.

LXII

  'Terence, this is stupid stuff:
You eat your victuals fast enough;
There can't be much amiss, 'tis clear,
To see the rate you drink your beer.
But oh, good Lord, the verse you make,
It gives a chap the belly-ache.
The cow, the old cow, she is dead;
It sleeps well, the horned head:
We poor lads, 'tis our turn now
To hear such tunes as killed the cow.

Pretty friendship 'tis to rhyme
Your friends to death before their time
Moping melancholy mad:
Come, pipe a tune to dance to, lad.'

Why, if 'tis dancing you would be,
There's brisker pipes than poetry.
Say, for what were hop-yards meant,
Or why was Burton built on Trent?
Oh many a peer of England brews
Livelier liquor than the Muse,
And malt does more than Milton can
To justify God's ways to man.
Ale, man, ale's the stuff to drink
For fellows whom it hurts to think:
Look into the pewter pot
To see the world as the world's not.
And faith, 'tis pleasant till 'tis past:
The mischief is that 'twill not last.
Oh I have been to Ludlow fair
And left my necktie God knows where,
And carried half way home, or near,
Pints and quarts of Ludlow beer:
Then the world seemed none so bad,
And I myself a sterling lad;
And down in lovely muck I've lain,
Happy till I woke again.
Then I saw the morning sky:
Heigho, the tale was all a lie;

The world, it was the old world yet,
I was I, my things were wet,
And nothing now remained to do
But begin the game anew.

Therefore, since the world has still
Much good, but much less good than ill,
And while the sun and moon endure
Luck's a chance, but trouble's sure,
I'd face it as a wise man would,
And train for ill and not for good.
'Tis true, the stuff I bring for sale
Is not so brisk a brew as ale:
Out of a stem that scored the hand
I wrung it in a weary land.
But take it: if the smack is sour,
The better for the embittered hour;
It should do good to heart and head
When your soul is in my soul's stead;
And I will friend you, if I may,
In the dark and cloudy day.

There was a king reigned in the East:
There, when kings will sit to feast,
They get their fill before they think
With poisoned meat and poisoned drink.
He gathered all that springs to birth
From the many-venomed earth;
First a little, thence to more,

He sampled all her killing store;
And easy, smiling, seasoned sound,
Sate the king when healths went round.
They put arsenic in his meat
And stared aghast to watch him eat;
They poured strychnine in his cup
And shook to see him drink it up:
They shook, they stared as white's their shirt:
Them it was their poison hurt.
– I tell the tale that I heard told.
Mithridates, he died old.

LXIII

I hoed and trenched and weeded,
  And took the flowers to fair:
I brought them home unheeded;
  The hue was not the wear.

So up and down I sow them
  For lads like me to find,
When I shall lie below them,
  A dead man out of mind.

Some seed the birds devour,
  And some the season mars,
But here and there will flower
  The solitary stars,

And fields will yearly bear them
    As light-leaved spring comes on,
And luckless lads will wear them
    When I am dead and gone.

From *Last Poems*

I

THE WEST

Beyond the moor and mountain crest
– Comrade, look not on the west –
The sun is down and drinks away
From air and land the lees of day.

The long cloud and the single pine
Sentinel the ending line,
And out beyond it, clear and wan,
Reach the gulfs of evening on.

The son of woman turns his brow
West from forty counties now,
And, as the edge of heaven he eyes,
Thinks eternal thoughts, and sighs.

Oh wide's the world, to rest or roam,
With change abroad and cheer at home,
Fights and furloughs, talk and tale,
Company and beef and ale.

But if I front the evening sky
Silent on the west look I,
And my comrade, stride for stride,
Paces silent at my side.

Comrade, look not on the west:
'Twill have the heart out of your breast;
'Twill take your thoughts and sink them far,
Leagues beyond the sunset bar.

Oh lad, I fear that yon's the sea
Where they fished for you and me,
And there, from whence we both were ta'en,
You and I shall drown again.

Send not on your soul before
To dive from that beguiling shore,
And let not yet the swimmer leave
His clothes upon the sands of eve.

Too fast to yonder strand forlorn
We journey, to the sunken bourn,
To flush the fading tinges eyed
By other lads at eventide.

Wide is the world, to rest or roam,
And early 'tis for turning home:
Plant your heel on earth and stand,
And let's forget our native land.

When you and I are spilt on air
Long we shall be strangers there;
Friends of flesh and bone are best:
Comrade, look not on the west.

II

As I gird on for fighting
  My sword upon my thigh,
I think on old ill fortunes
  Of better men than I.

Think I, the round world over,
  What golden lads are low
With hurts not mine to mourn for
  And shames I shall not know.

What evil luck soever
  For me remains in store,
'Tis sure much finer fellows
  Have fared much worse before.

So here are things to think on
  That ought to make me brave,
As I strap on for fighting
  My sword that will not save.

III

Her strong enchantments failing,
  Her towers of fear in wreck,
Her limbecks dried of poisons
  And the knife at her neck,

The Queen of air and darkness
  Begins to shrill and cry,
'O young man, O my slayer,
  To-morrow you shall die.'

O Queen of air and darkness,
  I think 'tis truth you say,
And I shall die to-morrow;
  But you will die to-day.

IV

ILLIC JACET

Oh hard is the bed they have made him,
  And common the blanket and cheap;
But there he will lie as they laid him:
  Where else could you trust him to sleep?

To sleep when the bugle is crying
   And cravens have heard and are brave,
When mothers and sweethearts are sighing
   And lads are in love with the grave.

Oh dark is the chamber and lonely,
   And lights and companions depart;
But lief will he lose them and only
   Behold the desire of his heart.

And low is the roof, but it covers
   A sleeper content to repose;
And far from his friends and his lovers
   He lies with the sweetheart he chose.

VII

In valleys green and still
   Where lovers wander maying
They hear from over hill
   A music playing.

Behind the drum and fife,
   Past hawthornwood and hollow,
Through earth and out of life
   The soldiers follow.

The soldier's is the trade:
  In any wind or weather
He steals the heart of maid
  And man together.

The lover and his lass
  Beneath the hawthorn lying
Have heard the soldiers pass,
  And both are sighing.

And down the distance they
  With dying note and swelling
Walk the resounding way
  To the still dwelling.

IX

The chestnut casts his flambeaux, and the flowers
  Stream from the hawthorn on the wind away,
The doors clap to, the pane is blind with showers.
  Pass me the can, lad; there's an end of May.

There's one spoilt spring to scant our mortal lot,
  One season ruined of our little store.
May will be fine next year as like as not:
  Oh ay, but then we shall be twenty-four.

We for a certainty are not the first
  Have sat in taverns while the tempest hurled
Their hopeful plans to emptiness, and cursed
  Whatever brute and blackguard made the world.

It is in truth iniquity on high
  To cheat our sentenced souls of aught they crave,
And mar the merriment as you and I
  Fare on our long fool's-errand to the grave.

Iniquity it is; but pass the can.
  My lad, no pair of kings our mothers bore;
Our only portion is the estate of man:
  We want the moon, but we shall get no more.

If here to-day the cloud of thunder lours
  To-morrow it will hie on far behests;
The flesh will grieve on other bones than ours
  Soon, and the soul will mourn in other breasts.

The troubles of our proud and angry dust
  Are from eternity, and shall not fail.
Bear them we can, and if we can we must.
  Shoulder the sky, my lad, and drink your ale.

X

Could man be drunk for ever
  With liquor, love, or fights,
Lief should I rouse at morning
  And lief lie down of nights.

But men at whiles are sober
  And think by fits and starts,
And if they think, they fasten
  Their hands upon their hearts.

XI

Yonder see the morning blink:
  The sun is up, and up must I,
To wash and dress and eat and drink
And look at things and talk and think
  And work, and God knows why.

Oh often have I washed and dressed
  And what's to show for all my pain?
Let me lie abed and rest:
Ten thousand times I've done my best
  And all's to do again.

XII

The laws of God, the laws of man,
He may keep that will and can;
Not I: let God and man decree
Laws for themselves and not for me;
And if my ways are not as theirs
Let them mind their own affairs.
Their deeds I judge and much condemn,
Yet when did I make laws for them?
Please yourselves, say I, and they
Need only look the other way.
But no, they will not; they must still
Wrest their neighbour to their will,
And make me dance as they desire
With jail and gallows and hell-fire.
And how am I to face the odds
Of man's bedevilment and God's?
I, a stranger and afraid
In a world I never made.
They will be master, right or wrong;
Though both are foolish, both are strong.
And since, my soul, we cannot fly
To Saturn nor to Mercury,
Keep we must, if keep we can,
These foreign laws of God and man.

XVII

ASTRONOMY

The Wain upon the northern steep
  Descends and lifts away.
Oh I will sit me down and weep
  For bones in Africa.

For pay and medals, name and rank,
  Things that he has not found,
He hove the Cross to heaven and sank
  The pole-star underground.

And now he does not even see
  Signs of the nadir roll
At night over the ground where he
  Is buried with the pole.

XIX

In midnights of November,
  When Dead Man's Fair is nigh,
And danger in the valley,
  And anger in the sky,

Around the huddling homesteads
  The leafless timber roars,
And the dead call the dying
  And finger at the doors.

Oh, yonder faltering fingers
  Are hands I used to hold;
Their false companion drowses
  And leaves them in the cold.

Oh, to the bed of ocean,
  To Africk and to Ind,
I will arise and follow
  Along the rainy wind.

The night goes out and under
  With all its train forlorn;
Hues in the east assemble
  And cocks crow up the morn.

The living are the living
  And dead the dead will stay,
And I will sort with comrades
  That face the beam of day.

XX

The night is freezing fast,
To-morrow comes December;
And winterfalls of old
Are with me from the past;
And chiefly I remember
How Dick would hate the cold.

Fall, winter, fall; for he,
Prompt hand and headpiece clever,
Has woven a winter robe,
And made of earth and sea
His overcoat for ever,
And wears the turning globe.

XXVII

The sigh that heaves the grasses
Whence thou wilt never rise
Is of the air that passes
And knows not if it sighs.

The diamond tears adorning
Thy low mound on the lea,
Those are the tears of morning,
That weeps, but not for thee.

XXIX

Wake not for the world-heard thunder
  Nor the chime that earthquakes toll.
Star may plot in heaven with planet,
Lightning rive the rock of granite,
Tempest tread the oakwood under:
  Fear not you for flesh nor soul.
Marching, fighting, victory past,
Stretch your limbs in peace at last.

Stir not for the soldiers drilling
  Nor the fever nothing cures:
Throb of drum and timbal's rattle
Call but man alive to battle,
And the fife with death-notes filling
  Screams for blood but not for yours.
Times enough you bled your best;
Sleep on now, and take your rest.

Sleep, my lad; the French are landed,
  London's burning, Windsor's down;
Clasp your cloak of earth about you,
We must man the ditch without you,
March unled and fight short-handed,
  Charge to fall and swim to drown.
Duty, friendship, bravery o'er,
Sleep away, lad; wake no more.

XXX

SINNER'S RUE

I walked alone and thinking,
  And faint the nightwind blew
And stirred on mounds at crossways
  The flower of sinner's rue.

Where the roads part they bury
  Him that his own hand slays,
And so the weed of sorrow
  Springs at the four cross ways.

By night I plucked it hueless,
  When morning broke 'twas blue:
Blue at my breast I fastened
  The flower of sinner's rue.

It seemed a herb of healing,
  A balsam and a sign,
Flower of a heart whose trouble
  Must have been worse than mine.

Dead clay that did me kindness,
  I can do none to you,
But only wear for breastknot
  The flower of sinner's rue.

XXXI

HELL GATE

Onward led the road again
Through the sad uncoloured plain
Under twilight brooding dim,
And along the utmost rim
Wall and rampart risen to sight
Cast a shadow not of night,
And beyond them seemed to glow
Bonfires lighted long ago.
And my dark conductor broke
Silence at my side and spoke,
Saying, 'You conjecture well:
Yonder is the gate of hell.'

Ill as yet the eye could see
The eternal masonry,
But beneath it on the dark
To and fro there stirred a spark.
And again the sombre guide
Knew my question, and replied:
'At hell gate the damned in turn
Pace for sentinel and burn.'

Dully at the leaden sky
Staring, and with idle eye
Measuring the listless plain,

I began to think again.
Many things I thought of then,
Battle, and the loves of men,
Cities entered, oceans crossed,
Knowledge gained and virtue lost,
Cureless folly done and said,
And the lovely way that led
To the slimepit and the mire
And the everlasting fire.
And against a smoulder dun
And a dawn without a sun
Did the nearing bastion loom,
And across the gate of gloom
Still one saw the sentry go,
Trim and burning, to and fro,
One for women to admire
In his finery of fire.
Something, as I watched him pace,
Minded me of time and place,
Soldiers of another corps
And a sentry known before.

Ever darker hell on high
Reared its strength upon the sky,
And our footfall on the track
Fetched the daunting echo back.
But the soldier pacing still
The insuperable sill,
Nursing his tormented pride,

Turned his head to neither side,
Sunk into himself apart
And the hell-fire of his heart.
But against our entering in
From the drawbridge Death and Sin
Rose to render key and sword
To their father and their lord.
And the portress foul to see
Lifted up her eyes on me
Smiling, and I made reply:
'Met again, my lass,' said I.
Then the sentry turned his head,
Looked, and knew me, and was Ned.

Once he looked, and halted straight,
Set his back against the gate,
Caught his musket to his chin,
While the hive of hell within
Sent abroad a seething hum
As of towns whose king is come
Leading conquest home from far
And the captives of his war,
And the car of triumph waits,
And they open wide the gates.
But across the entry barred
Straddled the revolted guard,
Weaponed and accoutred well
From the arsenals of hell;
And beside him, sick and white,

Sin to left and Death to right
Turned a countenance of fear
On the flaming mutineer.
Over us the darkness bowed,
And the anger in the cloud
Clenched the lightning for the stroke;
But the traitor musket spoke.

And the hollowness of hell
Sounded as its master fell,
And the mourning echo rolled
Ruin through his kingdom old.
Tyranny and terror flown
Left a pair of friends alone,
And beneath the nether sky
All that stirred was he and I.

Silent, nothing found to say,
We began the backward way;
And the ebbing lustre died
From the soldier at my side,
As in all his spruce attire
Failed the everlasting fire.
Midmost of the homeward track
Once we listened and looked back;
But the city, dusk and mute,
Slept, and there was no pursuit.

XXXII

When I would muse in boyhood
  The wild green woods among,
And nurse resolves and fancies
  Because the world was young,
It was not foes to conquer,
  Nor sweethearts to be kind,
But it was friends to die for
  That I would seek and find.

I sought them far and found them,
  The sure, the straight, the brave,
The hearts I lost my own to,
  The souls I could not save.
They braced their belts about them,
  They crossed in ships the sea,
They sought and found six feet of ground,
  And there they died for me.

XXXIII

When the eye of day is shut,
  And the stars deny their beams,
And about the forest hut
  Blows the roaring wood of dreams,

From deep clay, from desert rock,
  From the sunk sands of the main,
Come not at my door to knock,
  Hearts that loved me not again.

Sleep, be still, turn to your rest
  In the lands where you are laid;
In far lodgings east and west
  Lie down on the beds you made.

In gross marl, in blowing dust,
  In the drowned ooze of the sea,
Where you would not, lie you must,
  Lie you must, and not with me.

XXXIV

THE FIRST OF MAY

The orchards half the way
  From home to Ludlow fair
Flowered on the first of May
  In Mays when I was there;

And seen from stile or turning
  The plume of smoke would show
Where fires were burning

That went out long ago.
The plum broke forth in green,
The pear stood high and snowed,
My friends and I between
Would take the Ludlow road;
Dressed to the nines and drinking
And light in heart and limb,
And each chap thinking
The fair was held for him.

Between the trees in flower
New friends at fairtime tread
The way where Ludlow tower
Stands planted on the dead.
Our thoughts, a long while after,
They think, our words they say;
Theirs now's the laughter,
The fair, the first of May.

Ay, yonder lads are yet
The fools that we were then;
For oh, the sons we get
Are still the sons of men.
The sumless tale of sorrow
Is all unrolled in vain:
May comes to-morrow
And Ludlow fair again.

XXXVII

EPITAPH ON AN ARMY OF MERCENARIES

These, in the day when heaven was falling,
  The hour when earth's foundations fled,
Followed their mercenary calling
  And took their wages and are dead.

Their shoulders held the sky suspended;
  They stood, and earth's foundations stay;
What God abandoned, these defended,
  And saved the sum of things for pay.

XXXVIII

Oh stay at home, my lad, and plough
  The land and not the sea,
And leave the soldiers at their drill,
And all about the idle hill
  Shepherd your sheep with me.

Oh stay with company and mirth
  And daylight and the air;
Too full already is the grave
Of fellows that were good and brave
  And died because they were.

XXXIX

When summer's end is nighing
  And skies at evening cloud,
I muse on change and fortune
  And all the feats I vowed
  When I was young and proud.

The weathercock at sunset
  Would lose the slanted ray,
And I would climb the beacon
  That looked to Wales away
  And saw the last of day.

From hill and cloud and heaven
  The hues of evening died;
Night welled through lane and hollow
  And hushed the countryside,
  But I had youth and pride.

And I with earth and nightfall
  In converse high would stand,
Late, till the west was ashen
  And darkness hard at hand,
  And the eye lost the land.

The year might age, and cloudy
  The lessening day might close,
But air of other summers

Breathed from beyond the snows,
And I had hope of those.

They came and were and are not
And come no more anew;
And all the years and seasons
That ever can ensue
Must now be worse and few.

So here's an end of roaming
On eves when autumn nighs:
The ear too fondly listens
For summer's parting sighs,
And then the heart replies.

XL

Tell me not here, it needs not saying,
What tune the enchantress plays
In aftermaths of soft September
Or under blanching mays,
For she and I were long acquainted
And I knew all her ways.

On russet floors, by waters idle,
The pine lets fall its cone;
The cuckoo shouts all day at nothing

In leafy dells alone;
And traveller's joy beguiles in autumn
Hearts that have lost their own.

On acres of the seeded grasses
The changing burnish heaves;
Or marshalled under moons of harvest
Stand still all night the sheaves;
Or beeches strip in storms for winter
And stain the wind with leaves.

Possess, as I possessed a season,
The countries I resign,
Where over elmy plains the highway
Would mount the hills and shine,
And full of shade the pillared forest
Would murmur and be mine.

For nature, heartless, witless nature,
Will neither care nor know
What stranger's feet may find the meadow
And trespass there and go,
Nor ask amid the dews of morning
If they are mine or no.

XLI

FANCY'S KNELL

When lads were home from labour
  At Abdon under Clee,
A man would call his neighbour
  And both would send for me.
And where the light in lances
  Across the mead was laid,
There to the dances
  I fetched my flute and played.

Ours were idle pleasures,
  Yet oh, content we were,
The young to wind the measures,
  The old to heed the air;
And I to lift with playing
  From tree and tower and steep
The light delaying,
  And flute the sun to sleep.

The youth toward his fancy
  Would turn his brow of tan,
And Tom would pair with Nancy
  And Dick step off with Fan;
The girl would lift her glances
  To his, and both be mute:
Well went the dances

At evening to the flute.
Wenlock Edge was umbered,
And bright was Abdon Burf,
And warm between them slumbered
The smooth green miles of turf;
Until from grass and clover
The upshot beam would fade,
And England over
Advanced the lofty shade.

The lofty shade advances,
I fetch my flute and play:
Come, lads, and learn the dances
And praise the tune to-day.
To-morrow, more's the pity,
Away we both must hie,
To air the ditty,
And to earth I.

Agnes Miller Parker, illustration to *LVI* in *A Shropshire Lad*, 1940.

Agnes Miller Parker, illustration to *LVIII* in *A Shropshire Lad*, 1940.

From *More Poems*

They say my verse is sad: no wonder;
Its narrow measure spans
Tears of eternity, and sorrow,
Not mine, but man's.

This is for all ill-treated fellows
Unborn and unbegot,
For them to read when they're in trouble
And I am not.

I

EASTER HYMN

If in that Syrian garden, ages slain,
You sleep, and know not you are dead in vain,
Nor even in dreams behold how dark and bright
Ascends in smoke and fire by day and night
The hate you died to quench and could but fan,
Sleep well and see no morning, son of man.

But if, the grave rent and the stone rolled by,
At the right hand of majesty on high
You sit, and sitting so remember yet

Your tears, your agony and bloody sweat,
Your cross and passion and the life you gave,
Bow hither out of heaven and see and save.

II

When Israel out of Egypt came
  Safe in the sea they trod;
By day in cloud, by night in flame,
  Went on before them God.

He brought them with a stretched out hand
  Dry-footed through the foam,
Past sword and famine, rock and sand,
  Lust and rebellion, home.

I never over Horeb heard
  The blast of advent blow;
No fire-faced prophet brought me word
  Which way behoved me go.

Ascended is the cloudy flame,
  The mount of thunder dumb;
The tokens that to Israel came,
  To me they have not come.

I see the country far away
  Where I shall never stand;
The heart goes where no footstep may
  Into the promised land.

The realm I look upon and die
  Another man will own;
He shall attain the heaven that I
  Perish and have not known.

But I will go where they are hid
  That never were begot,
To my inheritance amid
  The nation that is not.

V

DIFFUGERE NIVES

Horace: Odes iv 7

The snows are fled away, leaves on the shaws
  And grasses in the mead renew their birth,
The river to the river-bed withdraws,
  And altered is the fashion of the earth.

The Nymphs and Graces three put off their fear
  And unapparelled in the woodland play.
The swift hour and the brief prime of the year
  Say to the soul, *Thou wast not born for aye.*

Thaw follows frost; hard on the heel of spring
  Treads summer sure to die, for hard on hers
Comes autumn, with his apples scattering;
  Then back to wintertide, when nothing stirs.

But oh, whate'er the sky-led seasons mar,
  Moon upon moon rebuilds it with her beams:
Come *we* where Tullus and where Ancus are,
  And good Aeneas, we are dust and dreams.

Torquatus, if the gods in heaven shall add
  The morrow to the day, what tongue has told?
Feast then thy heart, for what thy heart has had
  The fingers of no heir will ever hold.

When thou descendest once the shades among,
  The stern assize and equal judgment o'er,
Not thy long lineage nor thy golden tongue,
  No, nor thy righteousness, shall friend thee more.

Night holds Hippolytus the pure of stain,
  Diana steads him nothing, he must stay;
And Theseus leaves Pirithöus in the chain
  The love of comrades cannot take away.

VIII

Give me a land of boughs in leaf,
  A land of trees that stand;
Where trees are fallen, there is grief;
  I love no leafless land.

Alas, the country whence I fare,
  It is where I would stay;
And where I would not, it is there
  That I shall be for aye.

And one remembers and forgets,
  But 'tis not found again,
Not though they hale in crimsoned nets
  The sunset from the main.

IX

When green buds hang in the elm like dust
  And sprinkle the lime like rain,
Forth I wander, forth I must,
  And drink of life again.
Forth I must by hedgerow bowers
  To look at the leaves uncurled,
And stand in the fields where cuckoo-flowers
  Are lying about the world.

XIII

I lay me down and slumber
  And every morn revive.
Whose is the night-long breathing
  That keeps a man alive?

When I was off to dreamland
  And left my limbs forgot,
Who stayed at home to mind them,
  And breathed when I did not?

. . . . .

– I waste my time in talking,
  No heed at all takes he,
My kind and foolish comrade
  That breathes all night for me.

XIV

The farms of home lie lost in even,
  I see far off the steeple stand;
West and away from here to heaven
  Still is the land.

There if I go no girl will greet me,
  No comrade hollo from the hill,
No dog run down the yard to meet me:
  The land is still.

The land is still by farm and steeple,
  And still for me the land may stay:
There I was friends with perished people,
  And there lie they.

XVI

How clear, how lovely bright,
How beautiful to sight
  Those beams of morning play;
How heaven laughs out with glee
Where, like a bird set free,
Up from the eastern sea
  Soars the delightful day.

To-day I shall be strong,
No more shall yield to wrong,
  Shall squander life no more;
Days lost, I know not how,
I shall retrieve them now;
Now I shall keep the vow
  I never kept before.

Ensanguining the skies
How heavily it dies
  Into the west away;
Past touch and sight and sound,
Not further to be found,
How hopeless under ground
  Falls the remorseful day.

XIX

The mill-stream, now that noises cease,
Is all that does not hold its peace;
Under the bridge it murmurs by,
And here are night and hell and I.

Who made the world I cannot tell;
'Tis made, and here am I in hell.
My hand, though now my knuckles bleed,
I never soiled with such a deed.

And so, no doubt, in time gone by,
Some have suffered more than I,
Who only spend the night alone
And strike my fist upon the stone.

XXI

The world goes none the lamer,
  For ought that I can see,
Because this cursed trouble
  Has struck my days and me.

The stars of heaven are steady,
  The founded hills remain,
Though I to earth and darkness
  Return in blood and pain.

Farewell to all belongings
  I won or bought or stole;
Farewell, my lusty carcase,
  Farewell, my aery soul.

Oh worse remains for others
  And worse to fear had I
Than here at four-and-twenty
  To lay me down and die.

XXII

Ho, everyone that thirsteth
  And hath the price to give,
Come to the stolen waters,
  Drink and your soul shall live.

Come to the stolen waters,
  And leap the guarded pale,
And pull the flower in season
  Before desire shall fail.

It shall not last for ever,
  No more than earth and skies;
But he that drinks in season
  Shall live before he dies.

June suns, you cannot store them
  To warm the winter's cold,
The lad that hopes for heaven
  Shall fill his mouth with mould.

XXIII

Crossing alone the nighted ferry
  With the one coin for fee,
Whom, on the wharf of Lethe waiting,
  Count you to find? Not me.

The brisk fond lackey to fetch and carry,
  The true, sick-hearted slave,
Expect him not in the just city
  And free land of the grave.

XXVI

Good creatures, do you love your lives
  And have you ears for sense?
Here is a knife like other knives,
  That cost me eighteen pence.

I need but stick it in my heart
  And down will come the sky,
And earth's foundations will depart
  And all you folk will die.

XXXI

Because I liked you better
  Than suits a man to say,
It irked you, and I promised
  To throw the thought away.

To put the world between us
  We parted, stiff and dry;
'Good-bye,' said you, 'forget me.'
  'I will, no fear', said I.

If here, where clover whitens
  The dead man's knoll, you pass,
And no tall flower to meet you
  Starts in the trefoiled grass,

Halt by the headstone naming
  The heart no longer stirred,
And say the lad that loved you
  Was one that kept his word.

XXXII

With seed the sowers scatter
  The furrows as they go;
Poor lads, 'tis little matter
  How many sorts they sow,
  For only one will grow.

The charlock on the fallow
  Will take the traveller's eyes,
And gild the ploughland sallow
  With flowers before it dies,
  But twice 'twill not arise.

The stinging nettle only
  Will still be found to stand:
The numberless, the lonely,
  The thronger of the land,
  The leaf that hurts the hand.

It thrives, come sun, come showers,
  Blow east, blow west, it springs;
It peoples towns, and towers
  About the courts of Kings,
  And touch it and it stings.

XXXIII

On forelands high in heaven,
  'Tis many a year gone by,
Amidst the fall of even
  Would stand my friends and I.
Before our foolish faces
  Lay lands we did not see;
Our eyes were in the places
  Where we should never be.

'Oh, the pearl seas are yonder,
  The amber-sanded shore;
Shires where the girls are fonder,
  Towns where the pots hold more.
And here fust we and moulder
  By grange and rick and shed
And every moon are older,
  And soon we shall be dead.'

Heigho, 'twas true and pity;
  But there we lads must stay.
Troy was a steepled city,
  But Troy was far away.
And round we turned lamenting
  To homes we longed to leave,
And silent hills indenting
  The orange band of eve.

I see the air benighted
  And all the dusking dales,
And lamps in England lighted,
  And evening wrecked on Wales;
And starry darkness paces
  The road from sea to sea,
And blots the foolish faces
  Of my poor friends and me.

XXXVI

Here dead lie we because we did not choose
  To live and shame the land from which we sprung.
Life, to be sure, is nothing much to lose;
  But young men think it is, and we were young.

XXXVIII

By shores and woods and steeples
  Rejoicing hearts receive
Poured on a hundred peoples
  The far-shed alms of eve.

Her hands are filled with slumber
  For world-wide labourers worn;
Yet those are more in number
  That know her not from morn.

Now who sees night for ever,
  He sees no happier sight:
Night and no moon and never
  A star upon the night.

XXXIX

My dreams are of a field afar
  And blood and smoke and shot.
There in their graves my comrades are,
  In my grave I am not.

I too was taught the trade of man
  And spelt the lesson plain;
But they, when I forgot and ran,
  Remembered and remain.

XL

Farewell to a name and a number
  Recalled again
To darkness and silence and slumber
  In blood and pain.

So ceases and turns to the thing
  He was born to be
A soldier cheap to the King
  And dear to me;

So smothers in blood the burning
  And flaming flight
Of valour and truth returning
  To dust and night.

XLII

A. J. J.

When he's returned I'll tell him – oh,
  Dear fellow, I forgot:
Time was you would have cared to know,
  But now it matters not.

I mourn you, and you heed not how;
  Unsaid the word must stay;
Last month was time enough, but now
  The news must keep for aye.

Oh, many a month before I learn
  Will find me starting still
And listening, as the days return,
  For him that never will.

Strange, strange to think his blood is cold
  And mine flows easy on,
And that straight look, that heart of gold,
  That grace, that manhood gone.

The word unsaid will stay unsaid
  Though there was much to say;
Last month was time enough: he's dead,
  The news must keep for aye.

XLIV

Far known to sea and shore,
  Foursquare and founded well,
A thousand years it bore,
  And then the belfry fell.
    The steersman of Triest
    Looked where his mark should be,
    But empty was the west
    And Venice under sea.

From dusty wreck dispersed
  Its stature mounts amain;
On surer foot than first
  The belfry stands again.
    At to-fall of the day
    Again its curfew tolls
    And burdens far away
    The green and sanguine shoals.

It looks to north and south,
  It looks to east and west;
It guides to Lido mouth
  The steersman of Triest.
    Andrea, fare you well;
    Venice, farewell to thee.
    The tower that stood and fell
    Is not rebuilt in me.

XLVII

FOR MY FUNERAL

O thou that from thy mansion,
  Through time and place to roam,
Dost send abroad thy children,
  And then dost call them home,

That men and tribes and nations
  And all thy hand hath made
May shelter them from sunshine
  In thine eternal shade:

We now to peace and darkness
  And earth and thee restore
Thy creature that thou madest
  And wilt cast forth no more.

XLVIII

PARTA QUIES

Good-night; ensured release,
Imperishable peace,
    Have these for yours,
While sea abides, and land,
And earth's foundations stand,
    And heaven endures.

When earth's foundations flee,
Nor sky nor land nor sea
    At all is found,
Content you, let them burn:
It is not your concern;
    Sleep on, sleep sound.

From *Additional Poems*

II

Oh were he and I together,
  Shipmates on the fleeted main,
Sailing through the summer weather
  To the spoil of France or Spain.

Oh were he and I together,
  Locking hands and taking leave,
Low upon the trampled heather
  In the battle lost at eve.

Now are he and I asunder
  And asunder to remain;
Kingdoms are for others' plunder,
  And content for other slain.

III

When Adam walked in Eden young,
  Happy, 'tis writ, was he,
While high the fruit of knowledge hung
  Unbitten on the tree.

Happy was he the livelong day;
  I doubt 'tis written wrong:
The heart of man, for all they say,
  Was never happy long.

And now my feet are tired of rest,
  And here they will not stay,
And the soul fevers in my breast
  And aches to be away.

VI

Ask me no more, for fear I should reply;
  Others have held their tongues, and so can I;
Hundreds have died, and told no tale before:
  Ask me no more, for fear I should reply –

How one was true and one was clean of stain
  And one was braver than the heavens are high,
And one was fond of me: and all are slain.
  Ask me no more, for fear I should reply.

VII

He would not stay for me; and who can wonder?
  He would not stay for me to stand and gaze.
I shook his hand and tore my heart in sunder
  And went with half my life about my ways.

XII

AN EPITAPH

Stay, if you list, O passer by the way;
Yet night approaches; better not to stay.
  I never sigh, nor flush, nor knit the brow,
  Nor grieve to think how ill God made me, now.
Here, with one balm for many fevers found,
Whole of an ancient evil, I sleep sound.

XIII

Oh turn not in from marching
  To taverns on the way.
The drought and thirst and parching
  A little dust will lay,
  And take desire away.

Oh waste no words a-wooing
  The soft sleep to your bed;
She is not worth pursuing,
  You will so soon be dead;
  And death will serve instead.

XVII

The stars have not dealt me the worst they could do:
My pleasures are plenty, my troubles are two.
But oh, my two troubles they reave me of rest,
The brains in my head and the heart in my breast.

Oh grant me the ease that is granted so free,
The birthright of multitudes, give it to me,
That relish their victuals and rest on their bed
With flint in the bosom and guts in the head.

XVIII

Oh who is that young sinner with the handcuffs on his wrists?
And what has he been after that they groan and shake their fists?
And wherefore is he wearing such a conscience-stricken air?
Oh they're taking him to prison for the colour of his hair.

'Tis a shame to human nature, such a head of hair as his;
In the good old time 'twas hanging for the colour that it is;
Though hanging isn't bad enough and flaying would be fair
For the nameless and abominable colour of his hair.

Oh a deal of pains he's taken and a pretty price he's paid
To hide his poll or dye it of a mentionable shade;
But they've pulled the beggar's hat off for the world to see and stare,
And they're haling him to justice for the colour of his hair.

Now 'tis oakum for his fingers and the treadmill for his feet
And the quarry-gang on Portland in the cold and in the heat,
And between his spells of labour in the time he has to spare
He can curse the God that made him for the colour of his hair.

XXII

R. L. S.

Home is the sailor, home from sea:
 Her far-borne canvas furled
The ship pours shining on the quay
 The plunder of the world.

Home is the hunter from the hill:
 Fast in the boundless snare
All flesh ties taken at his will
 And every fowl of air.

'Tis evening on the moorland free,
 The starlit wave is still:
Home is the sailor from the sea,
 The hunter from the hill.

Many people have helped me
with their comments and advice.
I would like to thank, in particular,
Melanie Peeke, Zoë Jasko, Nicolas Bell, Todd Swift and
Alex Wylie. Also Nick Purser for his cover illustration,
Edwin Smet for the book design and Trinity College,
Cambridge for kind permission to reproduce the two
sketches of A. E. Housman by H. Lamb and
W. Rothenstein.

HSJ: Housman Society Journal

Aldington, R., *A.E. Housman and W.B Yeats: Two Lectures*, 1st edition, The Peacock Press, 1955.

Allsop, J., *The Land of Lost Content*, 1st edition, Shropshire Books, 1995.

Anderson de Navarro, M., *A Few More Memories*, 1st edition, Hutchinson, 1936.

Anon., 'Notes and News,' *Oxford Magazine*, 26 January, 1911.

Anon., *Bookman*, August 1896.

Anon., *Classical Review*, 1900.

Anon., *Classical Review*, 1900.

Anon., *New Statesman*, 1 January, 1938.

Anon., *The Academy*, February 24, 1900.

Anon., *The Times Literary Supplement*, 20 March, 1953.

Anon., *Times Literary Supplement*, 24 October 1936.

Anon., *Waifs and Strays; a Terminal Magazine of Oxford Poetry*, 1881.

Attwood, T., *The Complete Guide To Asperger's Syndrome*, 2nd edition, London and Philadelphia, Jessica Kingsley Publishers, 2007.

Bayley, J., 'Three Views of Some Housman Poems', *HSJ*, vol.17, 1991, pp.27-31.

Behrman, S.N., *Portrait of Max*, 1st edition, New York, Random House, 1960.

Benêt, W.R., 'A.E. Housman's Last Poems', *The Bookman*, March 1923, pp.83-85.

Bennet, A., *Untold Stories*, 1st edition, London, Faber & Faber, 2006.

Betjeman, J., 'The influence of AEH', *HSJ*, vol. 7, 1981, p.16.

Blocksidge, M., 'A.E. Housman's Early Biographers', *HSJ*, vol.42, 2016, pp.33-61.

Bloomfield, R., 'A.E. Housman and Enoch Powell', *HSJ*, vol. 24, 1998, pp.30-36.

Bloomfield, R., 'Charles Brink', *HSJ*, vol.27, 2001, pp.74-76.

Blotner, J., *Faulkner: A Biography*, 1st edition, London, Chatto & Windus, 1974.

Blunt, W.S., *My Diaries*, Part II, New York, Alfred A. Knopf, 1921.
Bourne, J., 'Housman in the Air', *HSJ*, vol.23, 1997, pp.42-45.
Bourne, J., *Westerly Wanderer*, 1st edition, Housman Society, 1996.
Bowra, C.M., 'An Appreciation', *Spectator*, Oxford, 19 June, 1936.
Bradbury, J.L., 'Poetry and Place in A.E. Housman', *HSJ*, vol.5, 1979, pp.11-18.
Brink, C. O., *Housman Society Publication*, 1996.
Brink, C.O., 'Historical Reflections on Bentley, Porson and Housman,' *English Classical Scholarship*, 1986.
Burnett, A. (ed.), *The Letters of A.E. Housman*, 1st edition, Oxford, 2007.
Burnett, A., Letters (review), *HSJ*, vol. 33, 2007, pp.104-109.
Burnett, A., 'The Housman Lecture', *HSJ*, vol.33, 2007, pp.8-24.
Burns Haber, T. (ed.), *The Manuscript Poems of A.E. Housman*, University of Minnesota, Minnesota Press and OUP, 1955.
Burns Haber, T., 'A.E. Housman', in S. Bowman (ed.), *Twayne's English Authors Series*, XLVI, 1967.
Burns Haber, T., 'Heine and Housman', *JEGP xlii*, 1944, pp. 326-32.
Butterfield, D., 'Housman's Cambridge Lectures', *HSJ*, vol. 35, 2009, pp.122-148.
Butterfield, D., 'Housman's Public Use of Reproof', *HSJ*, vol.36, 2010, pp158-170.
Butterfield, D., 'Your affectionate but inefficient godfather': The letters of A.E. Housman to G.C.A. Jackson, *HSJ*, vol.42, 2016, pp.89-10.
Carter, J. (ed.), *A.E. Housman: Selected Prose*, 1st edition, Cambridge, Cambridge University Press, 1961.
Cecil, D., *Max: A Biography*, 1st American edition, Boston, Houghton Mifflin, 1965.
Clemens, C., 'An Evening with Cyril Clemens', *HSJ*, vol.41, 2015, pp.104-112.
Coleridge, H.N., (ed.), *Specimens of the small oak Table talk of Samuel Taylor Coleridge*, vol.1, 1835.
Connolly, C., 'A.E. Housman: A Controversy' in C. Ricks (ed.), *A Collection of Critical Essays*, Englewood Cliffs NJ, Prentice-Hall, 1968.
Craft, J. (ed.), *Selected Letters*, New York, 1981.

Darling, W., *The Private Papers of a Bankrupt Bookseller*, Oliver and Boyd, 1931.

Davies, M., 'Housman and Murray: A Syncrisis', *HSJ*, vol.41, 2015, pp.68-100.

Dexter, C., 'The Housman Lecture, by Colin Dexter, Hay Festival', *HSJ*, vol.30, 2004, pp. 7-17.

Dexter, C., 'Halley's Comet: No Sighting Yet', *HSJ*, vol.17, 1991, p.9.

Dexter, C., 'Housman's Wordsworth', *HSJ*, vol. 32, 2006, pp.50-55.

Diggle, J. and Goodyear, F.R.D. (eds.), *The Classical Papers of A.E. Housman*, 1st edition, Cambridge, Cambridge University Press, 1972.

Dudley Smith, T., 'Snakes and Ladders,' *Hymn Society of Great Britain and Ireland*, Occasional Paper 3rd ser.1. 2008.

Eayrs, J.G., *Greenpeace and her enemies*, 1st edition, Toronto, Anansi Press, 1973.

Eliot, T.S., 'The Use of Poetry and Use of Criticism: Studies in the Relation of Criticism to Poetry in England', *The Charles Eliot Norton Lectures*, Harvard University Press, 1933.

Eliot, T.S., in *The Criterion*, October, 1933.

Farjeon, E., *Edward Thomas the Last Four Years*, 1st edition, London, Faber & Faber, 1958.

Firshow, P.E., 'The Land of Lost Content: Housman's Shropshire', *Mosaic*, XIII chapter 2, winter 1980, pp.103-122.

Fitzgerald, M., *The Genesis of Artistic Creativity: Asperger's Syndrome and the Arts*, Jessica Kingsley, 2005.

Forster, E.M., *The Listener*, 11 November, 1936.

Forsyth, M., *The Elements of Eloquence*, 1st edition, Icon Books, London, 2013.

Garrod, H.W., 'Housman', Essays & Studies, XXV, 1939, pp.7-21.

Garrod, H.W., 'Mr. A.E. Housman', *HSJ*, vol. 40, 2014, pp.104-116.

Garrod, H.W., *Scholarship: Its Meaning and Value: The J. H. Gray Lectures for 1946*, Cambridge University Press, 1946.

Garrod, H.W., 'The Profession of Poetry and other Lectures', Oxford, 1929.

Goldring, D., *The Nineteen-Twenties*, 1st edition, Nicolson & Watson, 1945.

Goodison, N., 'A Poet's Argyllshire Holiday,' *HSJ*, vol.36, 2010, pp.54-57.
Gow, A.S.F., *A.E. Housman: A Sketch*, Macmillan, 1936.
Gow, A.S.F., *Oxford Magazine*, 56, 11 November 1937.
Gow, A.S.F., 'A Sketch', *HSJ*, vol. 34.
Gow, A.S.F., *Trinity Review Lent Term*, 1967.
Graves, R.P., *A.E. Housman The Scholar-Poet*, 1st edition, Faber & Faber, 1979.
Harder, M., *Illustrated Glimpses of Aspergers*, copyright Marie Harder, 2010.
Haslam II, J. *The Vices of Integrity: E.H. Carr 1892-1982*, 1st edition, London, Verso, 2000.
Hawkins, M., *A.E. Housman: The Man behind the Mask*, 1st edition, Chicago, 1955.
Haynes, E., 'Housman's Shropshire', *HSJ*, vol.20, 1994, pp.17-20.
Hickey, W., (Thomas Driberg), 'An Appreciation' at the time of Housman's Death, *Daily Express*, May, 1936.
Holden, A. & B., *Poems That Make Grown Men Cry*, 1st edition, Simon and Schuster, 2014.
Holland, M. (ed.), *Complete Letters of Oscar Wilde*, 2nd edition, 1962, Rupert Hart-Davis Fourth Estate, 2000.
M. Holroyd, *The Best of Hugh Kingsmill: Selections from his Writings*, 1970.
Hopkins, S., 'Housman and Votes for Women', *HSJ*, vol.26, 2000, pp.62-72.
Hopkins, S., on A.E. Housman's 'De Amicitia', *HSJ*, vol. 26, 2000.
Housman Symons, N.V., 'Some Recollections of the Victorian Housmans', *HSJ*, vol.7, 1981, pp. 5-15.
Housman, A.E., *Collected Poems and Selected Prose*, 1988.
Housman, A.E. (ed.), *M. Manili Astronomicon Liber Primus*, London, 1903.
Housman, A.E., *Last Poems*, 1st edition, New York, Henry Holt & Co., 1922.
Housman, L., *A.E. Housman's De Amicitia*, 1942.
Housman, L., *A.E.H: Some Poems, Some Letters and A Personal Memoir by his Brother*, 1st edition, Jonathan Cape, 1937.
Housman, L., *The Unexpected Years*, Jonathan Cape, London, 1st edition,1937.

Howarth, T.E.B. Howarth's, *Cambridge between Two Wars*, 1st edition, London, HarperCollins, 1978.

Jackson, A., *Pivotal Friendship*, *HSJ*, vol. 36, 2010, pp.34-53.

Jebb, K., *A. E. Housman*, 1st edition, Bridgend, Seren, 1992.

John, A., *Chiaroscuro*, 1st edition, London, Cape, 1952.

Larkin, P., *Required Writing Miscellaneous Pieces: 1955-1982*, Faber & Faber 1983, pp.263-5.

Lawrence, T.E., *Seven Pillars of Wisdom*, privately printed, 1922.

Loos, A., *The International Mark Twain Society*, 1937, Historical Series 6.

Maas, H. (ed.), *The Letters of A.E. Housman*, 1st edition, London, Rupert Hart-Davis, 1971.

Markel, M. H., 'A.E. Housman's Modern Love Poetry,' *HSJ*, vol.2, 1975, pp.36-41.

Marlow, N., *A.E. Housman: Scholar and Poet*, 1st edition, London, Routledge & Keegan Paul, 1958.

Montgomery-Hyde, H., *The Trials of Oscar Wilde*, Dover, 1973.

Naiditch, P.G., *A.E. Housman at University College London*, 1st edition, Brill, Leiden, 1988.

Naidtich, P.G., 'Problems in the life and writings of A.E Housman', *HSJ*, vol.12, 1987.

Navarro, M.A. de, *A Few More Memories*, Hutchinson, 1936.

Orwell, G., *Inside the Whale and Other Essays*, 1st edition, Victor Gollancz, 1940.

Page, N., 'Housman as a comic writer', *HSJ*, vol. 17, 1991, pp. 10-14.

Page, N., *AE Housman: A Critical Biography*, 2nd edition, Palgrave MacMillan,1996.

Palgrave, F.T., *The Golden Treasury*, 1861.

Palmer, C., *Herbert Howells: A Centenary Celebration*, 1st edition, Thames & Hudson, 1992.

Parker, P., 'The Housman Lecture: May 2016, The Name and Nature of Poetry', in *HSJ*, vol.42, 2016, pp.5-24.

Parker, P., *Housman Country*, 1st edition, Little, Brown, 2016.

Pevsner, N., *Buildings of England – Shropshire*, 1st edition, Yale, Yale University Press, 1958.

Platt, A., *Nine Essays With a Preface by A.E. Housman*, Cambridge, Cambridge University Press, 1926.

Poole, A. and Leighton, A. (eds.), *Trinity Poets: An Anthology of Poems by members of Trinity College*, Carcanet, 2017.

Powell, E., 'A Personal Recollection of A.E. Housman', *HSJ*, vol.1, 1974, pp.27-29.

Priestley, J.B., 'The Poetry of A.E. Housman,' London Mercury, VII, December 1922, pp.171-184.

Pugh, J., *Bromsgrove and the Housmans*, Housman Society, 1974.

Reiwald, J.G. (ed.), *Rhymes and Parodies of Max Beerbohm*, 1st edition, Stephen Greene Press, 1963.

Richards, G., *Housman 1897-1936*, 1st edition, London, Oxford University Press, H. Milford, 1941.

Ricks, C., (ed.), *A.E. Housman Collected Poems and Selected Prose*. 1st edition, 1998.

Roberts, S.C., *Adventures with Authors*, 1st edition, Cambridge University Press, 1966.

Roberts, S.C., *The Family: The History of a Dining Club*, Printed for the club, Cambridge, 1963.

Robertson D.S., in *The Classical Review*.

Rose Benêt, W., 'A.E. Housman's Last Poems', *The Bookman*, March 1923, pp.83-85.

Rothenstein, W., *Men and Memories: Recollections of William Rothenstein*, vol.1, London, 1931.

Shackleton Bailey, D.R., 'Reviewing Classical Papers', *Cambridge Review*, 1973.

Shaw, R., *Housman's Places*, 1st edition, Housman Society, 1995.

Sisley, P., 'Malt does more than Milton can', *HSJ*, vol.30, 2004, pp.18-33.

J. Sparrow & J. Carter (eds.), *A. E. Housman, an Annotated Handlist*, 1st edition London, Rupert Hart-Davis, 1952.

Symons, K. (ed.), *Alfred Edward Housman Recollections*, 1st edition, London, Bromsgrove School,1936.

Tait, M.S., 'Hell-fire and the beauties of Shropshire', *HSJ*, vol.31, 2005, pp.41-52.

The Times obituary, May, 1936.

Thomson, J., 'Reminiscences' in G. Richards, *Housman 1897–1936*, 1st edition, London, Oxford University Press, H. Milford, 1941.

Thornton, R.K.R (ed.), *Ivor Gurney Collected Letters*, Carcanet, 1991.

Vincent, E., *A. E. Housman: Hero of the Hidden Life*, 1st edition, Boydell & Brewer, 2018.

Vincent, E.,'With affection', *Times Literary Supplement*, 30 September 2016.

Wain, J., *Preliminary Essays*, 1st edition, Macmillan, 1957.

Waine, P., and Hilliam, O., *22 Ideas That Saved The English Countryside*, 1st edition, Frances Lincoln, 2016.

Watson, G., *A.E. Housman; A Divided Life*, 1st edition, Rupert Hart-Davis, 1957.

Watson, G., *Never One's for Theory: England and the War of Ideas*, 1st edition, James Clake & Co, Ltd., 2000.

White, W., 'A. E. Housman on Blunt and Kipling', *N&Q*, CLXXXI, chapter 22, 29 November 1941.

Willey, B., *Cambridge and other Memories 1920–1953*, London, Chatto & Windus, New York, Norton, 1970.

Wilson, D., *Gilbert Murray OM 1866–1957*, Oxford, Oxford University Press, 1987.

Withers, P., *New Statesman* 36, 1936.

Withers, P., *A Buried Life: Personal Recollections of A.E. Housman*, 1st edition, London, Jonathan Cape, 1940.

Young, B., 'The Queen of Air and Darkness and a Letter on Genesis', *HSJ*, vol.33, 2007, p.97.